PIONEER

American edition

intermediate B1

H. Q. Mitchell – Marileni Malkogianni

student's book

JN126081

mm
publications

PIONEER INTERMEDIATE B1 CONTENTS

Reading	Listening	Speaking (Pronunciation/Intonation*)	Writing
• A magazine page with three short texts: *My unusual house* • A magazine article: *Feeling at home when living abroad: The 4 phases of culture shock*	• People talking in different situations • Three people talking about their experiences abroad	• Pair work: Talking about where you live • Pair work: Role play requesting information • Class discussion about living abroad • Pair work: Discussing and making a decision: Matching a person to a city * Intonation of direct and indirect questions	• An informal e-mail (I) **Developing skills:** • Focusing on the features of an informal letter/e-mail (layout, language, content)
• Three newspaper clippings describing survival stories • A magazine article: *The Dakar Rally*	• A radio interview about a survival story • A live radio report of a cycling endurance race	• Class discussion about survival stories • Class discussion about the weather • Pair work: Role play: Simulating a conversation between a reporter and an eyewitness to an accident • Pair work: Narrating a bad experience and responding by showing concern * Using stress to emphasize important facts	• A story with a given sentence **Developing skills:** • Focusing on the features of a story (tenses, tips to make it more exciting, etc.) • Using time linkers to indicate the sequence of events • Brainstorming and organizing ideas with the help of an outline
• An article: *The history of round-the-world trips* • Short descriptions of apps	• People talking in different situations • A conversation about traveling apps	• Class discussion about traveling • Group work: Comparing three different types of vacations • Class discussion about apps • Pair work: Discussing and making a decision: Choosing between two tours	• An article describing a place **Developing skills:** • Focusing on the features of an article • Using different ways to attract the reader's attention (e.g. descriptive language) • Brainstorming and organizing ideas with the help of an outline
• A volunteer teacher's blog • A quiz: *Find the perfect job for you*	• People talking in different situations • Four people talking about advice they were given	• Class discussion about volunteer work • Group work: Role play situations related to employment • Group work: Discussing different professions • Pair work: Speculating about a picture * Intonation of modal verbs in sentences	• A semi-formal e-mail asking for and giving information **Developing skills:** • Focusing on content and stylistic features of a semi-formal letter/ e-mail
• A magazine article: *Whistled Languages* • Three warning signs	• A conversation about a social media site • People talking in different situations	• Group work: Talking about communication • Pair work: Talking about the meaning of different signs • Pair work: Role play asking for and giving directions * Intonation of non-defining relative clauses	• An informal e-mail (II) **Developing skills:** • Focusing on language and content
• A magazine article: *Winners / Losers* • An article: *Fearless Felix*	• A talk about *The Marshmallow Experiment* • A radio quiz about world records	• Class discussion about dreams, goals and ambitions • Pair work: Discussing the advantages and disadvantages of two options and making a decision * Intonation of conditional sentences	• An essay (discussing advantages and disadvantages) **Developing skills:** • Focusing on layout, language and content • Using linking words/phrases to list/add points, to express contrast and to sum up

	Vocabulary	Grammar	Functions
7 p.67 **H₂O**	• Geographical features • Animals • Verbs + prepositions	• Past Perfect Simple - Past Perfect Progressive • Articles	• Sequencing past actions and events • Narrating • Discussing facts • Guessing the meaning of unknown words/phrases • Expressing doubt and confidence • Commenting on something someone has said • Paraphrasing what someone has said
8 p.77 **Green living**	• Words/Phrases related to the environment • Verbs easily confused • Phrasal verbs • Lexical set: food and food substances	• Passive Voice I • Passive Voice II	• Talking about environmental issues • Emphasizing an action rather than the doer of the action • Guessing the meaning of unknown words/phrases • Stating accepted facts • Talking about healthy eating habits • Expressing and supporting an opinion • Comparing two pictures

Task 7 & 8: Developing environmental self-awareness p.130

	Vocabulary	Grammar	Functions
9 p.87 **Preferences**	• Words/Phrases related to shopping • Word building: negative words beginning with *dis-*, *mis-*, ending in *-less* • Words/Phrases related to books	• Full/Bare Infinitive • -ing form • prefer, would prefer, would rather	• Expressing preference • Talking about shopping habits • Guessing the meaning of unknown words/phrases • Understanding online advertisements and reviews • Changing the meaning of a sentence through word stress • Talking about books
10 p.97 **Let's go!**	• Idiomatic expressions • Words related to sports and fitness • Prepositional phrases with *in* and *out of* • Collocations with *lose* and *miss*	• Reported Speech: Statements, Questions, Commands, Requests	• Talking about various forms of entertainment and spare-time activities • Guessing the meaning of unknown phrases • Talking about staying in shape • Reporting • Describing events

Task 9 & 10: Collaborating with a group to organize a fund-raiser p.131

	Vocabulary	Grammar	Functions
11 p.107 **Night**	• Words related to medical issues • Words easily confused • Phrasal verbs with *up* • Word building: adjectives ending in -ous, -al, -ful, -able, -ive, -ing	• Clauses of concession and purpose • all / both / neither / none / either • both... and... / neither... nor... / either... or...	• Talking about sleeping habits and problems • Guessing the meaning of unknown words/phrases • Distinguishing between words easily confused • Expressing contrast, purpose, reason and result • Emphasizing what you are saying • Indicating that you are following what someone is saying • Analyzing problems and proposing solutions
12 p.117 **By chance**	• Expressions with *chance* • Words used both as verbs and as nouns • Expressions with *time* • Idiomatic expressions	• Conditional Sentences Type 3 • Wishes and Unreal Past	• Guessing the meaning of unknown words/phrases • Talking about imaginary and hypothetical situations in the past • Expressing wishes and regret about something in the past • Showing sympathy and being encouraging • Discussing problems • Asking for and giving advice • Editing your own work

Task 11 & 12: Preparing for and taking part in a debate p.132

Reading	Listening	Speaking (Pronunciation/Intonation*)	Writing
• An extract from a novel: *Twenty Thousand Leagues Under the Sea* • A Q&A column of a magazine: H_2O	• A TV documentary about marine animals • A radio interview about World Water Day	• Pair work: Recounting a story • Class discussion: Predicting the continuation of a story • Pair work: Discussing facts • Group work: Speculating and making up a story using prompts * Pronunciation of *the*	• A story with a given sentence and prompts **Developing skills:** • Using "strong" adjectives • Using adverb and adjective collocations
• A feature article: *The Green Wall of China* • A magazine article: *To Meat or Not To Meat*	• A radio interview about wind turbines • People talking in different situations	• Class discussion about the problems created by pollution • Group work: Discussing headlines and proposing solutions to problems • Class discussion about healthy eating habits • Comparing two photographs of places to eat	• An essay expressing an opinion **Developing skills:** • Using topic sentences
• A magazine article: *Decisions, Decisions...* • Four online product reviews	• People talking in different situations • A conversation between a man and a customer service representative	• Class discussion about decision making • Class discussion about shopping habits • Pair work: Talking about what to buy and reaching a decision based on specific criteria • Class discussion about products and services • Class discussion about book preferences • Pair work: Choosing which books to read * Stress and meaning	• A book review **Developing skills:** • Focusing on language and content • Brainstorming and organizing ideas with the help of an outline
• A magazine article: *Xpogo!* • A walkthrough: *Tales of Simiaz II*	• People talking in different situations • An interview with a video game designer	• Class discussion about extreme sports • Pair work: Role play situations • Class discussion about video games • Pair work: Talking about events and coming to a decision • Class discussion about events you like to attend	• An article describing an event **Developing skills:** • Focusing on text cohesion and paragraphing • Brainstorming and organizing ideas with the help of an outline
• A problem page: *Solving your sleep problems* • An article: *Northern lights, a spectacular display*	• Four people describing dreams • A scientist talking at a planetarium	• Class discussion about sleeping problems • Pair work: Discussing dreams • Class discussion about natural phenomena • Group work: Analyzing city problems and expressing reason and result • Group work: Proposing solutions * Silent letters	• A letter (to the editor) expressing an opinion **Developing skills:** • Focusing on language and content • Brainstorming and organizing ideas with the help of a mind map
• A magazine page: *Oops! Accidental discoveries* • A magazine article: *I never want to see that number again*	• People talking in different situations • A radio show about identical twins	• Speculating about a picture • Class discussion about coincidences • Pair work: Talking about things you wish were different in your life • Pair work: Discussing problems and asking for and giving advice	• An informal e-mail (III) **Developing skills:** • Focusing on language and content • Using correction techniques

American and British English p. 158
Task Listening Transcripts p. 167

Listening Transcripts p. 159
Word List p. 168

DON'T MISS...

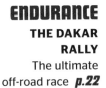

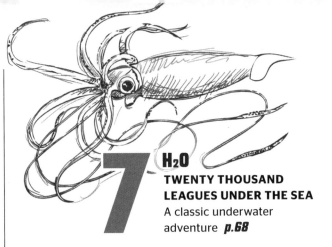

Home is where
the heart is

Home Sweet Home

Live out of
a suitcase

Discuss:

- Read the phrases. Do you understand what they mean?

- Do you agree with what they are trying to say?

- What things are important when making a home?

- What's the difference between a "house" and a "home"?

MAKE YOURSELF AT HOME

A HOME AWAY FROM HOME

HAVE
A ROOF
OVER
YOUR
HEAD

There's no place
like home

In this module you will learn...

- to distinguish between permanent and temporary situations
- different ways to say where you live
- to form different types of questions
- to ask for information formally and informally
- to give information
- to ask for somebody's opinion and express opinion
- to express agreement and disagreement
- to give news
- to respond to news by showing enthusiasm
- to write an informal e-mail

1a

Reading 🔊

A. Discuss.

- What unusual places can you think of to live in?
- Would you like to live somewhere unusual? Why? / Why not?

My unusual house

B. Read the texts A-C. What do the people think of their homes? Choose a, b, c or d.

a. They regret moving into their unusual home.

b. They don't want to change anything in their home.

c. They are satisfied with their home but are facing certain difficulties.

d. They aren't satisfied with their home but they have to stay.

C. Read again and answer the questions below. Write A, B or C.

1. Who doesn't find his/her home comfortable or easy to live in? ☐

2. Who mentions that the place will be his/her home for a short time? ☐

3. Who has to spend more money than before? ☐

4. Who has more space than he/she really needs? ☐

5. Who has to sometimes cope with loneliness? ☐

6. Who uses the place for recreational purposes? ☐

7. Who wants other people to know about his/her experiences? ☐

8. Who mentions making changes to the place? ☐

A. I live in an old fire station that I converted into a house last year, when I moved out of my dorm. My friends thought I was out of my mind at first, but now they love it, too. It's a spacious building, so I have plenty of room to put all my belongings. I even have my own gym and entertainment room! My friends often drop by, so I never get lonely living here. The only drawback is that I have more expenses than before, for heating during the winter and furniture to fill up the space. Most people want to know if I use the fire pole. The answer is all the time!

B. People usually wonder why I chose to live in a lighthouse. The truth is I wanted first-hand experience as I'm currently writing a book about living in a lighthouse. So I chose it as my temporary residence. I settled in very quickly and I try to enjoy every minute of it. I'm a long way away from stores and restaurants, but I don't mind, though. I love being so near the ocean. Every morning I climb the spiral stairway to the top of the tower and drink my coffee while admiring the view. That's when I remember how lucky I am at the moment. Of course, there are days when it seems like the loneliest and most isolated place in the world, but at least I have access to the Internet and I can stay in touch with my friends and family.

C. A few months ago my wife and I bought a houseboat. In the beginning, we only stayed for a few days at a time, but now we've decided to make it our permanent home and we're moving in at the end of this week. The truth is that we face many difficulties and we're still trying to get used to it. For one thing, it's a little bit cramped, and we have to use space wisely. Also, we don't have electricity all the time and when we buy groceries, we can't buy a lot, because it's a long walk to the boat with heavy bags. We might be far from stores, but we're in a great location and we still have our peace and quiet. Not many people wake up and see swans outside their window or "float away" if they get tired of the view!

D. Find words/phrases in the texts and match them with the definitions below:

1. crazy (text A)

2. the things that you own and can carry with you (text A)

3. disadvantage (text A)

4. at the present time (text B)

5. a place where sb. lives (text B)

6. a tall narrow building or part of a building (text B)

7. far away from other buildings, towns, etc. and difficult to reach (text B)

8. lasting for a long time, not temporary (text C)

9. to have to deal with a problem or situation (text C)

E. Discuss.
- Which of the three unusual homes would you like to live in?
- Which home do you think is the strangest one to live in? Why?

Vocabulary

A. Read the sentences below from the texts A-C. What do the adjectives in bold mean?

*For one thing, it's a little bit **cramped**, and we have to use space wisely.*

*It's a **spacious** building, so I have plenty of room to put all my belongings.*

B. Read the sentences and match the adjectives in bold with the definitions a-c.

1. I want to rent a **furnished** apartment, because I don't have money to buy my own things. ☐

2. Our hotel room was very **luxurious**, with a large bed and bathroom and a breathtaking view. ☐

3. It was an **inviting** garden with beautiful flowers. ☐

a. attractive, makes you feel welcome
b. containing furniture
c. comfortable, expensive and beautiful

Grammar Present Simple vs. Present Progressive, Stative verbs
→ *p. 146*

A. Look at text B and answer the questions.

1. What does the writer do every morning? Which tense is used? Why?

2. What is the writer writing? Which tense is used? Why?

3. What do people usually wonder about this person? Which tense is commonly used with adverbs of frequency (e.g. usually, often)?

B. Read about the uses of the Present Simple and the Present Progressive and think of one more example for each use.

The **Present Simple** is used for:
1. permanent situations, e.g. *He **lives** in an old fire station.*
2. repeated habitual actions, e.g. *My friends often **drop by**.*
3. general truths, e.g. *Birds **fly** south in the winter.*

The **Present Progressive** is used for:
1. actions happening now, e.g. *He **is having** breakfast right now.*
2. temporary situations, e.g. *I **am** currently **writing** a book about my experiences.*
3. future arrangements, e.g. *We**'re moving** in at the end of this week.*

C. Read the examples from the texts A-C. Which tense is used and why? Can you find more examples in the texts?

- I even **have** my own gym...
- ...now they **love** it, too.
- Most people **want** to know if...
- We **don't have** electricity...
- ...it **seems** like the loneliest...

Stative verbs (see, notice, like, need, believe, know, belong, etc.) are not usually used in the Present Progressive.

D. Complete with the Present Simple or the Present Progressive of the verbs in parentheses.

1. **A:** Whose coat is this?

   B: It's Samantha's. She 1 _____ (stay) with us for the weekend.

   A: Really? Where is she? I really 2 _____ (want) to talk to her and find out how she 3 _____ (cope) in London.

   B: She's fine. I 4 _____ (think) she 5 _____ (get) used to her new life. She also 6 _____ (have) a part-time job. Anyway, you can ask her for yourself. She 7 _____ (make) chocolate cake with Patricia in the kitchen. The two of them 8 _____ (always / like) to spend time together.

2. **A:** So, when 9 _____ you _____ (visit) your friend in Boston?

   B: Next week. I 10 _____ (leave) on Sunday afternoon. Are you sure you 11 _____ (not want) to come with me?

   A: Positive. You 12 _____ (know) how much I 13 _____ (hate) traveling by plane.

   B: It's only a two-hour flight. Come on!

   A: No, thanks. Anyway, I'm pretty busy this weekend. Jack and I 14 _____ (paint) the apartment.

   B: You are? I 15 _____ (hope) you do a good job. I'll drop by to see it when I come back.

Vocabulary

A. Read and talk in pairs. Tell each other about where you live.

I live...

in

the U.S. *(country)*

Florida *(state)*

Howard County *(county)*

London *(city)*

the suburbs of....

a suburban/rural/urban area

the country(side)

an apartment downtown

a cabin/cottage/bungalow

on

Rainbow Street/Road/
Avenue/Lane, etc.

the outskirts of...

the third floor

campus

at

5605 N. Webster St.
(address)

NEW MEXICO

BERNALILLO

ALBUQUERQUE

- COUNTRY
- STATE
- COUNTY
- ★ CITY
- STREET

B. Read the sentences and match the phrasal verbs in bold with their meanings.

> A phrasal verb consists of a verb (e.g. *get. break*) and an adverb (e.g. *back*) and/or one or more prepositions (e.g. *for. on. with*). The meaning of the phrasal verb is different from the meaning of the verb and the adverb/preposition(s) it includes.

1. Their school seemed a little scary at first but they soon **settled in**.
2. Could you **put** me **up** when I come to Rome?
3. All guests should **check out** by noon.
4. Janice doesn't live with her parents anymore. She **moved out** a long time ago.
5. We **checked in** at a luxurious hotel by the beach.
6. My friend was in the neighborhood so she **dropped by**.
7. **A:** I found a new roommate!
   B: Really? When is she **moving in**?

a. to get used to a new place, job, etc.

b. to make a short visit

c. to let sb. stay in your house

d. to start living in your new home

e. to report that you have arrived at a hotel or airport

f. to leave a hotel after paying the bill

g. to leave your home for another one

Grammar Question words, Subject-Object questions, Indirect questions → *p. 146*

A. Complete the questions below with question words.

1. **A:** _____ is your new office?
   B: Downtown.
2. **A:** _____ are you talking to?
   B: A colleague.
3. **A:** _____ much did you pay for that?
   B: Only $60.
4. **A:** _____ did you bring us from Peru?
   B: Lots of souvenirs.
5. **A:** _____ far is the airport?
   B: About 10 miles.
6. **A:** _____ carry-on is this?
   B: Jake's. He just arrived.
7. **A:** _____ can you pay me back?
   B: Tomorrow.
8. **A:** _____ sport should I take up, swimming or volleyball?
   B: I think swimming.
9. **A:** _____ is your new roommate like?
   B: She's pretty easygoing.
10. **A:** _____ did you sell your car?
    B: I needed the money.

B. Read the examples and answer the questions 1-3.

> • **A:** Who **lives** on campus?
>   **B:** Leslie (lives on campus).
> • **A:** Who **does** Leslie live with?
>   **B:** (She lives with) Karen, her roommate.

1. Which question asks about the subject of the verb?
2. Which question asks about the object of the verb?
3. In which question is the verb in question form?

C. Write questions. The words in bold are the answers.

1. **A:** What _____?
   B: I ordered **a milkshake and a donut** at the coffee shop.
2. **A:** Which _____?
   B: Greg bought **the red** jacket.
3. **A:** Who _____?
   B: **Peter** is going bowling with Mark.
4. **A:** Who _____?
   B: I want to visit **Barney** tomorrow afternoon.
5. **A:** What _____?
   B: **A motorcycle** crashed into that tree.

D. Read the examples and answer the questions.

Direct Questions	Indirect Questions
What time does the train leave?	Would you tell me **what time the train leaves**?
Can we check out later than 12 p.m.?	I'd like to know **if/whether we can check out later than 12 p.m.**

1. What is the difference in word order between direct and indirect questions?

2. How are indirect questions formed when the direct question does not begin with a question word?

Intonation 🔊

Listen and repeat. Is the intonation rising ↗ or falling ↘?

1. What kind of movies do you like?

2. Could you inform me what time the class starts?

3. Can you tell me how I can get to Green Avenue?

4. Where's the new coffee shop?

5. Do you know if Andy has changed his cell number?

6. Who lives in that cottage?

Listening 🔊

You will hear people talking in six different situations. For questions 1-6, choose the best answer a, b or c.

1. Where does Will live?
   a. On campus.
   b. In an apartment downtown.
   c. In a house in the suburbs.

2. Where is Julie going to go next?
   a. to Susie's house
   b. to the bank
   c. to the supermarket

3. How long did it take Pam to get used to living in the countryside?
   a. one month
   b. 2-3 months
   c. one year

4. What is the man doing at the hotel reception?
   a. checking in
   b. checking out
   c. complaining

5. What is NOT true about the apartment?
   a. It's on the fifth floor.
   b. It has two bedrooms.
   c. It's fully-furnished.

6. What is Linda's neighbor like?
   a. helpful
   b. annoying
   c. friendly

E. Read the direct questions and form indirect questions.

1. How long will the meeting last?
   Excuse me, do you know _____?

2. Where does Miss Davis live?
   Could you _____?

3. Is the apartment furnished?
   I'd like to _____.

4. When did you graduate?
   Can you _____?

5. Do I need to buy any books for the French course?
   I was wondering _____.

Speaking

Talk in pairs.

Student A: Imagine that you are looking for a new roommate. Student B is looking for a place to live and calls you. Ask him/her questions and hold a conversation to find out about him/her and see if he/she is suitable to become your new roommate. Discuss the ideas in the box and use a combination of direct and indirect questions.

personal information (age, nationality, family, etc.) personality   studies   job daily habits   spare time

Student B: Imagine you are looking for a place to live. Student A is looking for a roommate and you call him/her. Answer his/her questions requesting information about you and ask questions to find out about the house/apartment. Discuss the ideas in the box and use a combination of direct and indirect questions.

type of accommodations   exact location number of rooms   public transportation nearby if it's spacious/furnished, etc.

TIP

When asking for information, indirect questions are usually more polite and appropriate for formal situations. Begin your indirect questions with some of the following phrases:

Can / Could / Would you tell me...?
Can / Could / Would you inform me...?
Can / Could / Would you let me know...?
Do you know...?
I'd like to know...
I was wondering...

Reading 🔊

A. Discuss.

- Would you like to move to another country?
- What kind of problems do you think you would come across?

B. Read the first paragraph of the text and the box showing the 4 phases of culture shock. What do you think people should do to get over the problems caused by culture shock? Read the rest of the text and compare your answers.

Feeling at home when living abroad

When people decide to move abroad for work or study, they might experience culture shock at first. This is the phenomenon of disorientation people feel when they move to a country with a different lifestyle and culture. Studies have shown that there are four phases a person goes through when they have to adjust to an unfamiliar environment.

The 4 phases of culture shock

Honeymoon phase
(0→3 months): This phase occurs when you first move to a new culture. You observe your new environment and make new discoveries. You are fascinated by everything – the food, the lifestyle, the language and the cultural differences.

Negotiation phase
(3→6 months): The initial enthusiasm turns into anxiety. You become aware of the differences between the old and new culture as well as the difficulties in the language, and you often get frustrated. Feelings of loneliness and homesickness are common.

Adjustment phase
(6→12 months): Things start to feel normal, and you start thinking positively. You get used to the new culture, which you can now understand and appreciate.

Mastery phase
(12 months+): This phase occurs when you start feeling like a "local." You finally feel comfortable and you no longer have communication problems. You can participate in more aspects of the new culture without forgetting your own.

HELPFUL TIPS

Keep in mind that there are many new and positive experiences waiting for you in the new culture. Culture shock can cause problems, however, remember that there are things you can do to get over these problems.

MAKE YOURSELF AT HOME: Decorate your new home with familiar things that remind you of your old culture. This can include furniture, paintings and photographs of friends and family.

KEEP IN TOUCH: It can sometimes be difficult to stay in touch with loved ones if you're in a different time zone. However, phone calls, e-mail and Skype are all ways that can help you catch up on their news and make you feel like you are not missing out on important events in other people's lives.

EXPLORE NEW SURROUNDINGS: After finishing with the sightseeing, go out and explore your new neighborhood. Walk around or ride a bicycle to discover every corner of it and get to know it better.

DEVELOP A NEW ROUTINE: This helps you get used to the new lifestyle in a shorter period of time. Go to a coffee shop that you like every morning for breakfast or visit the same bakery. Small things like this can make you feel less "foreign."

GET INVOLVED IN THE LOCAL COMMUNITY: Join the local library or book club. Find out about any interesting entertainment events. Sign up for classes or sports that will help you meet new people and discover new hobbies. Also, take classes to learn the language if it is different from your native one.

C. Read again and answer the questions.

1. What can contact with an unfamiliar lifestyle cause some people to feel?

2. During which phase do people have the most negative feelings?

3. During which phase do people start recognizing the good qualities of a new culture?

4. How long does it take for people to get used to a new culture?

5. Does keeping in touch with family and friends make people feel more homesick?

6. Why does the writer suggest doing activities like riding a bike in the new neighborhood?

7. What does the writer mean by *Small things like this can make you feel less "foreign"*?

8. How can you make new friends when living abroad?

D. Look at the highlighted words in the text and match them with their meanings.

1. adjust ☐	4. initial ☐	7. get over ☐
2. observe ☐	5. anxiety ☐	8. surroundings ☐
3. fascinated ☐	6. frustrated ☐	9. native ☐

a. very interested

b. related to the place where you were born

c. happening at the beginning

d. annoyed or impatient because you can't achieve what you want

e. to become familiar with a new situation by changing the way you think and behave

f. everything that is around a person; the environment

g. to find a way to deal with sth. difficult

h. to watch sth. carefully and learn more about it

i. a worried feeling you have about sb. or sth.

E. Discuss.

• Do you think the text gives useful advice?

• Which advice would you follow if you had to move abroad?

Vocabulary

Read the note and the sentences. What does "get" mean in these examples?

> The verb **"get"** can be found in a variety of phrases, expressions and phrasal verbs and has many different meanings. Below are four broad categories to help you remember what it means:
>
> **OBTAIN:** buy, receive, bring, begin to have, etc.
> *(get some milk, get an invitation, get the kids, get a cold)*
>
> **BECOME / START TO BE**
> *(get frustrated, get ready, get older, get in trouble)*
>
> **MOVE:** arrive, reach, leave, enter, rise, etc.
> *(get to, get home, get off, get into, get up)*
>
> **IDIOMS**
> *(get rid of, get down to business)*

1. It is also a good idea to **get involved** in the local community.

2. Walk around or ride a bicycle to discover every corner of your new neighborhood and **get to know** it better.

3. I accepted the job because I want to **get** some teaching **experience**.

4. When you **get out of** the subway station, turn right and go down Maple Road. My house is number 4899.

5. Please call me when you **get there**.

6. I always **get excited** when I **get e-mail** from family and friends now that I'm living abroad.

Listening 🔊

A. Listen to three people talking about the problems they had when they moved abroad. Match the speakers with the statements a-e. There are two extra statements which you do not need to use.

Speaker 1 ☐   Speaker 2 ☐   Speaker 3 ☐

a. I didn't expect to like my new life.

b. I had difficulty understanding the language.

c. I didn't get much help from my friends in the beginning.

d. Learning about the culture helped me settle in.

e. I discovered ways to stop feeling homesick.

B. Discuss.

• Have you ever lived abroad?

• If yes, what problems did you face and how did you get over them?

• If not, what problems do you think you'd have abroad? What would you do to get over them?

Speaking

Talk in pairs. Pierre Clermont has decided to study in one of the three cities below. Read his profile and the information about the three U.S. cities. Discuss the cities and decide which is the most suitable for him. Give reasons for your choices. Use the phrases in the box.

Pierre Clermont

Age: 24
Nationality: French
Likes: eating out, sports, art, reading, cycling
Dislikes: shopping, swimming

Washington, D.C.
- museums and galleries
- fascinating sights to visit
- lots of theaters & movie theaters

Miami, Florida
- great beaches
- fantastic sports facilities
- peaceful parks

Los Angeles, California
- great beaches and activities
- lots of shopping malls
- huge variety of restaurants

Expressing opinion
I think...
Personally, I believe...
In my opinion,...
It seems that...
The way I see it,...
If you ask me, he should(n't)...

Agreeing/Disagreeing
I agree/disagree with you.
I think so, too. / I don't think so.
You're right/wrong about that.
You have a point.
I'm not so sure about that.
Very true, but...

Asking a question
What do you think?
What is your opinion?
Don't you think that...?
Don't you agree that...?

66 *I think the most suitable city for Pierre is... because he's interested in...*
I disagree. I think the ideal city for him is... because...
Very true, but he'll probably enjoy... more because...
Yes, but don't you agree that...? 99

TIP
- Express your opinion giving reasons. Don't worry if you disagree with your partner. Remember, no answer is right or wrong as long as it is justified.
- If one of you gets stuck, help each other by asking a question, for instance.

Writing An informal e-mail (I)

A. Read the two e-mails and find:
1. features that make them informal.
2. set phrases used to begin and end them.

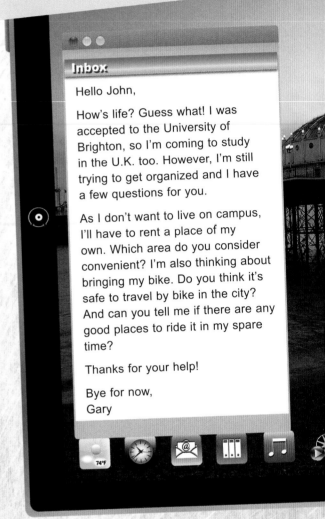

Inbox

Hello John,

How's life? Guess what! I was accepted to the University of Brighton, so I'm coming to study in the U.K. too. However, I'm still trying to get organized and I have a few questions for you.

As I don't want to live on campus, I'll have to rent a place of my own. Which area do you consider convenient? I'm also thinking about bringing my bike. Do you think it's safe to travel by bike in the city? And can you tell me if there are any good places to ride it in my spare time?

Thanks for your help!

Bye for now,
Gary

74°F

B. Read the e-mails again and answer the questions.
1. Why is Gary writing to John?
2. Does John answer all his questions?
3. Does he give him extra information?
4. In which e-mail are the following functions expressed? Write 1 or 2.
   a. giving information ☐
   b. expressing opinion ☐
   c. asking for an opinion ☐
   d. expressing enthusiasm ☐
   e. asking for information ☐
   f. giving news ☐

Hey Gary!

I've been meaning to get back to you since yesterday, and I finally managed today. Anyway, that's great news! I'm really glad you're going to study here.

If you ask me, I think you should live in Hanover or Preston Park. These areas are great for students as they're both close to the downtown area as well as the university. Don't worry about anything! I'll show you around and you'll soon get the hang of it.

Of course, you should definitely bring your bike. Brighton is a bicycle-friendly city with many bicycle lanes that allow you to ride safely. There are also lots of parks and a beautiful beach. When the weather's nice, I go riding along the shoreline, so I'm sure you'll love it too! Cycling is difficult in the winter, but don't worry. There are many buses that run all day and a few night buses as well.

I'm really excited about you coming here. Keep me posted!

See you soon,
John

Send

When writing an informal e-mail:

- use the appropriate layout (see page 136).
- organize it into paragraphs and use set phrases as shown in the plan.
- use informal language and expressions (*e.g. well, of course, anyway, you know, you see, actually, by the way*).
- use standard grammar and spelling conventions. Don't use forms such as *wanna, CU L8R,* etc.
- use short forms (*e.g. I'm, don't*).
- use exclamations (*e.g. Guess what!*) and direct questions (*e.g. What have you been up to?*).
- read the rubric and the e-mail you are replying to carefully. Make sure you understand why you are writing (to give information, to express your opinion, etc.) and respond to all the requests suitably.
- use appropriate expressions/phrases to express enthusiasm, give news, express your opinion, etc.

TIP

C. Read the expressions/phrases below and the situations 1-4. How would you reply?

Giving news

Guess what! I've recently...

Did I tell you about...? Let me fill you in.

You won't believe what happened to me!

I haven't told you the latest, have I?

Just thought I'd drop you a line to let you know that...

Expressing enthusiasm

Wow! That's great/awesome news!

How exciting/wonderful!

I am/was happy/glad/pleased to hear that...

I couldn't believe it when I read that...

1. I haven't told you the latest, have I? I bought a motorcycle!
_____
_____

2. Guess what! I have some time off work and I was thinking of going hiking or skiing. What do you think?
_____
_____

3. Guess what! I got a job at the Chinese restaurant downtown. I know where it is, but can you tell me the best way to get there from our area?
_____
_____

4. I'm finally moving out! Can you believe it? I only have one problem. Should I rent a furnished apartment or not?
_____
_____

D. Imagine you have received the following e-mail from a friend. Write a reply. Use the TIP and the plan on page 133.

new e-mail

Hi,

Just thought I'd drop you a line to let you know that I'm coming to study there! Yep, it's true! I just need to get organized and I need some help.

Do you think it'll be easy for me to work part-time while studying? And if so, do you know of any places where I can find a job as a waiter or anything else? The other thing I'm worried about is getting bored. What entertainment options are there? Where do you hang out?

Well, that's all for now. Get back to me soon.

A. Circle the correct words.

1. She lives in a nice cabin in the forest. However sometimes she feels kind of **cramped / isolated** because she's far from town.
2. It took Billy a few months to **adjust / occur** to his new school, but now he loves it.
3. Mary went out with Anna and they **missed / caught** up on each other's news.
4. One of the **surroundings / drawbacks** of living downtown is the traffic and noise.
5. I don't have a big suitcase, so I will have to pack my things **currently / wisely**.
6. Don't be so **impatient / fascinated**. Dinner will be ready in 20 minutes!
7. I live in a city that has many bicycle **lanes / avenues** so I use my bike all the time.

B. Complete the sentences with the correct preposition. (in, out, up, of, with, on)

1. I really want to get rid _____ all our old furniture.
2. Jake's roommate moved _____ because they didn't get along.
3. I don't think you're aware _____ the expenses of living alone.
4. It took us a few months to settle _____, but now we love our new apartment.
5. Carl put me _____ for the night, because I didn't have anywhere else to stay.
6. Tina finds it difficult to cope _____ the stress at work.
7. Our house is _____ the outskirts of the city.
8. I'm going to sign _____ for the creative writing course at college.

C. Complete with the Present Simple or the Present Progressive of the verbs in parentheses.

1. **A:** This weekend we _____ (have) a barbecue at our house. _____ you _____ (want) to come?
   B: Sure, that sounds great! Is it a special occasion?
   A: Not really, we just _____ (like) inviting friends over. We _____ (do) it often.
2. **A:** So, when _____ you _____ (leave) for France?
   B: Next month. I _____ (enjoy) taking trips during the fall. I am very excited about it.
3. **A:** I heard about your new job. _____ you _____ (live) in Toronto now?
   B: Well, yeah. I _____ (stay) at my cousin's house for a few days but I _____ (look) for an apartment in the downtown area.
4. **A:** Where's Dan? Don't tell me he _____ (work) again this weekend!
   B: No, he _____ (shop) for some furniture.
   A: He should go to *Cozy Couch*. It's a furniture store that _____ (sell) nice and cheap furniture.

D. Write questions. The words in bold are the answers.

1. **A:** _____
   B: I'm moving **next Saturday**.
2. **A:** _____
   B: I took a picture of **the lighthouse**.
3. **A:** _____
   B: **Mark** dropped by this morning.
4. **A:** _____
   B: My new apartment is **spacious**.
5. **A:** _____
   B: Well, it takes me **about half an hour** to get to work.
6. **A:** _____
   B: We usually invite **our neighbors** to our barbecues.

E. Match. Choose from the responses a-h. There are two extra responses which you do not need to use.

1. Could you tell me what happened at the meeting yesterday? ☐
2. I'd really like to live in a location with some peace and quiet. ☐
3. Guess what! I got accepted to the University of Chicago! ☐
4. The car is filthy! When are you going to clean it? ☐
5. I was wondering how far the art gallery is from here. ☐
6. If you ask me, this coffee maker is useless! ☐

a. I couldn't believe it when I heard it.
b. Wow! That's awesome news.
c. You'll soon get the hang of it.
d. Well, then I suppose somewhere in the suburbs will suit you.
e. I think living on the outskirts of the city is boring.
f. It's about ten minutes by bus.
g. Let me fill you in.
h. I know. I've been meaning to do it.

Self-assessment
Read the following and check the appropriate boxes. For the points you are unsure of, refer back to the relevant sections in the module.

NOW I CAN...
- distinguish between permanent and temporary situations ☐
- say where I live in different ways ☐
- form different types of questions ☐
- ask for information formally and informally ☐
- give information ☐
- ask for somebody's opinion and express opinion ☐
- express agreement and disagreement ☐
- give news ☐
- respond to news by showing enthusiasm ☐
- write an informal e-mail ☐

hold a tarantula

climb up a rope

Discuss:

- Can you do any of the things shown in the pictures?
- Which do you think is the hardest?
- Are you good at endurance activities?

bungee jump

hold your breath underwater for 1 minute

run a marathon

go without food for 24 hours

In this module you will learn...

- to read and locate important facts in newspaper clippings
- to distinguish between words easily confused
- to talk about past events and habits
- to describe weather conditions
- to emphasize important facts when speaking
- to narrate past events/experiences
- to report incidents
- how suffixes are used to form nouns that refer to people
- to respond to bad news and show concern
- to use time linkers
- to write a story

17

Reading 🔊

A. Read "The Rule of 3" and discuss.
- How important is it to prepare for trips in the wild?
- What are the most important things to have with you?
- Do you think you would be good at surviving in the wild?

B. Read the headlines of the newspaper clippings below. What do you think happened?

C. Skim through the newspaper clippings and find information to complete the table below. Then read the clippings more carefully and check your answers.

THE RULE OF 3

In extreme conditions you cannot survive for more than...

3 minutes without oxygen
3 hours without shelter
3 days without water
3 weeks without food

	A	B	C
Who?			
Where?			
How long?			

B
Feb 19th 2012

MAN SURVIVES 2 MONTHS IN SNOW-COVERED CAR

Doctors treating a Swedish man who survived two months in a snow-covered car, say he is awake and able to communicate. But they are stunned he is alive at all. Peter Skyllberg, 44, was found by passersby near the northeastern town of Umeå. They thought his vehicle was an abandoned, crashed car, and dug down through about three feet of snow. To their surprise, they found Skyllberg lying on the back seat. He could barely move or speak. His car had broken down on December 19th and during the time he was trapped, temperatures dropped to -22°F. He only ate snow and kept inside his warm clothes and sleeping bag. Doctors believe the only reason Skyllberg survived against all odds was because his car formed a natural igloo. This kept his body temperature high enough to survive.

A
September 16th 2011

HIKER CRAWLS THROUGH DESERT WITH BROKEN LEG FOR 4 DAYS

Amos Richards, 64, was rescued on Monday after spending four days crawling through the Utah Desert with a broken leg. Richards was camping in Canyonlands National Park and went for a day hike in Little Blue John Canyon, an area that is about a five-hour drive from the national park. While he was climbing, he fell and broke his leg in several places. With no one around to help him and no one knowing his location, he was forced to drag his body through the desert. He had no warm clothing for the cold nights nor a map, and only 10 pints of water and two power bars. Richards tried to follow his footprints back to his car and managed to cover 5 miles before he was found. Luckily, the national park rangers sent out search parties when they discovered his abandoned campsite. A helicopter took him to Moab Regional Hospital where he's expected to recover very soon.

C
January 4th 2005

TSUNAMI SURVIVOR FOUND OUT AT SEA

It has been over a week since the catastrophic tsunami in the Indian Ocean, but rescue teams are still finding survivors. An Indonesian man, Rizal Shahputra, 23, was found yesterday floating on a tree branch 100 miles off the coast. When the tsunami struck on December 26th, he was working on a building site in Banda Aceh on the northern tip of Sumatra. He was swept out to sea along with several others, but, one by one, they drowned. Rizal survived by eating floating coconuts and drinking rainwater. At least one ship passed by but didn't notice Rizal who was waving frantically. Eventually, a Japanese ship spotted him and took him to Port Klang in Malaysia.

D. Read the newspaper clippings again and the statements below. Which clipping do they refer to? Write A, B or C.

1. He had supplies with him. ☐
2. He survived a natural disaster. ☐
3. He was discovered by accident. ☐ ☐
4. He had appropriate clothes with him. ☐
5. In the beginning, he wasn't alone. ☐
6. He was injured. ☐
7. He was lucky to find food. ☐
8. He tried to signal for help, but it didn't work. ☐

E. Look at the highlighted words in the texts and match them with their meanings.

1. crawl ☐
2. ranger ☐
3. recover ☐
4. stunned ☐
5. passersby ☐

6. abandoned ☐
7. strike ☐
8. drown ☐
9. spot ☐

a. to die from being underwater and unable to breathe

b. people who are walking past sb./sth. by chance

c. a person whose job is to look after a park or forest

d. to happen suddenly and cause harm or damage

e. extremely surprised or shocked

f. to notice sb./sth. especially when it is not easy to do so

g. left by the people who owned or used it

h. to move on hands and knees

i. to get better after an illness, accident, shock, etc.

F. Discuss.

• Which of the three situations do you think would be the most difficult to survive in?

• Have you heard of any other survival stories?

Vocabulary

Complete the sentences with the correct form of the words in the boxes. In some cases, there may be more than one answer.

| harm   hurt   injure |

1. I was skiing all day and now my knees _____.

2. Pollution can _____ our health.

3. Only two people were seriously _____ in the accident.

| damage   destroy   ruin |

4. The bad weather _____ our plans to go on a picnic in the countryside.

5. Several buildings were completely _____ by the fire.

6. Don't put that hot pot on the table. You'll _____ the surface.

| carry   pull   drag |

7. We couldn't lift the bookcase, so we _____ it to the other side of the room.

8. A complete stranger helped me _____ the shopping bags to my car.

9. The scuba diver _____ the rope to show that he wanted to go back up to the surface.

Grammar Past Simple, used to → p. 147

A. Read the examples and answer the questions.

> They **thought** his vehicle **was** an abandoned, crashed car.
>
> He **could** barely move or speak.
>
> At least one ship **passed** by but **didn't notice** Rizal.

1. How do we form the Past Simple of regular and irregular verbs?

2. Which verb do we use to form the negative and question forms?

3. What's the Past Simple of the verbs *be* and *can*?

4. What kind of actions does the Past Simple describe?

B. Read the examples below. Do they mean the same thing? In which cases can we use either the Past Simple or *used to*?

> I **went** rock climbing a lot when I was younger.
>
> I **used to go** rock climbing a lot when I was younger.

C. Complete the dialogues with the Past Simple of the verbs in parentheses. Use *used to* where possible.

1. **A:** 1 _____ (you / know) that Mark 2 _____ (go) hiking every weekend before he 3 _____ (move) to the city?

   B: Yes. Don't tell me that you 4 _____ (not know) that!

2. **A:** I 5 _____ (not mind) driving in extreme weather conditions before I 6 _____ (have) the accident. Now, I never drive if the weather is bad.

   B: Good for you.

3. **A:** 7 _____ (your uncle / live) in an igloo when he 8 _____ (be) in Alaska?

   B: Don't be silly. Inuits don't live in igloos. My uncle 9 _____ (stay) in an igloo for a couple of days during his hunting trips.

   A: Wow! It sounds like a great experience.

   B: It is. When I 10 _____ (visit) him last winter, we 11 _____ (go) hunting together once and we 12 _____ (spend) a night in an igloo. It 13 _____ (be) awesome!

Vocabulary

A. Read through the groups of weather words in the table below and label them using the words in the box.

SUN	RAIN	STORM
TEMPERATURE	CLOUD	WIND

mild chilly freezing boiling	shine clear skies	shower drizzle pour wet

blow breeze	foggy overcast dull	thunder lightning blizzard

B. Circle the correct words.

1. You don't need an umbrella. It's only **pouring / drizzling**.

2. It will be **overcast / mild** all day tomorrow without any sunshine, and with the possibility of showers in the afternoon.

3. We were sitting outside and a light **blizzard / breeze** was blowing. It was very pleasant.

4. There was a violent storm during the night and lots of trees were struck by **lightning / thunder**.

5. Winters here are usually mild, but you sometimes get some **boiling / freezing** cold days in January.

C. Discuss.

- What different types of weather do you have in your country?
- What's the weather like today?
- Is it normal for this time of year?
- What's your favorite type of weather?
- What's the worst weather you've ever experienced? Where were you? What did you do?

Grammar Past Progressive, Past Simple vs. Past Progressive → p. 147

A. Read the examples and notice the words in blue. Then match them with the rules about the uses of the Past Progressive a-c.

1. The men **were working** on a building site when the tsunami struck. ☐

2. I **was holding** the ropes while my friend **was climbing**. ☐

3. It **was pouring** and we couldn't find shelter. ☐

The Past Progressive is used:

a. to give background information

b. for an action in progress in the past which was interrupted by another action

c. for actions that were happening at the same time in the past

B. Read the examples and answer the questions.

a. Richards **was climbing** when he **fell**.

b. When the rescue team **found** Richards, they **took** him to the hospital.

1. In which example did the two actions happen one after the other?

2. In which example did one action happen while another action was in progress?

C. Complete the text with the Past Simple or the Past Progressive of the verbs in parentheses.

Last weekend, I 1 _____ (go) hiking with my friend Janice. As we 2 _____ (walk) near some cliffs, I 3 _____ (hear) someone calling for help. We 4 _____ (look) down and 5 _____ (see) a man at the bottom. His leg was injured. Janice immediately 6 _____ (call) for help. While she 7 _____ (talk) on the phone, I 8 _____ (try) to find something like a branch so I 9 _____ (can) pull the man up. While I 10 _____ (look) around, I 11 _____ (slip) on some loose rocks. Luckily, I 12 _____ (not fall) all the way down and my friend 13 _____ (help) me up. A rescue team 14 _____ (arrive) quickly and 15 _____ (save) the man.

Listening 🔊

A. Listen to a radio interview and choose the correct newspaper headline.

TWO MEN DISCOVER CRASHED PLANE IN JUNGLE

JUNGLE PLANE CRASH SURVIVOR DISCOVERED

NO SURVIVORS AFTER JUNGLE PLANE CRASH

B. Listen again and answer the questions.

1. Where did the plane crash?
   a. In Peru.
   b. In Brazil.
   c. In Bolivia.

2. Why did the plane crash?
   a. There was engine trouble.
   b. The plane was struck by lightning.
   c. The pilot couldn't see in the storm.

3. What was the first thing Conrad found?
   a. Other survivors.
   b. A river.
   c. The plane.

4. Who found Conrad?
   a. A rescue helicopter.
   b. Two fishermen.
   c. A man from a village.

5. How many people initially survived the plane crash?
   a. 9
   b. 89
   c. 1

6. How does Conrad feel about going back to the crash site?
   a. He's excited.
   b. He's terrified.
   c. He doesn't really want to.

Intonation 🔊

A. Listen to the following extract from the listening activity above and underline the words that the speaker stresses. Why do you think he does this?

"Three years ago tomorrow, a young man survived an airplane crash and then lived ten days in the jungle before he was rescued."

> We stress words in a sentence usually when we want to emphasize, compare, correct or clarify something. The words we stress are important to understanding and bring out the meaning of the sentence.

B. Read the sentences below. Which words would you stress? Listen and compare your answers.

1. I was driving through a terrible storm.

2. We didn't go swimming because the water was freezing.

3. Twenty houses were completely destroyed in the earthquake.

4. We were walking through the forest for three hours.

5. The accident happened on Bell Avenue, not on Chrysler Avenue.

Speaking Role play

A. Read the news article below and talk in pairs.

BUS CRASHES INTO STORE WINDOW

Kingston residents waiting at a bus stop on Market Road yesterday morning were shocked to see a bus slide right past them on the icy road and crash into a bookstore just a few feet away. Fortunately, there were no bystanders on the sidewalk and the store had not opened yet. However, the bus overturned and landed on its side, blocking all the doors of the bus. Emergency services were quick to come and get all the passengers out safely through the windows. Luckily, very few were injured and only two of them seriously. According to the weather forecast, more icy weather is expected.

Student A: Imagine that you are a reporter. Interview Student B, an eyewitness, about the accident. Use the prompts below and keep notes.

> Where / you / be / and / what / you / do?
> What / weather / be / like?
> What / exactly / happen?
> What / you / think / when / first / see / accident?
> How / people / rescue?
> What / you / think / cause / accident?

Student B: Imagine that you were an eyewitness to the accident. Student A is a reporter. Answer his/her questions using the information in the news article, your imagination and some of the words/phrases in the box.

| snowstorm | skid | lose control | panic |
| helpless | break windows | ambulance |

B. Report what happened to the class.

> When reporting an incident, be sure to use the facts as well as your own wording. Also, try to report the events in chronological order so that it is easy for others to understand. **TIP**

Reading 🔊

A. Discuss.

- What car or motorcycle races do you know of?
- Do you find them adventurous or dangerous? Why?
- Look at the poster and picture below. What do you know or can you guess about this race?

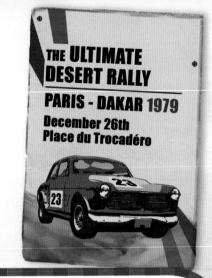

THE **ULTIMATE DESERT RALLY**
PARIS - DAKAR 1979
December 26th
Place du Trocadéro

B. Read the text quickly. Which of the following topics are discussed?

1. The most well-known riders and drivers.
2. The companies involved.
3. Who can take part.
4. What competitors have to endure.
5. The location of the race.
6. The risks involved.
7. The future of the Dakar Rally.
8. How it all started.

TheDakarRally

or simply The Dakar is the ultimate off-road race that combines adrenaline thrills and endurance skills in an event that takes place in the breathtaking landscape of the world's most impressive deserts. Riders and drivers of motorcycles, quads, cars and trucks from all over the world take part in an annual race that tests their endurance and racing abilities.

This exciting challenge was the idea of the motorcycle racer, Thierry Sabine, in 1977. He was competing in a race when he got lost in the Ténéré Desert and suddenly realized that it would make the perfect location for a rally. He made his dream a reality a year later, in December 1978. He is considered the founder and main organizer of the Paris-Dakar, a race starting in Europe and finishing in Africa.

For almost thirty years, competitors raced across the two continents, covering thousands of miles. Most of the events were from Paris, France to Dakar, Senegal with the routes often changing. However, in 2008, the race was canceled due to security reasons. Since then, it has been taking place in South America and more specifically in Argentina, Peru, Chile and Bolivia. The name of the race has remained the same.

The Dakar Rally is not a conventional rally, but an off-road race for professionals as well as amateurs. Riders and drivers have to cross tough terrain such as sand dunes, mud, rocks, etc. and may have to cover distances of up to 500-560 miles per day during the 15-day challenge. It is an extraordinary experience; both a race and a test of skills and endurance. For participants, reaching the finish line is the challenge of a lifetime.

Unfortunately, this long-distance race is an adventure which has also proven to be dangerous. According to some, it is one of the most dangerous motorsports on Earth. There have been quite a few fatal accidents, the majority of which involved motorcyclists. Security measures are taken even for spectators, as many unfortunate incidents have occurred throughout the years.

The Dakar Rally continues to attract millions of people from all over the world. It brings together about fifty nationalities each year; people who share the same enthusiasm for racing.

C. Read again and write T for True or F for False.

1. The first race Thierry Sabine organized was in 1977. ☐
2. The Dakar Rally doesn't necessarily have the same route every year. ☐
3. The 2008 race took place in South America. ☐
4. The name of the race changed when it moved to South America. ☐
5. You don't have to be a professional to take part in the Dakar Rally. ☐
6. Competitors have to travel about 500 miles a day. ☐
7. The race lasts just over a week. ☐
8. For many competitors winning is not very important. ☐
9. Quite a few motorcycle racers have died in the Dakar Rally. ☐

D. Look at the highlighted words in the text and match them with their meanings.

1. combine ☐   5. amateur ☐
2. founder ☐   6. terrain ☐
3. competitor ☐   7. fatal ☐
4. conventional ☐   8. incident ☐

a. causing death
b. an event, especially one that is unpleasant or unusual
c. join together
d. an area of land, when considering its natural features
e. sb. who starts a business, organization, etc.
f. sb. who takes part in a competition
g. sb. who is not a professional
h. usual, traditional

> **TIP**
>
> When trying to guess the meaning of an unknown word, always look for clues in the context (the words before and after it as well as the previous and following sentences). Also look for clues in the word itself. See if it is similar to any other words that you know and try to analyze it into its parts – root, ending, prefix, suffix. Then try to determine:
> • what part of speech it is (verb, noun, adjective, etc.)
> • if it has a positive, negative or neutral meaning.
> • what general topic it is related to.
> • what it means approximately.

E. Discuss.

• Would you ever participate in an endurance race?
• Would you like to be a spectator at the Dakar Rally? Why? / Why not?

Vocabulary

A. The nouns *racer, competitor, motorcyclist* and *participant* appear in the text in the reading activity. Which words do they come from? Can you find more nouns referring to people in the text?

> Many nouns that refer to people are formed by adding a suffix (-er, -or, -ist, -ant, etc.) to nouns or verbs.

B. Complete the table with nouns that refer to people. Use the words in the box and a suitable suffix. Make any necessary changes.

cycle	instruct	contest	survive	final	lose
journal	train	attend	lead	edit	assist

-er	-or	-ist	-ant

Listening 🔊

You are going to listen to a live radio report of the final stage of a cycling endurance race in three parts. The first part is before the race, the second one is during the race and the third one is after the race. Listen to each part and answer the questions that follow.

Before the race

1. How many miles do competitors have to cover on the last day of the race?
   a. 10
   b. 80
   c. 800

2. Why couldn't Alex take part in the Extreme Bicycle Race last year?
   a. He was in a race in Australia.
   b. He didn't have time to train for it.
   c. He was injured.

During the race

3. What is true about Michael Phillips?
   a. He is an amateur cyclist.
   b. He is a doctor.
   c. He is a professional cyclist.

4. Who has won the race?
   a. Daniel Kent.
   b. Michael Phillips.
   c. Alex Tyler.

> **TIP**
>
> • Read the options quickly before you hear each part.
> • Don't work on a question when the next part is being spoken.

After the race

5. How many cycling races has the winner won?
   a. 3
   b. 4
   c. 5

6. What is he going to do in the future?
   a. Train for the Tour de France.
   b. Become a cycling trainer.
   c. Take part in more competitions.

Speaking

A. Talk in pairs.

Student A: Imagine you found yourself in a dangerous situation and luckily you managed to survive. Tell Student B about your experience, explaining what happened, what you did and how you felt. Answer any questions he/she may have. Use some of the words/phrases in the box.

hiking	bear	chase	shake with fear	slip
hang off	hold on	edge	cliff	terrified	panic
shout	be in luck	rescue	pull up	relieved

Student B: You see your friend (Student A) who doesn't look very well. Ask him/her what is wrong, listen to him/her carefully and respond appropriately. Ask questions to find out more about his/her unfortunate experience. Use some of the phrases in the box.

Responding to bad news and showing concern

How awful/unlucky!
Really? That's terrible!
What? Are you serious?
Oh my!
Poor you!
That's so scary!
What a frightening experience!
You're joking/kidding, right?
And then what? Didn't you...?
Don't tell me you...?
Are you all right?
Is everything OK?
Is there anything I can do to help?
You aren't hurt, are you?
Don't worry. It's over.

TIP

In conversation, it is important for the listener to respond to what the speaker is saying by showing interest, surprise, concern, sympathy, etc. You can respond by:

- making exclamations (*How awful!, Poor you!, That's so scary!*).
- asking different types of questions (*Is there anything I can do?, Who rescued you?*) as well as negative questions (*Wasn't anyone with you?*) and tag questions (*You aren't hurt, are you?*).

66 *What's up with you? You don't look very well.*
   You won't believe what happened to me yesterday. As I was hiking in the woods...
What? Are you serious?
   Yeah, I'm still in shock! 99

B. Discuss.

- What's the most dangerous or unusual situation you have ever been in?
- How did you react?
- How did you feel?

MENU   ∧   ∨   CANCEL

Writing A story (I)

A. Read the writing task and the story that follows and answer the questions.

An international magazine has organized a short story competition and you have decided to enter. The competition rules say that the story must begin with the following sentence:

Paul and Frank looked around and wondered where they were.

Paul and Frank looked around and wondered where they were. They got out of their car into the thick fog. They were in the middle of nowhere without any gas or signal on their cell phones. It was freezing and getting darker. They felt helpless!

They decided to search for a gas station or a house nearby. Unfortunately, as they were walking, Paul tripped over a branch and sprained his ankle. As soon as he tried to walk on it, he realized it was impossible. Frank had no choice. He had to carry him.

After a while, Frank stopped. "I'm exhausted!" he said. So, they decided to light a fire and camp in the forest for the night. Paul fell asleep immediately. His ankle was swollen and was hurting him a lot. Suddenly, Frank heard something. He was scared stiff. A moment later, he saw flashes of light coming towards them. He was so relieved when he saw a forest ranger.

The ranger took them to the nearest medical center where a doctor bandaged up Paul's ankle. "What were you doing out in that fog?" the ranger asked. "You're lucky I found you!" Yes, they had been lucky.

1. Has the writer begun the story appropriately?
2. What tenses does the writer use throughout the story?
3. Why does the writer use the highlighted words/ phrases?
4. Why does the writer use Direct Speech in the story?

B. Read the note. Then use the words/phrases in parentheses to link the sentences given.

Use time linkers to indicate the sequence of events:
when, while, as, as soon as, before, after, after that, after a while, at first, in the beginning, during, soon, later, then, at that moment, a moment later, just as, till/until, immediately, finally, in the end, etc.

---

1. Amanda thought there was someone in the house. She realized it was her cat.　　(at first, but then)

_____

2. The swimmer was waving for help for a long time. Somebody saw him.　　　　　　　　(and, finally)

_____

3. I was driving to work. I had an accident.　　(while)

_____

4. The athlete crossed the finish line. He began feeling dizzy.　　　　　　　　　　　　　　(when)

_____

5. Ann saw help coming. She started crying. (as soon as)

_____

6. Mark saw the bear running towards him. He knew what to do.　　　　　　　(when, immediately)

_____

C. Read the writing task below and complete the outline for the story.

An international magazine has organized a short story competition and you have decided to enter. The competition rules say that the story must begin with the following sentence:
Tina thought it would be a typical Monday morning, but she was wrong.

INTRODUCTION
How must you begin your story?
_____
Where was Tina?
_____
What was the place/weather/etc. like?
_____
Was anyone with Tina? Who?
_____

MAIN PART
What was Tina expecting that Monday morning to be like?
_____
What was it like? / What happened?
_____
What did Tina (and the other people involved) do/see/hear/say?
_____
How did Tina (and the other people involved) feel?
_____

CONCLUSION
What happened in the end?
_____
How did Tina feel afterwards?
_____

D. Read the TIP below and the plan on page 133. Then use your ideas from the outline above and write the story.

TIP

When writing a story:
- always keep the given sentence in mind and plan your story around it. Do not change the given sentence.
- use past tenses (Past Simple, Past Progressive, Past Perfect).
- use linking words/phrases to indicate the sequence of events (see activity B).
- use Direct Speech, to make a situation seem real.
- use questions or exclamation marks, to make the story more exciting.
- use expressions/phrases like:
I couldn't believe my eyes/ears!
(Un)luckily...
(Un)fortunately...
All of a sudden/Suddenly...
To my surprise...
I was in luck/shock.
It was a real shock.

A. Choose a, b or c.

1. I fell down the stairway and I ____ my ankle.
   a. injured   b. harmed   c. damaged

2. There is a ____ of rain, so don't forget your umbrella.
   a. reality   b. majority   c. possibility

3. After searching for a while, we found ____ in a cave.
   a. landscape   b. challenge   c. shelter

4. The ____ cheered the bicycle racer on, as he passed by.
   a. spectators   b. participants   c. competitors

5. The sky was ____ and it began to drizzle.
   a. wet   b. overcast   c. clear

6. The temperature ____ ten degrees today.
   a. dropped   b. dragged   c. drowned

7. After a week in the hospital, George had ____ from his illness.
   a. recovered   b. remained   c. treated

8. It's ____ hot outside today, so we should go to the beach.
   a. mild   b. freezing   c. boiling

B. Complete the sentences with the words in the box.

> ranger amateur chilly spotted
> annual relieved landed

1. It's kind of _____ tonight so you should put on a coat before you go out.

2. I was _____ to see that John was safe in the end.

3. Peter won a photography competition and he's only a(n) _____ photographer.

4. We would like to thank everyone who participated in Covington's 15th _____ Bicycle Ride.

5. As we were walking, we _____ a bear in the distance.

6. The airplane _____ at the nearest airport due to an engine problem.

7. The park _____ told us not to light a fire.

C. Complete the dialogues with the Past Simple of the verbs in parentheses. Use *used to* where possible.

1. A: When I _____ (be) younger, I _____ (play) basketball on the school team.
   B: Really? I _____ (not know) that! I never _____ (like) basketball that much.

2. A: I _____ (camp) with my friends on this beach every summer.
   B: That's nice. I _____ (not go) to the beach very often, because it _____ (be) pretty far from where I _____ (live).

3. A: _____ you _____ (participate) in the marathon that _____ (take) place last weekend?
   B: Yes and I also _____ (manage) to reach the finish line!

D. Complete the sentences with the Past Simple or the Past Progressive of the verbs in parentheses.

1. The police officer _____ (stop) me because I _____ (talk) on my cell phone while I _____ (drive).

2. The baby _____ (crawl) on the floor while Mary _____ (cook) in the kitchen.

3. The car _____ (hit) the side of the bridge and immediately _____ (overturn).

4. We _____ (try) to find our way through the fog when we _____ (hear) someone calling for help.

5. As soon as the ambulance _____ (arrive), the paramedics _____ (take) care of the injured.

E. Put the dialogue in order. Write 1-8.

☐ Tom, what are all those scratches on your arm?
☐ Poor thing? I'm the one with all the scratches!
☐ A cat attacked me.
☐ Yeah. It was stuck in a tree and I climbed up to save it.
☐ What? Are you serious?
☐ You're right. But why did it scratch you? Didn't it want to get down?
☐ The poor thing!
☐ I think it was scared. That's why it started scratching me.

Self-assessment
Read the following and check the appropriate boxes. For the points you are unsure of, refer back to the relevant sections in the module.

NOW I CAN...
- locate important facts in newspaper clippings ☐
- talk about past events and habits ☐
- describe weather conditions ☐
- emphasize important facts when speaking ☐
- narrate past events/experiences ☐
- report incidents ☐
- use suffixes to form nouns that refer to people ☐
- respond to bad news and show concern ☐
- use time linkers ☐
- write a story ☐

Task 1&2 p. 127

Discuss:
- Look at the map and match the cities below with the countries.

  Casablanca Warsaw Shanghai

  Acapulco Doha Lima

- Which of them are capital cities?
- Where would you like to travel in the world? Why?
- What does the phrase below mean? Do you agree with it?

  Travel broadens the mind.

China

Qatar

Poland

Morocco

Peru

Mexico

In this module you will learn...

- to talk about vacations and traveling experiences

- to use appropriate tenses to link the past with the present

- to distinguish between words easily confused

- to form nouns (ending in *-ion*, *-ation* and *-ment*) from verbs

- to compare and contrast people and situations

- to express preference and make suggestions

- to use descriptive language

- to write an article describing a place

Reading 🔊

A. Discuss.
- Have you ever read any books or seen any movies featuring trips around the world?
- What modes of transportation were used?

B. Read the text quickly and choose the most appropriate title a, b or c.

a. The history of round-the-world trips

b. Discovering new places around the world

c. How people travel around the world

Ever since the first explorers circled the globe, more and more people have tried to do the same. Using a variety of modes of transportation, many brave globetrotters have succeeded in doing so, despite the difficulties and risks involved.

The first successful expedition to sail around the world was led by the Portuguese explorer Ferdinand Magellan. Magellan and his crew began a journey across the Atlantic, around South America and into an ocean which was unfamiliar at the time, the Pacific. The expedition took three years, from 1519 to 1522, but unfortunately Magellan himself did not complete the entire voyage, as he died during a battle in the Philippines. This incredible achievement proved that the Earth is round and also provided us with a name for the Pacific Ocean, which Magellan described as peaceful (pacific) when he first saw it.

American adventurer and writer Joshua Slocum was the first person to sail around the globe alone. He set sail from Boston in 1895 and returned more than three years later. The book he published of his experience *Sailing Alone Around the World* has become a classic in travel literature. Modern developments in sailboats have made it possible to sail around the world much faster. Francis Joyon, a French sailor and sailboat racer, currently holds the record for the fastest solo trip which took him just over 57 days in 2008.

Perhaps a more remarkable achievement is that of Laura Dekker from the Netherlands, who, at 16, became the youngest person to sail around the world on her own. Her attempt began in August 2010 and was successfully completed after 518 days in January 2012.

Sailing, however, is not the only way that people have chosen to travel. American globetrotter Dave Kunst managed the journey on foot between 1970 and 1974. He covered 14,450 miles and wore out 21 pairs of shoes. Others have attempted the journey by bicycle. Thomas Stevens from England was the first to succeed. He circled the globe from April 1884 till December 1886 on a penny-farthing.

In recent years, people have been attempting stranger ideas, like hitchhiking around the world or using social media to help them travel. In 2009, Paul Smith from the U.K. set himself a challenge: to travel as far as he could in 30 days using only Twitter. The rules were that he couldn't spend any money on travel or accommodations, and could only accept offers from his Twitter followers. The "Twitchiker" managed to travel to New Zealand, on the other side of the world. Since then, he has been writing travel articles in newspapers and has also been giving presentations on the benefits of social media. As for the future of round-the-world trips, only time will tell.

C. Read again and write T for True, F for False or NM for Not Mentioned.

1. It took Magellan and his crew 3 years to cross the Pacific. ☐
2. The Pacific Ocean is named after an explorer. ☐
3. Joshua Slocum managed to sail around the world by himself in less than three years. ☐
4. Joshua Slocum became famous from his book *Sailing Alone Around the World*. ☐
5. Francis Joyon is the youngest person to sail around the world. ☐
6. Dave Kunst walked around the globe. ☐
7. Thomas Stevens started his journey from England. ☐
8. Paul Smith managed to travel around the world in 30 days. ☐

D. Look at the highlighted words in the text and match them with their meanings.

1. brave ☐
2. complete (v.) ☐
3. achievement ☐
4. sailor ☐
5. solo ☐
6. remarkable ☐
7. wear out ☐
8. attempt (v.) ☐

a. a person who works on a boat or sails a boat

b. to try to do sth. difficult or dangerous

c. unusual or surprising

d. facing difficult or dangerous situations without showing fear, but courage

e. to use sth. so much that it can no longer be used

f. to finish doing sth.

g. done alone

h. sth. important that sb. has done successfully

E. Discuss.

• Would you like to go on a trip around the world? Why?/Why not?

• If yes, how would you travel?

Vocabulary

Complete the sentences with the correct form of the words in the boxes.

trip	voyage	cruise	journey	flight

1. Captain James Cook made three important _____ to the Pacific Ocean.

2. Their dream vacation is going on a _____ around the Mediterranean.

3. The _____ to Moscow was delayed so we had to wait for three hours at the airport doing nothing.

4. Mark is away on a business _____ in Kuala Lumpur, Malaysia.

5. The _____ through the mountains was long and exhausting.

tour	expedition	excursion

6. The _____ through the jungle was more difficult than the explorers expected.

7. My family and I went on an all-day _____ to the beach.

8. As soon as Jake and Lisa arrived in Paris, they went on a(n) _____ of the city.

Grammar Present Perfect Simple vs. Past Simple, Present Perfect Simple - Present Perfect Progressive → p. 147

A. Read the examples. What's the difference between *has entered* and *entered*?

> My uncle **has entered** many sailboat races.
> My uncle **entered** a sailboat race in 2013 and won.

B. Read the examples and answer the questions.

> Modern developments in sailboats **have made** it possible to sail around the world much faster.

1. What is important, the result of the action or the time of the action? Which tense is used?

> Ever since the first explorers circled the globe, more and more people **have tried** to do the same.

2. Are people still trying to do the same? Which tense is used?

> Since he completed his project, he **has been writing** travel articles in newspapers.

3. Has he stopped writing articles? Which tense is used?

C. Complete the rules by circling the correct words.

• Use the **Present Perfect Simple / Past Simple** for an action which happened in the past, but the exact time is not mentioned.

• Use the **Present Perfect Simple / Present Perfect Progressive** for an action or state which started in the past and continues up to the present (emphasis on the action).

• Use the **Present Perfect Simple / Present Perfect Progressive** for an action or state which started in the past and continues up to the present (emphasis on the duration).

D. Complete with the Present Perfect Simple, the Present Perfect Progressive or the Past Simple of the verbs in parentheses.

I 1 _____ (always / like) traveling and experiencing new things, which is why, two months ago, I 2 _____ (decide) to try something different. For the past five years, Mark, a friend of mine, 3 _____ (travel) to different countries while working at the same time. So far, he 4 _____ (visit) ten different countries, including countries like Finland and Argentina. I 5 _____ (choose) to go to New Zealand. I 6 _____ (work) here for two months now and I feel like it's a unique way to learn about a different culture without spending a lot of money. I'm working on a horse farm and I 7 _____ (learn) how to take care of horses as well as how to ride a horse, of course! I 8 _____ (never / live) on a farm before, so this experience 9 _____ (be) very educational for me. For the past few days, I 10 _____ (think) about where to go next year. I think that South America sounds pretty interesting!

Vocabulary

A. Find nouns in the text in the reading activity which derive from the verbs below. Which suffixes are added to the verbs?

accommodate _____

transport _____

present _____

achieve _____

develop _____

> Many nouns are formed by adding a suffix such as *-ion*, *-ation* and *-ment* to a verb. Pay attention to spelling irregularities:
>
> decide – decision   describe – description
> introduce – introduction   explain – explanation

B. Complete with the correct form of the words in capitals.

1. I've noticed a great _____ in your work.   **IMPROVE**

2. There were many flight _____ due to extreme weather conditions.   **CANCEL**

3. I'm having problems with my Internet _____. Who should I call?   **CONNECT**

4. The lecture I attended was on space _____.   **EXPLORE**

5. I want to put an _____ to sell my car in the local paper.   **ADVERTISE**

6. Please call the restaurant and make a _____ for tonight.   **RESERVE**

7. I would like to make an important _____. Jane and I are getting married.   **ANNOUNCE**

8. Please complete the _____ form and send it to us by next Monday at the latest.   **APPLY**

Grammar Adjectives, Adverbs of Manner, Comparisons → *p. 148*

A. Read the examples below. Which of the words in blue is an adjective and describes a noun and which is an adverb of manner and describes how something happens?

> • The first **successful** expedition to sail around the world was led by the Portuguese explorer Ferdinand Magellan.
> • Her attempt began in August 2010 and was **successfully** completed after 518 days in January 2012.

B. Read the examples and answer the questions.

> • The journey lasted **longer than** we expected.
> • Magellan thought the Pacific Ocean was **more peaceful than** the Atlantic Ocean.
> • Laura Dekker is **the youngest** person to sail around the world on her own.
> • **The most difficult** part of the trip was when we ran out of water.

1. How are the comparatives and superlatives of one-syllable adjectives and adverbs formed?

2. How are the comparatives and superlatives of multi-syllable adjectives and adverbs formed?

3. Which form is used to compare two people, things or actions?

4. Which form is used to compare one person, thing or action with several of the same kind?

C. Read the examples and answer the questions. Choose a, b or c.

> • In my opinion, traveling by train is **as tiring as** traveling by car.
> • It was raining this morning but now the weather is getting **better and better**.

1. What does **as... as...** mean?
   a. more than
   b. less than
   c. the same as

2. What does **better and better** indicate?
   a. a continual change
   b. a comparison between two actions
   c. the result of an action

D. Complete with the correct form of the adjectives or adverbs in parentheses. Add *the* and *as* where necessary.

Would you like to travel the world without leaving the comfort of your home? Vacations are becoming 1 _____ and _____ (expensive); that's why some people are choosing virtual traveling. All you need is a computer and an Internet connection. Virtual tours consist of videos, panoramic photos, sounds and descriptions of some of 2 _____ (popular) destinations in the world. Virtual traveling is 3 _____ (cheap) than a regular vacation and you can travel to other countries 4 _____ (quickly) than flying by plane. Just a few clicks and you're visiting the Eiffel Tower or the Taj Mahal. However, lots of people strongly disagree with the idea of virtual traveling. They believe that nothing is 5 _____ (good) than or 6 _____ (exciting) as the experience of actually visiting a place.

Listening 🔊

You will hear people talking in six different situations. For questions 1-6, choose the best answer a, b or c.

1. On which date did the woman book her flight?
   a. March 14th
   b. March 15th
   c. March 16th

2. What time will the two men take the train on Saturday?
   a. 4:45
   b. 5:30
   c. 7:00

3. According to the announcement, which of the following is true?
   a. The train is coming from Chicago.
   b. The train is arriving at platform 1.
   c. The train is arriving at 2:45.

4. What are the two friends going to do today?
   a. rent bicycles
   b. go on a bus tour
   c. go shopping

5. What is the man's problem?
   a. He doesn't have travel insurance.
   b. He didn't prepare his presentation.
   c. His luggage got lost.

6. What is the man trying to do?
   a. cancel his reservation
   b. make a second reservation
   c. confirm his reservation

TIP
- Read the questions and options carefully before you hear each extract.
- Listen to the extracts carefully. Don't try to understand every single word or phrase; focus on the whole message.
- Choose the option which best answers the question. Don't choose an option just because words or phrases included in the extract appear in it.

Speaking

A. Discuss.
- Where do you usually go on vacation?
- What type of vacation do you usually go on?
- What type of accommodations do you usually choose?
- What type of vacation have you never tried but would like to? Why?

B. Talk in groups. Look at the pictures showing three different types of vacation. Compare them and discuss the questions. You can use the words/phrases in the boxes.

safari

camping

cruise

- What are the advantages and disadvantages of each vacation?
- What kind of people do you think prefer to go on each vacation?
- Which vacation would you prefer to go on?

exotic destinations   wildlife   scenery   explore nature
dangerous   safe   adventurous   relaxing   exhausting
convenient   comfortable   boring   exciting
environmentally friendly   (in)expensive   luxurious
organized   guided tour   supplies   equipment
campground   on board   stress-free

When going camping / on a safari / on a cruise,...
One of the best/worst things about... is that...
The main advantage/disadvantage of... is...
Another advantage/disadvantage is...
In my opinion, ... is better/worse than...
I agree, but... isn't as... as...
I think that... are ideal for...
Personally, I believe that more and more people are choosing...
I'd really like to go...
I'd prefer to go...

Reading 🔊

A. Discuss.

- Do you download apps for your cell phone or tablet?
- What sort of apps do you use?
- What is the most useful app you know of?

B. Read the information about the five people below. Match each person with one of the apps on the right that you think would suit him/her the most. Write a-h. There are three extra apps which you do not need to use.

TIP

First read the descriptions of the people carefully. Then scan each text and look for the specific information mentioned in each of the descriptions.

1 ☐

Wendy is studying to be a reporter and travels abroad frequently to find topics to write about. She enjoys keeping a digital record of her experiences.

2 ☐

Roger takes a lot of domestic flights because of his job. His company pays for all his travel expenses but he prefers to use public transportation to get around and rarely takes a cab or rents a car. It's important for him to arrive on time for meetings.

3 ☐

Jessica loves traveling and whenever she can afford to, she books a trip. She has traveled to lots of cities and is now looking for more unusual places to visit. Since she's unemployed at the moment, she has no time restrictions. Anytime she comes across a bargain, she can take it.

4 ☐

John has been reading about other cultures for years, but finds traveling a hassle. The only times he has traveled abroad was to stay with friends. He really enjoyed this because he felt safe and relaxed. He would like to start seeing the world on his own, but feels anxious about it.

5 ☐

Natasha used to be a tour guide. She loves going abroad with her family, but it can be a struggle as she has four children. Just trying to remember everything each of them needs and packing it all makes her exhausted! As a result, she often has a lot of anxiety before a trip but once she's away, she has a great time.

appmarket

🔍 [   ] **search**

| Home | New | Games | Apps | About us | Portfolios | Cart | Contact |

New > Apps > Editor's Collection

SkyFinder

You can always count on SkyFinder to find the right flight for you. Compare flight prices and then book directly with the airline through the app. Flexible when you fly? This app has unique search tools to find the best prices over a month. It is available in 128 languages and 61 currencies, and also has a section where you can search for car rentals.

Made by *JordanB*
Released *05/14/2013*

a

$2.99

Public Trans-buddy

You will be impressed by this app. You can find information about bus routes, subways, streetcars, etc. for all major cities in the world. There are also live updates about changes in schedules or delays. It works with GPS, so it can find the nearest bus stops and stations from your location. It works both on smartphones and tablets.

Made by *Mickey*
Released *09/29/2013*

b

FREE

Rights For Flyers!

Have you ever been stuck on the tarmac for more than three hours on a domestic flight? Did you know this was illegal? Well, the new RFF app lets you know all your legal rights as a passenger. It also has a section showing arrivals and departures at most international airports. Plus, it searches for the next available flight, if yours is canceled or you missed it. An essential app for frequent flyers.

Made by *Charlie Nock*
Released *04/05/2013*

c

FREE

MyJournal

This is a handy app for keeping a journal while traveling. Through GPS you can record your location when a picture is taken. You can easily take notes, record voice messages and even videos and store them on a daily schedule. Then, you can upload your journal to social media sites to show to your friends. It's an app you simply can't do without!

Made by Vicky
Released 01/25/2013

$0.79

Local M8

Have you ever wanted to create your own personalized travel guide? Just enter your destination and how long you plan to stay and Local M8 recommends places, things to do and how to get around. It's just like staying with a local. What's more, you can share info and photos directly with social media sites. You can even access this app offline if you're somewhere without a signal.

Made by OfficeBox
Released 11/16/2012

$0.99

TaxiCall

Convenient, practical, useful! All the taxi drivers who work with TaxiCall appear on a map. With the press of a button you can book the taxi closest to you and save money on calls. What's more, you can even pick which driver you'd like! Look at the drivers' profiles and the reviews TaxiCall customers have given and choose.

Made by Black Cat
Released 02/07/2013

$1.99

B4 U go

Are you fed up with forgetting things when going on a trip? Well, this app helps you get organized, makes sure you pack everything, and creates useful "to do" lists. It also remembers previous trips and uses them as templates. Or you can choose from business, leisure, family vacation, etc. It will also remind you when to do things. If you have a trip coming up, it's an essential app to download B4 U go.

Made by Norman Colt
Released 12/12/2012

$1.99

Landmarx

With a complete list of 900 famous landmarks, this app is ideal for globetrotters. It includes information and over 650 photographs. There's an interactive world map and you also have the ability to check the landmarks you have visited. Have pictures of your own? Save them in the photo gallery. This app works with GPS so it can inform you about landmarks that are nearby. Perfect for those who want to explore the world.

Made by AppTribe
Released 06/28/2013

$4.99

C. Find words/phrases in the texts that mean the same as the following:

1. sth. that annoys you or causes problems for you (John)
2. relating to a particular country; not foreign (text c)
3. not allowed by the law (text c)
4. necessary and important (text c)
5. useful (text d)
6. not able to manage without having sth. (text d)
7. annoyed or bored with sth. that you have experienced for too long (text g)
8. to be happening soon (text g)

D. Discuss.
- Would you like to have any of these apps?
- When would you use them?

Listening 🔊

A. Listen to a conversation between two people. Which three apps did the woman download for her trip?

B. Listen again and write T for True or F for False.

1. The woman is meeting some friends in Beijing. ☐
2. The woman traveled to Moscow last year. ☐
3. The man is worried about using an app on the plane. ☐
4. The woman's app finds a restaurant that the man has been to. ☐
5. The woman was an organized person even before she downloaded the apps. ☐
6. The man already has one of the woman's apps. ☐

33

Speaking

Talk in pairs. Imagine that you and your partner are in Cairo, Egypt and have enough time to go on only one of the tours below. Discuss and decide which one, using the information you have and giving reasons. Use some of the words/ phrases in the boxes.

Giza Pyramids & Camel Ride

Tour includes:
- English-speaking tour guide
- Visit to the Step Pyramid of Zoser (the first Pyramid built)
- Drive to Memphis, the capital of ancient Egypt
- Lunch in Giza at local restaurant
- Camel ride (approximately 2 hours)
- Visit to the Great Pyramids and the Sphinx

Duration: 6 hours
Price: 60 dollars per person

Felucca Ride on the Nile & Egyptian Museum

Tour includes:
- English-speaking tour guide
- Felucca ride on the Nile (two hours): enjoy spectacular views of Cairo and buffet lunch with local dishes
- Private tour of the Egyptian Museum which has the largest collection of ancient Egyptian artifacts in the world: See the famous treasures of King Tutankhamun

Duration: 5 hours
Price: 40 dollars per person

historic   ideal   enjoyable   adventurous
impressive   educational
spectacular/magnificent/breathtaking views
unforgettable experience   great opportunity
get seasick   too tiring

Making recommendations/suggestions:
I think we should go... because...
Let's choose...
If we choose..., we can/will see/enjoy...
Why don't we...?
Why not visit...?
What/How about...?
What if we...?
We can/could... What do you say?

Agreeing/Disagreeing with a suggestion:
I agree. It'll be fun.
Yes, let's.
Why not?
(That's a) good idea!
Don't you think we'd enjoy... more?
I don't think so.
I think we'd enjoy going to... more because...

Expressing preference:
I'd prefer (not) to... because...
I'd rather (not)... because...

Writing An article describing a place

A. The following announcement was published in an international magazine. Read it and underline the key words.

Write an article for
worldsights.com!

Tell us about a sight or interesting place you have visited. Describe the place, say what attracts visitors to it and refer to any other special features of the place. The most interesting articles will be published in the next issue.

B. Read the article one visitor to worldsights.com wrote and answer the questions.

1. Which of the two titles below is more suitable? Why?
   a. Discover the Exotic Jardim Botânico
   b. The Rio de Janeiro Botanical Garden

2. What kind of information does the writer give in each paragraph?

When I travel, I like to visit places that aren't typical tourist attractions. So, when I went to Rio de Janeiro, I spent a day at the Jardim Botânico, or Botanical Garden. It was an unforgettable experience!

Originally, the Garden was a place to grow spices and was opened to the public in 1822. This large, impressive park lies at the foot of Rio's famous Corcovado Mountain. From the entrance, you walk down the magnificent Avenue of Royal Palms which is lined with 134 tall palm trees and leads into the Garden. The Garden contains more than 6,000 different species of tropical plants and trees, both Brazilian and imported. Have you ever seen a carnivorous plant? Well, I saw some really weird ones!

In the Garden you can also find about 140 species of birds. They have become used to humans and are much easier to see than in the wild. It was an amazing experience to see colorful toucans swooping over my head. I believe the highlight of the Garden, however, is the massive Victoria water lilies in the Lago Frei Leandro pond. Some are 10 feet across! It's like something out of a sci-fi movie!

If you're a nature lover, Jardim Botânico is the perfect place for you. Seeing the wonders of the Amazon jungle from up close is a once-in-a-lifetime experience. Why not plan a trip there and see for yourself?

C. When we write an article, we want to attract and keep the reader's interest. We can do that by:

1. having a title that catches the reader's attention.

2. using descriptive language, e.g. colorful adjectives.

3. addressing the reader personally.

4. asking rhetorical questions.

Find examples of these in the article and underline them.

D. Read the note. Then rewrite the sentences 1-6 using the adjectives in the box to make them more lively. There is more than one correct answer.

When describing something, think about the following:
- **sight**: color, shape, size (e.g. *green, colorful, square, round, huge, tiny*)
- **sound**: type and volume (e.g. *quiet, peaceful, noisy, loud, soft*)
- **smell**: scent and strength (e.g. *sweet, pleasant, disgusting, strong*)
- **taste**: flavor and strength (e.g. *delicious, spicy, strong, tasteless*)
- **touch**: texture and temperature (e.g. *soft, hard, cool, cold, warm, hot*)
- **emotions**: (e.g. *fascinated, impressed, excited*)
- **general opinion**: (e.g. *ideal, magnificent, luxurious, isolated*)

spectacular	peaceful	sweet-smelling
impressive	enjoyable	noisy	massive
mouth-watering	fascinating	

1. You can taste some local dishes at the market.

_____

2. The square is full of flowers and children running around.

_____

3. In the middle of this town there's a building with a tower.

_____

4. People visit this place for the view.

_____

5. I spent an afternoon walking by the river.

_____

6. Beijing is a city for anyone who is interested in Chinese culture.

_____

E. Think of an interesting place you have visited and know well and complete the outline below.

TITLE
What title are you going to give your article?

_____

INTRODUCTION
What's the name of the place?

_____

Where is it?

_____

What is the place well-known for?

_____

MAIN PART
Do you know anything about its history?

_____

Which sights/attractions are you going to describe?

_____

What do you know about them?

_____

What else can you see and do there?

_____

CONCLUSION
What is your impression of this place?

_____

Why do you think it's worth visiting?

_____

F. Read the announcement in activity A again and use your ideas from the outline above to write an article. Make sure you read the TIP below and the plan on page 134.

When writing an article describing a place, you want to catch the reader's attention and interest. You should:
- use a catchy title.
- write about a place you are familiar with; for example, one you have been to.
- think about the purpose of the article and who will read it in order to write in an appropriate style (formal, semi-formal, informal)
- organize the article in paragraphs which expand on, describe or give examples of the topic.
- use the Present Simple to describe the place and the Past Simple to talk about its history.
- use lively colorful language (e.g. a variety of words/phrases/expressions, direct and indirect questions, exclamation marks)

A. Complete the sentences with the words in the box.

benefits remarkable destinations insurance
illegal essential seasick

1. Richard enjoys traveling to exotic _____, like Indonesia and Guatemala.
2. Travel _____ usually covers things like lost luggage.
3. In many countries, it is _____ for 17-year-olds to drive a car.
4. I don't like sailing, because I often get _____.
5. Exercising a few times a week has many _____.
6. Kate has a _____ talent for learning languages. She can already speak four languages fluently.
7. Equipment like tents and sleeping bags are _____ when going camping.

B. Circle the correct words.

1. It was the sailor's first **cruise / voyage** at sea and it lasted 9 months.
2. The Casa Batlló in Barcelona is a very **inexpensive / impressive** building. You should go see it.
3. I **compared / developed** the flight prices, and Express Airlines has the cheapest flights.
4. Did you hear the **announcement / accommodations**? There is going to be a delay!
5. The scientists went on an **excursion / expedition** to Antarctica to explore and do research.
6. Mary had to change her hotel reservations due to the flight **connection / cancelation**.

C. Complete the sentences with the Past Simple or the Present Perfect Simple of the verbs in parentheses.

1. **A:** _____ you ever _____ (travel) abroad?
   B: Yes, I _____ (be) to many different places and just last month I _____ (visit) Brazil.
   A: Amazing! _____ you _____ (like) it?
   B: It _____ (be) an unforgettable experience!
2. **A:** My cousin Jack _____ (arrive) from Houston last night. He _____ never _____ (come) to Australia before.
   B: Interesting! _____ you _____ (go) sightseeing today?
   A: No, he _____ (feel) tired but he _____ (already / decide) where he wants to go tomorrow!

D. Complete using the Present Perfect Simple or the Present Perfect Progressive of the verbs in parentheses.

1. **A:** I think the salesperson _____ (forget) us. We _____ (wait) here for 20 minutes.
   B: Yes, but he _____ (help) other customers too, so I'm sure he'll come in a little while.
   A: I guess we can wait a little longer.

2. **A:** _____ you _____ (finish) with the tablet? You _____ (play) on it for hours. I want to download a new app.
   B: Which one?
   A: It's a travel app that keeps a record of all the places you _____ (be) to and organizes all the photos that you _____ (take).
3. **A:** How long _____ you _____ (work) at the travel agency as a guide?
   B: For about 5 years. So far, I _____ (travel) to 15 countries.

E. Choose a, b or c.

1. Going on a safari was ____ exciting thing I have ever done.
   a. the most **b.** more **c.** as
2. Our house by the beach is ____ peaceful than the one we have downtown.
   a. the more **b.** much more **c.** much
3. Teenagers get bored ____.
   a. very easy **b.** easier **c.** easily
4. Alice's daughter is getting taller and ____ every day!
   a. more tall **b.** tallest **c.** taller
5. I don't think that traveling by ship is ____ frightening as traveling by plane.
   a. as **b.** more **c.** so much

F. Complete the dialogue with the phrases a-e.

| a. You have a point.
| b. This is a once-in-a-lifetime experience.
| c. I think we should go tomorrow.
| d. Why don't we go to the Louvre?
| e. I'd rather not go today. |

A: I'm so glad we chose to visit Paris this summer!
B: Me too. 1 ____
A: You can say that again! What are we going to do now?
B: 2 ____ We can't leave Paris without visiting it.
A: 3 ____ But it's 3 p.m. and the museum closes at six today.
B: So, let's go.
A: 4 ____
B: Why not?
A: 5 ____ That way, we'll have the whole day ahead of us and we'll get to see more.
B: That's a good idea!

Self-assessment
Read the following and check the appropriate boxes. For the points you are unsure of, refer back to the relevant sections in the module.

NOW I CAN...
- talk about vacations and traveling experiences ☐
- use appropriate tenses to link the past with the present ☐
- form nouns ending in –ion, –ation and –ment ☐
- compare and contrast people and situations ☐
- express preference and make suggestions ☐
- write an article describing a place ☐

Exam Practice Modules 1-3 p. 138

work environment

Discuss:

- Look at the pictures. Which do you think people consider important when looking for a job?

- Can you think of other things that are important?

- What would your ideal job be?

Gross Pay TD
...ss for Tax TD
Tax paid TD
Earnings For NI TD
National Insurance TD
Pension TD (Inc AVC)

prospects

work/life balance

salary

colleagues

benefits

In this module you will learn...

- to express obligation, lack of obligation, and prohibition

- to express strong advice, threat and warning

- to express regret, disapproval and criticism

- to talk about jobs and employment

- to express possibility, certainty and make deductions in the present/future and in the past

- to write a semi-formal e-mail asking for and giving information

Jane's Borneo Blog

About | **Gallery** | **Contact**

Reading 🔊

A. Discuss.

- Have you ever done any volunteer work?
- If yes, what did you do and why?
- If not, would you like to?

B. Read the blog quickly. What is the purpose of the text?

a. To inform people about Borneo and its people.

b. To encourage people to visit Borneo.

c. To explain what it's like to be a volunteer in Borneo.

d. To advise people who are planning to travel to Borneo.

Log in [   ] ▶
Search [   ] ▶

Hi! I'm Jane Callaghan from Killarney, Ireland. I studied English Literature, but somehow found myself working in an office. My income was fairly good, but I wasn't satisfied. I had long working hours and my job was stressful. One day, I had enough so I made the decision to take a career break and do something I would enjoy. That's when I learned about the volunteer programs in Borneo, and I was willing to try. So here I am, in Borneo, trying to make a difference in the lives of these people as a volunteer teacher. So far, it's been rewarding, and I've made plenty of friends along the way! If you wish to sponsor me, you should subscribe to this blog.

At last, I got an Internet connection and I can write about my experience in Tawau, where I'm teaching English to 24 local teens. They must have really needed me at the school here because, as soon as I got off the bumpy bus from Kota Kinabalu, the principal put me in a classroom! "You can't be serious," I said to him, but he was.

After a sleepless night on a crowded bus, teaching was the last thing on my mind, but I made an effort to do my best. In return, the students immediately made me feel at home. "Welcome, Miss Jane! You are our family now," they sang together. You should have seen the smiles on their faces. They made me feel so important!

When they greeted me into their "family," they sure meant it! We are all one big family here as we study, cook, eat, clean, play sports and share happy moments together even when not in school. Also, because we interact in English, they're benefiting even more. These young cheerful teens are great teachers as well as enthusiastic students. They are always so eager to teach me about their culture and customs.

Being in a classroom with students who are so motivated to learn is a wonderful experience. It's not all work, work, work, though. A few days ago, the principal encouraged me to take a trip to Sepilok Orangutan Sanctuary. I was delighted! Orangutans are fascinating creatures, and I was allowed to feed a baby orangutan!

My first two weeks in Tawau have passed by quickly, and I'm sure the next three will fly by. I really shouldn't have arranged to leave so soon. I'm going to try to make the most of my short stay, but when I leave, I'm going to miss the school, the students, the other teachers, and the wonderful sounds of the mynah birds singing when the sun rises in the morning. I still don't know my plans for next year, so hopefully I may be able to come back again soon.

Leave a comment ▶ | *Click here to read all 32 comments* ▶

C. Read again and answer the questions. Choose a, b or c.

1. Why did Jane decide to volunteer?
   a. To get teaching experience.
   b. To make money from a blog.
   c. To help people in need.

2. Why did Jane feel that they must have really needed her at the school?
   a. The principal didn't waste time putting her in a class.
   b. They welcomed her so cheerfully into their "family."
   c. They made her come on an overnight bus in a hurry.

3. Why does Jane feel that the school is a "family"?
   a. She lives with some of the students.
   b. Everybody is always happy together, like a "family."
   c. Apart from teaching, teachers take part in other daily activities.

4. What does Jane think of her trip to the sanctuary?
   a. It can't be compared to her teaching experience.
   b. It was fun and enjoyable.
   c. Both of the above.

5. How long will Jane's stay in Tawau last?
   a. Two weeks.
   b. Three weeks.
   c. Five weeks.

6. What is true about Jane?
   a. She regrets not staying longer.
   b. She's planning to participate in another volunteer program.
   c. She has to leave earlier than planned.

D. Discuss.

- Would you consider traveling abroad to be a volunteer? Why?/Why not?
- Would you become a volunteer teacher? Why?/Why not?

Vocabulary

Complete with *make* or *do* to form phrases. Some of the phrases appear in the blog.

1. _____ a decision/guess
2. _____ my best
3. _____ up my mind
4. _____ as you please
5. _____ sb. a favor
6. _____ a difference
7. _____ an effort
8. _____ business
9. _____ a project
10. _____ the most of sth.
11. _____ research
12. _____ a suggestion / an arrangement
13. _____ a mistake
14. _____ my hair
15. _____ some exercise
16. _____ sense
17. _____ well/badly
18. _____ a good/bad impression
19. _____ plans
20. _____ an experiment

Grammar Modals I (must/have to/need, should/ought to/ had better) → *p. 149*

A. Which of the verbs in the box can we use to replace the ones in blue in the sentences so that they have a similar meaning?

needn't	have to	had to	need to	mustn't	didn't need to	don't have to

1. You **must** be a native speaker to teach in Borneo.
2. You **don't need to** stay for the whole summer. It isn't necessary.
3. You **can't** take the students on a trip without asking the principal. You're not allowed.
4. I **needed to** send them a résumé before they accepted me.
5. You **didn't have to** bring warm clothes with you. It's very warm in Borneo.

B. Read the examples and find the modal verb that expresses a stronger piece of advice or threat/warning.

1. You **should** be on time for the staff meeting.
2. You **ought to** be at the staff meeting at seven.
3. You **had better not** be late for the staff meeting.

C. Read the dialogue and answer the questions.

Peter: I **should have worked** overtime today to finish my project.

Mark: I agree. You **shouldn't have left** work so early. Mr. Davis will be mad at you. You **should go** in early tomorrow and **work** overtime if you have to.

1. Which sentence(s) refer(s) to the past? Which verb form is used after the modal verb *should* in this case?
2. Did Peter work overtime today? How does he feel about it?
3. Does Mark think Peter did the right thing?

D. Circle the correct words.

1. Diane **needs / ought to** go to Mrs. Stevens' office right now. She called for her.
2. You **should have / must** been more careful while you were driving to work.
3. She **has / should** definitely apply for that job. It's perfect for her!
4. You **mustn't / didn't have to** bring this cake; I already made one!
5. He **had to / should have** finish his work before he left the office.
6. I **had better not / shouldn't have** stayed up late last night; now I'm sleepy.
7. Students at this school **should / must** wear uniforms. It's a rule.
8. Don't worry. You **don't need to / shouldn't** take the bus. I'll drive you to work.

Vocabulary

Circle the correct words.

1. I quit my job because the **income / salary** I was getting was too low.

2. Our only **income / salary** at the moment is the rent we receive from our apartment downtown.

3. Mr. Edison **hired / rented** three graphic designers this week.

4. Mr. Edison **hired / rented** an apartment near his office.

5. The company I work for always looks for the best person to fill the **position / job**.

6. Roger is very experienced. He's been doing the **position / job** for years.

7. Unfortunately, I don't have any **knowledge / experience** of history.

8. Peter has no previous **knowledge / experience** as an accountant.

Grammar Modals II (may/might/could, must/can't) → *p. 150*

A. Read the examples 1-3. Which one refers to the present/future and which ones refer to the past? Then choose which of the statements a or b is closer in meaning.

1. Learning a foreign language **may/might/ could help** you get a better job.

a. It is likely to happen.

b. It will certainly happen.

2. Brad's late. He **may/might have had** an accident. Let's call him.

a. Brad definitely had an accident.

b. It is possible that Brad had an accident.

3. Without my GPS, I **could have gotten** lost in the mountains.

a. I was able to get lost.

b. There was a possibility I would get lost, but I didn't.

B. Read the examples. What do they mean? Choose a or b.

1. Jack **must be** good at his job, because he got a raise.

a. Jack has to be good at his job.

b. I believe Jack is good at his job.

2. She **can't be** the manager of the company. Look at how young she is!

a. I'm sure she isn't the manager.

b. She isn't able to be the manager.

C. Read the examples and answer the questions. Then come up with examples of your own.

- Tina **must have worked** overtime today because she still hasn't arrived home.
- Robert **can't/couldn't have gotten** the job in Paris. He doesn't speak a word of French!

1. Do the examples refer to the present/future or past?

2. What do the words in blue express in each example?

D. Circle the correct words.

Some people think that I **1 must / could** be crazy to do the job I do. Well sure, I **2 could have chosen / must have chosen** a safer way to earn a living, but when I'm hundreds of feet in the air, looking down at the beautiful view, I know it was the right choice. Washing the windows of skyscrapers **3 may have seemed / may seem** like a difficult and dangerous job, but for me it's fun and enjoyable. It **4 might have been / can't have been** much more dangerous in the past, but nowadays many safety measures are taken to make sure that window washers are safe. People often tell me: "It **5 mustn't / can't** be that perfect! Isn't it tiring?" Of course, it's pretty tiring at times but, like every job, it has its advantages and disadvantages.

Intonation 🔊

Listen and repeat. Notice the stressed words.

1. Natalie might come with us.

2. Daniel could have had a successful career but he didn't work hard enough.

3. Mary shouldn't have lied to her parents.

4. Albert can't become a paramedic. He doesn't have the qualifications.

5. Jack must have done very well in his interview because he got hired.

6. You can't have met the manager. He's away on a business trip.

Listening 🔊

You will hear people talking in six different situations. For questions 1-6, choose the best answer a, b or c.

1. Why does the woman believe Danny got fired?
   a. He was lazy.
   b. He was looking for a new job.
   c. He was often late.

2. What does Bill regret?
   a. Making a bad impression at an interview.
   b. Leaving his previous job without finding a new one first.
   c. Forgetting to call his cousin.

3. What made the applicant apply for the job?
   a. The salary.
   b. The job prospects.
   c. The working hours.

4. What doesn't Mark like about his job?
   a. The distance he has to travel.
   b. The salary.
   c. The people he works with.

5. What's wrong with Susan's new colleague?
   a. She isn't very willing to help.
   b. She's never worked at a computer company before.
   c. She doesn't know much about computers.

6. What is one of the requirements of the volunteer program?
   a. Paying for your own flight.
   b. Arranging your own accommodations.
   c. Being able to speak a second language.

Speaking

Talk in groups of three.

Student A: Choose one of the situations below and tell Students B and C what happened. Discuss what you think went wrong and what you should(n't) have or could have done instead. Use some of the phrases in the box.

- You've just lost your job because you were late every morning.
- Your boss told you off for taking too many breaks.
- You left your job without finding a new one and are now unemployed.
- Your boss offered you a more important position but you refused it.
- You went to a job interview but you didn't get the job.
- You complained about a colleague at work and they got fired.
- You were playing online games at work, and your computer got a virus.

Expressing regret	
I should have thought twice before...	I guess I could have just...
I shouldn't have reacted the way I did.	I don't have any excuses for my behavior.
I regret (not) doing...	I didn't mean to...
That was thoughtless/careless of me...	
I don't know what I was thinking.	

Students B and C: Listen to Student A and point out what he/she should(n't) have or could have done instead. Then give him/her advice on what he/she can do now. Use some of the phrases in the box.

Expressing disapproval and criticism	Giving advice
You did what?	If I were you, I'd...
That wasn't very wise of you.	You'd better...
What were you thinking?	I suggest you...
You shouldn't have done that!	You should definitely...
You know better than that!	I would strongly advise you to...
Why on Earth did you do that?	It might be a good idea to...
How thoughtless of you!	You ought to...
You know, you could have just...	

"You should check your e-mail more often. I fired you over three weeks ago."

Vocabulary & Speaking

A. Read the sentences. What do the adjectives in bold mean? Match them with the definitions a-j.

1. Mark is such a **sociable** young man. He can easily start a conversation with a complete stranger. ☐
2. You need to be **imaginative** to create something unique. ☐
3. Frank is a very **rational** person. He never lets his feelings affect his decisions. ☐
4. Andrew was very **courageous**. He ran into the burning house to save the girl. ☐
5. Olivia is the most **spontaneous** person I know. She doesn't think twice about anything. ☐
6. Karen is a very **honest** young lady. You should believe her. ☐
7. Whenever I'm in trouble, I go to my sister. She's the most **reliable** person I know. ☐
8. Nathan is an **ambitious** young man who will do anything to achieve what he wants. ☐
9. Liv is too **disorganized** to become a successful accountant. ☐
10. Our teacher is **patient**. She never gets angry with us. ☐

---

a. really wanting to become successful
b. able to think calmly and make decisions that are not based on emotions only
c. always telling the truth
d. able to stay calm for a long time
e. good at thinking of new and interesting ideas
f. enjoying meeting and talking with other people; outgoing
g. brave; showing courage
h. doing things without planning them first
i. can be trusted when needed for help or support
j. bad at arranging or planning things

B. Talk in groups. Look at the pictures. What characteristics do you need for these jobs? Why? You can use some of the phrases in the boxes and some of the adjectives from the vocabulary activity above.

a teacher

a firefighter

a secretary

be hard-working	To become a...
be a role model	If you want to become...
have good communication skills	People who want to become...
like helping other people	In my opinion, you have to be able to...
deal with emergencies	I think/believe you must have the ability to...
provide medical care	You definitely need to...
work well as part of a team	This job involves being...
be organized	

Reading 🔊

A. Do the quiz to find out what kind of job you are best suited for.

FIND THE

****

Extrovert or **I**ntrovert?

1. Working as part of a team feels:
- uncomfortable. I prefer working alone. (I)
- good. I feel more confident when others can help me with my ideas. (E)

2. Your idea of a perfect evening is:
- staying in with a book. (I)
- going out with friends and meeting new people. (E)

3. When you communicate:
- you take your time to think before you speak. (I)
- express yourself freely without thinking too much. (E)

E or **I** ? Which do you have more of?
****

Creative or **R**ational?

1. If a device or appliance breaks down:
- you are the person people call to fix it. (C)
- you're useless. You have to call a technician. (R)

2. At work, you prefer tasks to be:
- clear with rules and instructions. (R)
- without rules so that you have the freedom to be creative. (C)

3. You prefer to learn through:
- reading and research. (R)
- trying things out for yourself. (C)

C or **R** ? Which do you have more of?
****

Organized or **S**pontaneous?

1. You've made plans to meet a friend at 4 p.m. You're:
- on time, as always. (O)
- ten minutes late. Never mind. (S)

2. Your desk or the area in which you work is usually:
- well-organized and neat. (O)
- a mess. (S)

3. When you travel, how do you usually prepare?
- At the last minute. (S)
- I always know all the details for the entire trip before I leave. (O)

O or **S** ? Which do you have more of?
****

PERFECT JOB FOR YOU

YOU · LIFE · JOY · THE FUTURE →

CONFIDENCE · Brilliant IDEAS · CHAOS · STRESS

ENERGY

RESULTS ***

Which personality type are you?

E R O types are sociable, confident and comfortable working with other people. They are honest and organized. They usually like structure and working with rules and instructions.
Possible careers: lawyer, scientist, engineer, doctor, accountant

E R S types are usually confident, patient people who express themselves well and get along well with lots of different people. They hate routine and are more interested in complex issues than everyday concerns.
Possible careers: consultant, online business manager, journalist, sales manager

E C O types enjoy being in a variety of social situations. They are usually artistic or musical. They are reliable and organized, and they work well with deadlines.
Possible careers: graphic designer, music teacher, politician, marketing manager

E C S types are usually outgoing and need to feel free to express themselves. They are spontaneous and don't like planning or rules. They often come up with original ideas. They can get bored with routine or in structured environments.
Possible careers: musician, writer, performer, public speaker, director, actor

I R O types are quiet and hard-working. They read a lot and enjoy learning about a variety of things. They are well-organized and practical, and like to plan ahead. They are good at finding solutions to problems.
Possible careers: politician, engineer, lawyer, computer programmer, scientist, editor

I R S types are usually pretty quiet and shy. They like to follow instructions and are practical. They prefer to learn by reading. However, they like variety in life and do not like to plan into the future very much.
Possible careers: police detective, accountant, veterinarian, writer

I C O types are imaginative and usually good at working with their hands. They prefer to work on their own, in their own organized way, without having strict rules. They like testing new ideas.
Possible careers: architect, writer, artist, teacher, designer, mechanic

I C S types are usually shy people who are happier working alone. They have a creative imagination, but are often considered kind of disorganized by others because of the way they work.
Possible careers: musician, artist, interior designer, researcher, academic, scientist

B. Talk in groups. Find out which personality type your classmates are. Do you agree or disagree with the results? Discuss.

Listening 🔊

Listen to four people talking about advice they were given. Match the speakers with the statements a-f. There are two extra statements which you do not need to use.

Speaker 1 ☐   Speaker 3 ☐
Speaker 2 ☐   Speaker 4 ☐

a. This person was advised to be honest.

b. This person was advised to be sociable.

c. This person was advised to be spontaneous.

d. This person was advised to be patient.

e. This person was advised to be ambitious.

f. This person was advised to be organized.

Speaking

Talk in pairs. Look at the picture below and try to speculate what might have happened to the man and why he's upset. Use some of the ideas and phrases in the boxes.

- lose/delete important document
- get fired
- have to work overtime
- exhausted / out late last night

- have an argument with boss
- do a bad presentation
- not get promotion
- cannot make the deadline

Expressing possibility (we are not certain)
He may/might/could (have)...
He may not / might not (have)...
Maybe/Perhaps he...
It's hard to say, but it's possible that he...

Expressing probability (we are almost certain)
He must (have)...
He can't / couldn't (have)...
He probably...
It's probable that...
It's very (un)likely that...
I bet...
I guess he...
My guess is that...

66 *I think he must have deleted an important document by mistake. That's why he's upset. He's also probably thinking about...*
   I doubt it. That's very unlikely. I think he might have... 99

Writing A semi-formal e-mail asking for and giving information

A. Discuss.
- Have you ever been to a job fair?
- Do you think they are useful for finding a job?

B. Read the flyer about the job fair and the e-mail Tony wrote in response. Then answer the questions.

Riverdale Workforce and Development Network invite you to

Riverdale Community

JOB FAIR

Coby Wayde Recreation Center
Saturday, October 29th
9 a.m.

- Showcasing 50+ companies
- Candidates of all ages and experience levels welcome
- Companies will be looking to fill positions or offer internship opportunities
- Please come prepared with résumés and dress professionally

Guest speaker: **John Fitzwilliam** giving a talk on: **"Tips for finding a job"**

For information and to reserve a place contact:
Jane Rollins
966-555-1445
info@riverdalecommunity.net

New mail

To: info@riverdalecommunity.net

Dear Ms. Rollins,

I saw the flyer for the Riverdale Community Job Fair and I am very interested in attending this event.

My name is Tony Richards and I am 22 years old. I am a college student in my senior year. I am looking for ideas of what career to follow, so I believe the job fair will be an excellent opportunity for me. I am really looking forward to the event and I would like to reserve a place.

However, I would like to have some more information about the job fair. Firstly, I would like to know what time the fair closes. It is not mentioned on the flyer. Also, will companies be promoting full-time positions, or part-time as well? I was also wondering what "dress professionally" means. Do I have to wear a suit and tie?

Looking forward to your reply.

Yours sincerely,
Tony Richards

⟨ ⟩

1. How does Tony address the person he is writing to?
2. What information does Tony give about himself?
3. Do you find any of this information irrelevant?
4. What information does Tony ask for?
5. Does he use direct or indirect questions?
6. What is the topic of each of the paragraphs?
7. How does Tony sign off?

C. Below is another e-mail someone wrote in response to the flyer in activity B. Divide it into paragraphs and improve the underlined sections.

Dear Rollins,

I saw the flyer for the Riverdale Community Job Fair on my school bulletin board and I am very interested in attending. My name is Kelly White and I am 22 years old. I am a senior so I was very excited to read about the job fair. As I have never attended something similar before, it will give me the chance to learn what career opportunities are available with my major. So, I would really like to reserve a place. However, here are a few questions for you. First of all, I would like to know how much it costs to attend. This information is not mentioned on the flyer. Furthermore, why don't you mention what time Mr. Fitzwilliam's talk begins? Do I need to book a seat? I look forward to hearing from you.

Bye for now,
Kelly

D. You have seen the following flyer. You are interested in taking part but you need more information before you decide. You want to ask:

• about the cost
• if accommodations are provided
• how long the exchange program lasts

Write an e-mail to Mr. Collins giving any necessary information about yourself and asking for the information you want.

SIGN UP FOR AN UNFORGETTABLE SUMMER EXPERIENCE!
International Language Exchange Program

Each semester, ILEP connects hundreds of students from all over the world so they can help each other learn more about languages, cultures and customs. ILEP is a great opportunity to stay in touch with a language you have already learned or to learn a new one.

To sign up, contact James Collins, giving name, age and saying which country you are interested in going to.

Registration ends on May 7th.

AUTHENTIC SPEAKING OPPORTUNITIES FOR ALL STUDENTS!

Contact information:
James Collins
International Language Exchange Program
Ormond Road
TW11

TIP

A semi-formal letter/e-mail:
• is written to a person you don't know very well or when you want to be polite and respectful.
• begins with Dear Mr./Miss/Mrs./Ms./Dr. + last name or with Dear + first name and ends with Yours sincerely or Yours truly.
• is neutral in style (not too informal and not too formal).

When writing a semi-formal letter/e-mail asking for and giving information:
• write in an appropriate style.
• read the information given carefully and cover all the points required.
• organize the information into paragraphs.
• use standard grammar and spelling conventions.
• use a combination of direct and indirect questions.
• use linking words/phrases to list your questions

• *firstly, first of all, to begin with*
• *secondly, also, what is more, furthermore, in addition, apart from that*
• *finally, lastly*

A. Choose a, b or c.

1. Derek is a(n) _____ person and he doesn't usually plan things ahead.
   a. spontaneous   **b.** rational   **c.** ambitious

2. What do you do to _____ a living?
   a. earn   **b.** rise   **c.** get

3. Ted must have _____ a good impression, because he immediately got the job.
   a. made   **b.** had   **c.** done

4. Britney is new at work, but she is very _____ to learn new things.
   a. delighted   **b.** eager   **c.** honest

5. Olga is never afraid to _____ her feelings, whether she is happy or sad.
   a. react   **b.** express   **c.** interact

6. It's difficult to find _____ and hard-working employees nowadays.
   a. rewarding   **b.** courageous   **c.** reliable

7. A colleague at work got _____ because he was never on time.
   a. hired   **b.** rented   **c.** fired

8. Fred studied to be a(n) _____.
   a. accountant   **b.** applicant   **c.** candidate

B. Complete the sentences with the words in the box.

> trust   registration   sanctuary   incomes
> deadline   promotion   knowledge

1. Don't worry. You can _____ me to keep your secret.

2. There's a bird _____ near here. Do you want to visit it?

3. I have been working at this company for three years and I soon hope to get a _____.

4. I have just a few days to finish this project; the _____ is on Monday.

5. I was amazed at Tim's _____ of English literature.

6. To attend the seminar, you need to pay a _____ fee.

7. There are lots of people living on low _____ nowadays.

C. Circle the correct words.

1. I **may / must** go to the mall later today. If I do, do you need anything?

2. You **mustn't / don't have to** drive a car without a driver's license.

3. Tony **ought to / should have** apologized for his behavior.

4. You **didn't have to / needn't** tell him off. You **could / must** have explained what he did wrong politely.

5. Brian **can't / mustn't** be asleep. I can hear him talking.

6. Penny **ought / had better** to go on the volunteer program. It's a great opportunity.

7. You **don't have to / shouldn't** forget to make an appointment with the doctor.

D. Rewrite the sentences using the words given.

1. It's a good idea to dress professionally for the job interview.   **(better)**
   _____

2. It isn't necessary to call a technician for the printer.   **(need)**
   _____

3. I regret quitting my old job.   **(should)**
   _____

4. I'm pretty sure I left my cell phone at home.   **(must)**
   _____

E. Complete the dialogue with the phrases a-e.

> **a.** You should definitely apologize for your behavior.
> **b.** That wasn't very wise of you.
> **c.** I shouldn't have reacted the way I did.
> **d.** I doubt it.
> **e.** You know, you could have just repeated the question.

A: What's the matter, William?

B: I feel horrible. I got into a really bad argument with my colleague Robert.

A: 1 _____

B: You can say that again. I don't know what I was thinking.

A: What exactly happened?

B: I asked him a question about a project we're working on together and he didn't answer me.

A: 2 _____

B: Yeah, well I didn't, and I started shouting at him.

A: What were you thinking?

B: I know, but it's too late now! He's really mad at me. **3** _____ It was so thoughtless of me.

A: That's true. **4** _____ Maybe he'll forgive you.

B: 5 _____

Self-assessment

Read the following and check the appropriate boxes. For the points you are unsure of, refer back to the relevant sections in the module.

NOW I CAN...

▶ express obligation, lack of obligation, and prohibition	☐
▶ express strong advice, threat and warning	☐
▶ express regret, disapproval and criticism	☐
▶ talk about jobs and employment	☐
▶ express possibility, certainty and make deductions in the present/future and in the past	☐
▶ write a semi-formal e-mail asking for and giving information	☐

Task 3 & 4 p. 128

Get the message

5

pigeon post

smoke signals

semaphore flags

maritime flag signals

Morse code

sign language

Discuss:

• Look at the pictures. Do people still use these forms of communication?

• Where are/were they used?

• What sort of messages are/were sent with these forms of communication?

In this module you will learn...

• to define people, places, things and ideas and give additional information about them

• useful phrases that help you when you need more time to think

• useful phrases that help you when you want to politely interrupt someone or when you want to get back to the topic of discussion

• to understand warning signs

• how to say whether something is permitted or not

• to ask for and give directions

• to ask for clarification and repetition

• to ask if you have been understood

• to write an informal e-mail

47

Reading 🔊

A. Read the text quickly without paying attention to the missing sentences. Where would you find this text?

a. encyclopedia   b. blog   c. magazine   d. travel guide

Whistled Languages

There are more than 6,500 different languages in the world which all have one thing in common: we use our voices to speak them. What many people are not aware of, however, is that there are some languages that do not require speech at all. **1 [ ]** Less familiar are some other systems of communication found in small communities across the globe, whose origins still remain somewhat of a mystery.

On the Spanish island of La Gomera, off the coast of Africa, there is an unusual language that has been around since before the 15ᵗʰ century. **2 [ ]** The local landscape, which is hilly and mountainous and covered in mist, may explain why this whistling became so widely used. The sound created by whistling travels much further than the human voice, so it's an effective way to communicate quickly across valleys or long distances. Also, locals find that it can sometimes be convenient to be able to communicate in a secret way that outsiders cannot understand.

3 [ ] In Turkey there is a village where it's difficult to tell the difference between humans "talking" and birds "tweeting." At least, most foreigners would say so. It's called "Kuskoy," which means "Village of the birds." Here, like in La Gomera, whistling was beneficial for communicating across mountainous regions and long distances, when telephones and other methods were not available. Even today, when phones are more commonplace, there are people from older generations who still prefer to whistle. **4 [ ]**

Education in the fine art of whistling begins at an early age with the older generations passing down their skills to the young. It's not easy of course; in Kuskoy, for example, there are 29 separate whistled noises, one for each letter of the Turkish alphabet. **5 [ ]** Practice makes perfect and local children pick it up in the end.

In La Gomera, residents, who want to protect their tradition, have gone a step further and made learning whistling compulsory in schools. Unfortunately though, they complain that the everyday use of whistling is becoming rarer as modern technology takes over and younger generations move to towns and cities. **6 [ ]**

B. Read the text again. Complete the gaps 1-6 with the sentences a-g below. There is one extra sentence which you do not need to use.

TIP

- First read the whole text in order to get an overall idea.
- Carefully read the sentences before and after each gap and the given sentences (a-g).
- Look for clues in both the text and the given sentences. Pay attention to reference items (it, they, this, there, etc.) and identify what they refer to as well as sentence linkers (however, furthermore, therefore, etc.). This will help you understand the text.
- Remember: the correct option must logically complete the writer's meaning and grammatically fit the gap.

a. Whistled communities are also found in parts of Greece, Mexico, Turkey and France.

b. They find it much simpler and, of course, it does not cost anything.

c. Sign language, which uses hand gestures to communicate, is the most well-known of these.

d. When yelling, the message can travel about 1,600 ft., but it wouldn't be very clear.

e. As well as talking, people here whistle to communicate.

f. We will have to wait and see if efforts by locals to protect their unusual culture can survive the many changes of the modern world.

g. However, it's pretty much like learning to talk.

C. Look at the highlighted words/phrases in the text and match them with their meanings.

1. mist ☐
2. effective ☐
3. valley ☐
4. commonplace ☐
5. separate ☐
6. compulsory ☐
7. take over ☐

a. a low area of land between two hills or mountains

b. different

c. that must be done because of a law or rule

d. a light cloud close to the ground which makes it difficult to see

e. to take control of sth.

f. successful; producing the result that is wanted

g. existing in many places

D. Discuss.

• Would you be interested in learning a whistled language? Why? / Why not?

Vocabulary

A. Read the extracts from the text. What do the phrases in bold mean?

*...it's difficult to **tell the difference** between humans "talking" and birds "tweeting."*

*At least, most foreigners would **say so**.*

B. Complete the sentences with the correct form of *tell* or *say* to form collocations.

1. You should _____ **thank you** to Amanda for buying you such a nice gift.

2. I was in the neighborhood so I decided to stop by and _____ **hello**.

3. Rita would never _____ **a secret** that she promised to keep. You can trust her.

4. Tina _____ us **a joke** yesterday but I don't remember it.

5. I can't believe that Frank didn't _____ **sorry** after he accidentally pushed me. How rude!

6. Now that my younger brother has learned to _____ **time**, I'm going to buy him a watch.

7. Don't just sit there. _____ **something**!

8. OK, children. Let me _____ you **a story**.

9. I asked my brother if I could borrow his car and he _____ **yes**.

10. I always know when Jack is _____ **lies** and when he's _____ **the truth**.

Grammar
Relative pronouns (who, which, that, whose)
Relative adverb (where) → p. 150

A. Read the examples and answer the questions.

> a. There are some languages **which** do not require speech at all.
>
> b. Aiden is a student **who** has to learn whistling at his school.
>
> c. Sign language is something **which** you can learn quite easily.
>
> d. In Mexico there is a region **where** people use whistling to communicate.
>
> e. I was at college with a girl **whose** grandfather was a professor of chemistry.

1. Which of the words in blue refers to:
   • people?
   • places?
   • things and ideas?
   • possession?

2. In which of the examples can we replace the word in blue with *that*?

3. In which of the examples can we omit the word in blue?

B. Complete with *who*, *which*, *that*, *whose* or *where*. If they can be omitted, put them in parentheses.

A: Do you know a good language school 1 _____ I can learn Russian?

B: Yes. Actually, I have a colleague 2 _____ wife is a secretary at a very good language school downtown.

A: Great!

B: Hold on! I'm pretty sure you met him at my barbecue last summer. His name is George.

A: Is that the guy 3 _____ was making the sandwiches?

B: No, that was Brian. George is the one 4 _____ I was talking to about sports.

A: Oh, I remember him. The Mets fan.

B: Right! Well, I can give you his number and you can talk to his wife about the details. But why Russian?

A: It's a language 5 _____ has always fascinated me and it's something 6 _____ I've wanted to do since I visited Moscow.

B: You've been to Moscow? Wow! It's certainly a city 7 _____ is worth visiting.

A: You can say that again!

Vocabulary

A. What do the verbs in bold in the sentences mean? Match them with the definitions a-h.

1. I'm not sure where Frank is. He **mentioned** something about meeting Harry. ☐
2. My roommate and I keep **arguing** about who will wash the dishes. ☐
3. Can you please **explain** to me how this washing machine works? ☐
4. "Stop right there!" **yelled** the police officer. ☐
5. We need to **discuss** the problem with Sandra first. ☐
6. Lisa and Erica spend all their spare time **chatting** on Skype. ☐
7. Mark is **complaining** about his computer. I think it crashed again. ☐
8. It's not polite to **gossip** about other people. ☐

---

a. to shout

b. to talk about other people and their private lives

c. to talk informally, usually with a friend

d. to say that you are not pleased with sth.

e. to speak angrily because you disagree

f. to speak about or refer to sth. without using many words

g. to talk about sth. in order to come to a decision

h. to make sb. understand sth.

B. Complete with the verbs in the box.

> install   drop   shut down
> scroll   drag   tap   attach
> press   deactivate

1. Another way of saying "turn off" your computer is _____.
2. To make the keys on a keyboard or phone write letters, numbers, etc. you have to _____ them.
3. When you select part of a text or image, then move it and place it in its new position, you _____ and _____ it.
4. After you download a new program onto your computer, you need to _____ it.
5. The verb used instead of "press" or "click" on a touchscreen device is _____.
6. When you want to send an image or a separate document with an e-mail, you have to _____ it.
7. When you want to stop using an e-mail account, you _____ it.
8. When you move up or down a web page or document, you _____.

Grammar Relative Clauses → *p. 150*

A. Read the examples below, note the relative clauses in blue and answer the questions.

> • There are people from older generations **who still prefer to whistle**.
> • In La Gomera, residents, **who want to protect their tradition**, have gone a step further and made learning whistling compulsory in schools.

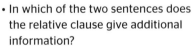

- Which of the two sentences is incomplete without the relative clause?
- In which of the two sentences does the relative clause give additional information?
- What is the difference in punctuation in the two sentences?

B. Read the rules below and decide which of the relative clauses in the examples in activity A is defining and which is non-defining.

Defining relative clauses:
- give necessary information without which the meaning of the sentence is incomplete.
- are not separated from the rest of the sentence by commas.

In defining relative clauses we can use *that* instead of *who* or *which*.

Non-defining relative clauses:
- give additional information about someone or something.
- are separated from the rest of the sentence by commas.

In non-defining relative clauses we **can't** use *that* instead of *who* or *which*.

C. Join the sentences using *who*, *which*, *that*, *whose* or *where*.

1. UNICEF is an organization. It helps take care of the health and education of children around the world.

   _____

2. Mrs. Sanders lives on the third floor. Her son is a gadget freak.

   _____

3. Mr. Henderson is my employer. He was on the news last night.

   _____

4. Toronto is a beautiful city. My cousin lives there.

   _____

5. You've met my aunt. She makes amazing pasta dishes.

   _____

6. Twitter is used by many people nowadays. It is an online social networking service.

   _____

Intonation 🔊

Listen and repeat. Notice the intonation and rhythm.

1. Basketball, which was invented in 1891, is very popular around the world.
2. Diane, who lives next door, works for a computer company.
3. Argentina, where my mother was born, is a beautiful country.
4. Greg, whose car is parked outside, had an accident yesterday.

Listening 🔊

Listen to two friends talking about a social media site and write T for True or F for False.

1. The boy deactivated his account with the site because there was a problem with it. ☐
2. The girl spends a lot of time on the site. ☐
3. The boy regrets not being able to keep in touch with all his old school friends. ☐
4. The boy isn't interested in what other people do all the time. ☐
5. The girl uses the site for a variety of activities. ☐
6. The boy doesn't care about learning the latest news instantly. ☐
7. The boy has also deactivated his e-mail account. ☐

Speaking

Discuss in groups. Use some of the words/phrases given.

- How do you communicate with the different people in your life?
- What are some popular social networking sites people your age use and what do they use them for?
- What are the advantages and disadvantages of smartphones?
- How has communication changed people's lives?
- What do you think the future of communication will be like?

> face-to-face   instant messaging   Skype   video chat   keep in touch
> download   upload   post   touchscreen   functions of a computer
> Internet access   apps   user-friendly   handy   practical   portable
> time-saving   time-consuming   viruses   (in)convenient   outdated
> costly   need to keep up to date   store huge amounts of data
> know latest news instantly   not socialize

Taking time to think
Well, let's see now…
Well, let me think…
Umm, give me a minute…
You know,…

Interrupting politely
Sorry to interrupt, but…
Can I add something?
Could I say something before you continue?
May I interrupt you for a second?
Hold on. Are you saying that…?

Getting back to the topic
Anyway, as I was saying…
Now, what was I saying?
Now, where was I?

TIP
- When discussing a topic, take turns to speak. Listen to what the other person is saying and try not to interrupt him/her frequently. If you need to interrupt, do it politely.
- When it's your turn to speak and you need more time to think about what to say, avoid long pauses. Use phrases which help you gain time.

5b

Reading

A. Discuss.

- Where are warning signs needed?
- How do warning signs or labels get the message across?

B. Look at the signs below and read through them quickly. Where would you find these signs?

C. Read again and choose from the sentences (a-e) on the next page the ones that are correct for each sign. There are two correct answers for each sign.

A

ON-BOARD EMERGENCY INSTRUCTIONS

ALWAYS	Use the passenger emergency intercom to contact a crew member. Listen for announcements.	
FIRE	Move to an unaffected car. Remain inside – tracks are electrified. Follow instructions of emergency workers. Fire extinguishers are located at the end of each passenger car.	
MEDICAL	If a passenger needs medical attention, notify a crew member. If you are medically qualified and able to assist, identify yourself to the crew.	
POLICE	Notify the crew of any unlawful or suspicious activity on board - they can contact the police.	
EVACUATION	Lift plastic cover above side door. Pull red handle down. Slide door open. Evacuate only when instructed by the crew.	

B

Warning Flag Meanings:

 **LOW HAZARD:** Calm conditions. Normal care and caution required.

 **CAUTION!** Moderate waves and/or currents. Use extra care.

 **HIGH HAZARD!** Large waves and/or strong currents. Swimmers are strongly advised not to enter the water.

 ATTENTION! DANGER! No swimming or surfing permitted.

C

SITE SAFETY

 All visitors and drivers must report to the site office and obtain permission before entering the site or any work area.

Wear protective equipment at all times on this site.

Wear eye, ear and hand protection where appropriate.

 Caution! Construction work in progress. Beware of trucks.

 Vehicles parked at owners' risk. Park only in the specified areas.

CAUTION
THIS SIGN HAS
SHARP EDGES
DO NOT TOUCH THE EDGES OF THIS SIGN

Sign A

a. In an emergency, always give instructions to other passengers to help them.

b. In case of fire, evacuate the train immediately.

c. If you are a doctor, you should inform the train crew in an emergency.

d. If you see someone behaving in an unusual or dangerous manner, call the police.

e. In an emergency, do not exit the train if the crew doesn't tell you to do so.

Sign B

a. When there is a red flag, swimming is considered dangerous.

b. When there are strong winds and waves, there is a green flag.

c. Surfers are allowed in the water only when there is a yellow flag with a black circle.

d. Swimmers are warned to keep out of the water when there is a yellow flag.

e. Swimmers are advised to enter the water only when there are green and yellow flags.

Sign C

a. If you see someone entering the site, notify the site office.

b. You can enter the work area only if you have permission.

c. Parking is not permitted.

d. Construction workers don't have to wear all the safety equipment shown at all times.

e. Trucks are not permitted on this site.

D. Find words in the signs that mean the same as the following:

1. to inform (sign A)
2. not legal (sign A)
3. to move out of a dangerous place to somewhere safe (sign A)
4. extreme care and attention (sign B)
5. not too big nor too small in amount or degree (sign B)
6. to get (sign C)
7. happening at this time (sign C)

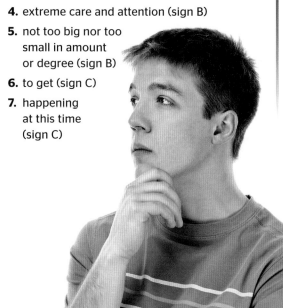

Listening & Speaking 🔊

A. Listen to five conversations and match them with the signs a-g below. Write 1-5. There are two signs which you do not need to use.

 a ☐

 c ☐

 e ☐

 f ☐

 b ☐

 d ☐

 g ☐

B. Look at the signs again and in pairs discuss what they mean. Use the phrases in the box.

Saying whether something is permitted or not

... is (not) allowed.

You're (not) allowed to...

... is (not) permitted.

... is strictly forbidden.

It's strictly forbidden to...

It's (not) illegal to...

... is (not) against the law.

People/You can/may/must/should (not)...

People/You are (not) supposed to...

Speaking
Talk in pairs.

Student A: Imagine that you are in an unfamiliar area. Ask Student B for directions to two of the following places: post office, police station, bus station, (name of) museum, (name of) restaurant. Make sure you understand the directions. If you don't, ask him/her for clarification and repetition. Use some of the phrases below.

Asking for directions

Excuse me, how can/do I get to the... from here?
I'm looking for the... Where exactly is it?
Can you tell me the way to the...?
Could you give me directions to the...?
Could you tell me where the... is?
Do you happen to know where the... is?

Asking for clarification and repetition

Excuse me? Did you say...?
So, I turn/go..., right?
Could you repeat that, please?
What was that again?
(I'm) sorry, I didn't catch/get that.
Sorry, I don't understand. Where do I turn left?
I'm not following you.

Student B: Imagine that you're walking down the street and a stranger (Student A) stops you for directions. Give him/her clear directions, using some of the phrases below.

Giving directions

Go up/down/along... Street/Road/Avenue.
Go straight for another hundred yards / until you come to...
Keep going for two blocks and then...
Walk/Go past/towards...
Turn left/right onto... Street/Road/Avenue.
Turn left/right at the intersection / traffic lights / stop sign.
Take the first/second, etc. left/right onto...
Cross at the crosswalk / traffic lights / footbridge.
It's on your/the left/right.
You'll see/find it on the left-/right-hand side.
It's on the corner of... / across from...

Asking if you have been understood

Is that/everything clear (now)...?
Do you understand (now)...?
Are/Were my directions clear enough?
Does that make sense?
I hope you're making some sense of what I'm saying.
I hope that's not too confusing.
Do you want me to say it again?

❝ *Could you tell me the way to the nearest post office?*
    Sure. Go up this road for two blocks and turn left onto Sanders Street.
Excuse me? What was the name of the street again?
    Sanders. Keep going and you'll find it on your right.
I see. So, it's on Sanders Street, right?
    Exactly. Is that clear?
Yes. You've been very helpful. Thank you. **❞**

Writing An informal e-mail (II)

A. Read the writing task below. Which of the functions listed do you think the receiver of the e-mail should include in the reply?

1. offering accommodations ☐
2. making suggestions ☐
3. congratulating ☐
4. giving advice ☐
5. expressing enthusiasm ☐
6. complaining ☐
7. giving directions ☐
8. making arrangements ☐

Beata, a foreign friend of yours, is visiting your city for the first time. Below is part of the e-mail she sent you. Read it and write a reply.

I'm coming on the 26th and leaving on the morning of the 28th. The seminar is taking place at the Business and Seminar Center downtown. You mentioned in an earlier e-mail that you work downtown. Well, I'll be free both evenings after 6 p.m. so, if you want to meet up, let me know when, where and how to get there. One more thing: I'd love to go to a museum, so please tell me which one not to miss.

B. Read the e-mail Amy has written in response. Which of the functions (1-8) from above are expressed in her e-mail? Has she included all the necessary information?

Dear Beata,

I'm so happy that you're coming, even if it's for such a short time. I'll get to see you again after all these years!

The hotel where I work is very close to the Business and Seminar Center. Unfortunately, I'm working on the 26th and can't get anyone else to work my shift. However, I get off work at 5:30 on the 27th, so we can meet at around 6:15 at a very nice coffee shop which is located in the old part of the city. The coffee shop is called "Coffee Beans" and it's very easy to find. Just follow my directions: when you get out of the Center, turn left and walk along Kent Street for about 200 yards. You'll see a pharmacy on the corner. Turn left again there and then take the third right onto Clark Road. "Coffee Beans" is on the corner of Clark Road and Maple Street. You can't miss it!

Well, I'd better finish off here.

See you soon,
Amy

C. Read the two paragraphs below and choose which is more suitable to complete the e-mail in activity B. Then decide where you would include this information. Why is the other paragraph not suitable?

a. There are so many things you can do here that I'm not even sure where to start from. Firstly, you should definitely walk through the old part of the city, which is beautiful in the evening. You can also visit one of the many museums. Then, why don't you have dinner at a traditional restaurant?

b. There are many places worth visiting but I think you'll enjoy the Archeological Museum more than any other, since you love history. It's not far from the downtown area, but it's best for you to take a taxi there so that you don't get lost.

D. Imagine that Beata is a friend of yours and is visiting your city. Read the writing task in activity A again, look at the map below and write an e-mail responding to her. You can use Amy's e-mail as a model, but you mustn't copy it. Use your own ideas and phrases giving directions from the speaking activity.

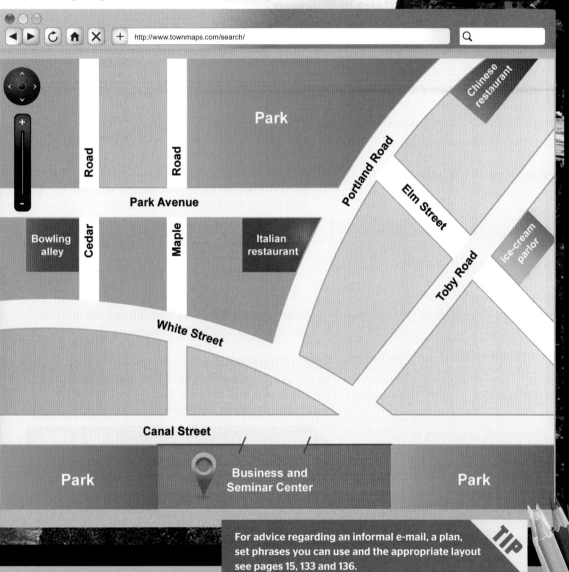

> **TIP**
> For advice regarding an informal e-mail, a plan, set phrases you can use and the appropriate layout see pages 15, 133 and 136.

A. Choose a, b or c.

1. Dylan might be at the mall, because he ____ something about going shopping.
   a. warned   b. mentioned   c. referred

2. I ____ a new antivirus program on my computer today.
   a. installed   b. scrolled   c. attached

3. The younger ____ uses social media sites much more often than mine does.
   a. generation   b. origin   c. shift

4. It is ____ for all drivers to wear seat belts.
   a. compulsory   b. qualified   c. protective

5. Jack's no good at ____ jokes. Nobody laughs when he does.
   a. saying   b. telling   c. explaining

6. This ____ gadget is very handy, since I can take it with me anywhere I go.
   a. effective   b. practical   c. portable

7. Everybody ____ the building because of the fire on the fifth floor.
   a. deactivated   b. obtained   c. evacuated

8. I ____ to the manager about the bad service at the restaurant.
   a. complained   b. gossiped   c. socialized

9. The boy asked for his mother's ____ to go to the park.
   a. gesture   b. law   c. permission

10. We walked through the construction site with extreme ____.
    a. warning   b. hazard   c. caution

B. Rewrite the sentences using the word given.

1. It is illegal to talk on your cell while driving. **law**

2. Smoking in this building is not allowed. **permitted**

3. You mustn't use the staff elevator. **forbidden**

4. I know I should be home in bed, but I came to work anyway. **supposed**

C. Circle the correct words and add commas where necessary.

1. George **whose / who** wife works as a teacher is coming over for dinner tonight.

2. We can meet at the coffee shop **where / which** is on Grandview Avenue.

3. Brenda **who / that** lives in Denver will visit me next week.

4. The hotel **which / where** we stayed was kind of far from the beach.

5. The elevator **where / that** is next to the reception desk is out of order.

6. Facebook **that / which** is a social media site is popular with young people.

D. Join the sentences using *who*, *which*, *that*, *whose* or *where*.

1. Mrs. Snyder is my new secretary. Her son is an accountant.

2. The bakery is on Ivy Creek Road. It's two blocks away from my house.

3. The man is a construction worker. He is wearing a yellow shirt.

4. You've been to the bookstore. My wife works there.

5. In case of fire, use the fire extinguisher. It is located in the hallway.

E. Put the dialogue in the correct order. Write 1-9.

`1` Excuse me, how can I get to the ice-cream parlor from here?

☐ Sorry, I didn't catch the name of the road. Could you repeat that, please?

☐ It's right next to the bank. You can't miss it.

☐ Exactly. Then keep going and take the second right. Does that make sense?

☐ Well, let me think. Umm, go down this street until you come to the stop sign. Then turn left and walk along Shelbourne Road for about 100 yards.

☐ I see. Thank you for your help.

☐ Shelbourne. After that, you'll see the post office on the corner. Turn right there and then take the second right onto Caramel Avenue.

☐ Yes. And is that where the ice-cream parlor is?

☐ Hold on. 100 yards down Shelbourne Road and then I have to turn right at the post office?

Self-assessment

Read the following and check the appropriate boxes. For the points you are unsure of, refer back to the relevant sections in the module.

NOW I CAN...

- define people, places, things and ideas and give additional information about them ☐
- use phrases to help me gain time when I need more time to think ☐
- use phrases to politely interrupt someone or to get back to the topic of discussion ☐
- understand warning signs ☐
- say whether something is permitted or not ☐
- ask for and give directions ☐
- ask for clarification and repetition ☐
- ask if I have been understood ☐
- write an informal e-mail ☐

being respected ☐

having a job ☐

being well-educated ☐

making history ☐

being famous ☐

being attractive ☐

being rich ☐

Discuss:

- Look at the pictures. What is success for you? Put the ideas in order of importance.

- What is considered successful in your culture?

- What do you consider yourself to be successful at?

- What would you like to be successful at?

In this module you will learn...

- to refer to the future using appropriate tenses

- to form opposites using prefixes (un-, in-, il-, ir-, im-)

- to express hypotheses about what is likely or unlikely to happen in the future

- to talk about your goals and ambitions

- to discuss the advantages and disadvantages of an issue

- ways to open a discussion

- to support your opinion

- to express contrast

- linking words/phrases used when listing/ adding points and when summing up

- to write an essay presenting advantages and disadvantages

Reading 🔊

A. Read the statements below. What do they mean?
Do you agree with them?

a. Winners are always part of the answer	← →	Losers are always part of the problem
b. Winners learn from mistakes	← →	Losers forget their mistakes
c. Winners see opportunities	← →	Losers have doubt
d. Winners find answers	← →	Losers only see difficulties
e. Winners follow their heart	← →	Losers settle for second best
f. Winners are a part of the team	← →	Losers are apart from the team

B. Read the text quickly and find the correct headings from above to match with the stories (1-4). There are two extra headings which you will not need to use.

Winners | Losers

Everybody enjoys winning. However the concept of victory is so mysterious. Those who are successful make it seem so simple that we are all curious about how it's done. Perhaps that's why we love success stories. Here are a few snippets of success:

1

A reporter once asked a bank president what the secret of his success was. "Two words," said the bank president. "Right decisions." When asked how he learned to make these, the bank president gave a one-word response. "Experience." Hoping for a more satisfying answer, the reporter asked him how he got his experience. "Two words," said the bank president. "Wrong decisions!"

2

In another interview, a farmer who grew award-winning corn revealed that he shared his best seeds with his neighbors. The reporter was surprised that the farmer was risking being outdone by his neighbors. "I know it seems irrational, but if I don't share, then the risk is greater," explained the farmer. "When the wind picks up pollen from the corn, it blows it from field to field. If my neighbors grow bad corn, I will too. Unless I help them, I won't be able to grow good corn. We are all connected."

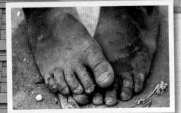

3

A shoemaker once sent two salesmen to investigate the market of a developing country. "Nobody will buy shoes here," said the first salesman confidently. "They don't wear them." "We will have sold thousands of shoes by the end of the year," reported the second salesman, a winner by nature. "They are all barefoot!"

4

In a fable by cartoonist James Thurber, there was a little moth that fell in love with a star. "If I were you, I wouldn't set such an unrealistic goal," said his mother. "You will be much happier if you fall in love with a candle."
"I'm going to reach my star!" said the little moth while the other moths made fun of him. Unaffected by their laughter, the dreamy moth left. He kept flying up high as the other moths below were getting burned by candles and street lights. The moth must have been miles and miles away when he looked down and realized that he was the only moth of his family that was still alive. "Without you I wouldn't exist now!" the moth said to the beloved star that had saved his life.

C. Read again and answer the questions. Choose a, b, c or d.

TIP

- Read each question carefully to get an idea of what you are looking for and underline the section in the text where the answer is found.
- When a question refers to the whole text, avoid options which are true but refer only to part of the text.
- Make sure you have chosen the correct answer by eliminating the wrong options.
- Avoid options which:
  - sound logical but are not mentioned in the text.
  - include a word/phrase from the text, but do not mean the same thing.
  - overgeneralize using words like *always, all, every*, etc.

1. Why does the writer suggest that we like success stories?
   a. They make us feel like winners.
   b. The lives of winners have secrets.
   c. We want to find out how to win.
   d. Their stories make us enthusiastic about winning.

2. What was it that made the bank president a successful man?
   a. Making decisions at the right time.
   b. Blaming others for mistakes.
   c. Learning from experience.
   d. It is not mentioned.

3. Why did the farmer give his best seeds to his neighbors?
   a. He didn't care about the competition.
   b. He liked challenges when competing.
   c. He was a good neighbor and a risk-taker.
   d. He wanted to be sure that he would get corn of the best quality.

4. Why was the second salesman a winner by nature?
   a. He refused to be realistic in his report.
   b. He saw the positive side of things.
   c. He did better research than the first.
   d. He sold more shoes to the people.

5. How did the moth survive?
   a. He took his mother's advice.
   b. He tried to avoid candles and street lights.
   c. He was helped by other moths.
   d. He went after his dream.

6. According to the whole text, which of the following people aren't winners?
   a. Those who believe in themselves and think they know everything.
   b. Those who aren't afraid of taking risks when others see danger.
   c. Those who keep trying and are eager to learn from their mistakes.
   d. Those who dream of achieving a goal that may not be realistic.

D. Discuss.
- What examples of successful people can you think of?
- Do you have the qualities of a winner?

Grammar Future Tenses → *p. 151*

A. Read the dialogue below and match the phrases in blue with their functions a-c.

> **A:** Next week I **am going to attend** a seminar on how to start a business. Why don't you come along? ☐
>
> **B:** Well, I have no plans, but it sounds pretty boring.
>
> **A:** Brad Garner, the guy who owns the computer company BigBytes, is going to reveal the secret of how he achieved success. It **will be** a very useful seminar! ☐
>
> **B:** Well, in that case, I**'ll come** with you. ☐

a. a future prediction
b. sth. that sb. has just decided to do
c. sth. that sb. has already planned to do

> - The **Present Progressive** is used for future plans and arrangements.
>   *We're traveling to New York this weekend.*
> - When referring to the future, use **will** in the main clause but use the **Present Simple** in the time clause (i.e. after *when, as soon as, until, till, before, after* and *by the time*).
>   *I'll get the groceries before I come home.*

B. Read the example from the text, answer the question and complete the rule.

> "We **will have sold** thousands of shoes by the end of the year," reported the second salesman.

When will it happen?
a. before the end of the year   b. after the end of the year

> The **Future Perfect** (will + _____ + past participle) is used for actions that will be completed _____ a specific time or another action in the future.

C. Complete the dialogue with the Future *will*, the Future *going to*, the Present Simple or the Future Perfect of the verbs in parentheses.

A: Susan, I have a meeting at 6 p.m., so I **1** _____ (get) home late.

B: Well, by the time you **2** _____ (get) back, I **3** _____ (leave).

A: Where are you going? To Tracy's?

B: Yes. We **4** _____ (work) on that college assignment for a while and then go for a run in the park.

A: Be careful.

B: Don't worry. I **5** _____ (make) sure I have my cell phone with me. I **6** _____ (call) you as soon as we **7** _____ (return) to Tracy's house.

Vocabulary

A. What are the opposites of the following words?
What do you notice about their formation?

suitable   convenient   legal   rational   possible

B. Complete the table forming the opposites of the adjectives in the box.

> The opposites of many English words are formed by adding a negative prefix (un-, in-, il-, ir-, im-) to the words. Notice the rules in the table below but keep in mind that there are exceptions: *e.g. lucky-unlucky, realistic-unrealistic, reliable-unreliable, pleasant-unpleasant, professional-unprofessional*

patient   literate   regular   secure   logical   correct   affected   mature   practical
aware   responsible   experienced   polite   kind   appropriate   relevant   willing

un-	in-	il- (+adj. starting with l)	ir- (+adj. starting with r)	im- (+adj. starting with m or p)

C. Complete the sentences with some of the opposites from the table above.

1. Mark may be seventeen, but I don't think he should get a driver's license yet. He's so __im__ for his age!

2. The politician was __un__ to answer the reporters' questions and got up and left.

3. Whether I think you're good at math or not is __ir__. The important thing is that you pass the exam.

4. What I'm going to say may sound crazy and __il__ but it's true.

5. Lots of teenagers are __in__ about their appearance. We need to help them feel confident about themselves.

6. Don't be __im__. I know it's a long line but it will be your turn soon.

Grammar Conditional Sentences Type Zero, 1, 2 → *p. 151*

A. Read the examples and answer the questions.

> If/When ice melts, it turns into water.

1. Does this sentence refer to sth. that is likely to happen or to a general truth/fact?

> If my neighbors grow bad corn, I will grow bad corn, too.

2. Does this sentence refer to the present/future or past?
3. Does the speaker think that this is likely to happen?

> If I were a scientist, I would try to find a solution to the problem of global warming.

4. Is the speaker a scientist?
5. Is it likely that the speaker will find a solution?
6. Does the sentence refer to the present/future or past?

B. Read the examples again and complete the rules below.

> **Conditional Sentences Type Zero** are used to talk about general truths/facts.
>
> If/When + _____ Simple → _____ Simple

> **Conditional Sentences Type 1** express something which is likely to happen in the present or future.
>
> If + _____ ↗ will, can, must, may, might, should + base form
> ↘ Imperative

> **Conditional Sentences Type 2** express something imaginary/unreal or unlikely to happen in the present or future.
>
> If + Past Simple → _____, could + base form

> **Unless** can be used instead of **if... not**.
> *You won't reach your goal **unless** you work hard.*
> *You won't reach your goal **if** you **don't** work hard.*

C. Complete the dialogue with the correct form of the verbs in parentheses.

A: What would you do if you suddenly **1** _____ (win) a lot of money and became rich?

B: Well, if I **2** _____ (be) rich, I **3** _____ (travel). I love traveling. When you **4** _____ (travel), you **5** _____ (learn) so much about other countries and cultures without realizing it.

A: That's true, but if I **6** _____ (have) a lot of money, I **7** _____ (start) my own business.

B: Like what?

A: Well, if I **8** _____ (have) the chance to do anything I liked, I **9** _____ (open) a restaurant. My dream is to become a famous chef.

B: A chef? That's impossible! You don't know how to cook anything.

A: I can easily learn anything if I **10** _____ (decide) to. If I **11** _____ (become) a chef, I **12** _____ (be) very successful, I'm sure.

B: I'm sure of one thing: you **13** _____ (not become) a chef unless you **14** _____ (take) some courses. So, start studying harder if you **15** _____ (want) to go to college.

Intonation 🔊

Listen and repeat. Notice the intonation and rhythm.

1. If you ever need help, just give me a call.
2. Unless we hurry, we'll miss the bus.
3. When you believe in success, you succeed.
4. If I were you, I wouldn't make fun of people.
5. If Mary lived closer, we'd visit her more often.
6. If you eat a lot of junk food, you put on weight.

Listening 🔊

A. Discuss.

- Do you think it's possible to predict if a person will be successful from a young age?
- Have you ever heard of the "Marshmallow Experiment"? Can you guess what it involves?

B. Listen to a psychologist giving a talk about the "Marshmallow Experiment" and complete the notes.

TIP

Read the notes carefully before listening to the recording. This will give you some idea of what you are going to hear and what kind of answers you are looking for.

The Marshmallow Experiment

When?: 1 _____ and 2 _____

The concept: Success is not just about intelligence but also about whether people are able to 3 _____ themselves and delay gratification*.

The experiment: A group of 4 _____ year-olds had to choose between 2 options: eat one marshmallow only or wait for 5 _____ to get a second one.

Results: 6 _____ out of 7 _____ children was able to wait for a second marshmallow.

15 years later: The children who had waited to get a second marshmallow were more 8 _____ than the other children later on in their lives.

gratification: the state of feeling satisfied

Speaking

Think of your dreams, goals and ambitions and discuss the questions below. Use some of the phrases given.

- What goals have you set in your life?
- How do you plan to achieve them?
- Have you achieved any so far?
- In your opinion, is it important for people to go after their dreams? Why?/Why not?
- Is there anything you would like to do but consider impossible?
- What do you think you will have accomplished in ten years' time?
- If you could be anyone in the world, who would you choose to be? Why?

I want to...
I'd like to...
I'm planning to/on...
I intend to...
I'm going to...
I'm thinking of...
I'm hoping to...
As soon as I finish school/college, I'll...
My dream has always been to...
If I (don't) succeed in..., I will (not)...
If I ever manage to..., I'll...
After I accomplish that, I'll...
If I had the chance to..., I'd...
I'd never choose to be... because...

Reading 🔊

A. Discuss.

- Do you know of or have you heard of any record-breaking achievements?

B. Read the text quickly. What is the purpose of this text?

a. to describe an important event in the history of skydiving

b. to explain what extreme skydivers go through

c. to compare the lives of Joe Kittinger and Felix Baumgartner

d. to discuss the history and future of skydiving

Fearless Felix

Felix Baumgartner 127,851 ft.

Joe Kittinger 102,800 ft.

weather balloon 80,000 ft.

Boeing 747 46,000 ft.

STRATOSPHERE

Mt. Everest 29,029 ft.

On August 16th, 1960, a man named Joe Kittinger jumped from a height of 102,800 ft. (19.5 miles). He fell for 4 minutes and 36 seconds, reaching a top speed of 614 mph before opening his parachute at 18,000 ft. In a matter of minutes, Kittinger had made history. He set records for highest ascent*, highest parachute jump and fastest velocity*. 52 years later, Kittinger was first on the list of a highly-experienced crew when skydiver Felix Baumgartner decided to break the record and go even higher.

Felix Baumgartner was born on April 20th, 1969 in Salzburg, Austria. He is a professional BASE jumper and skydiver, and has accomplished many amazing feats. In 1999, he claimed the world record for the highest parachute jump from a building after leaping 1,479 ft. from The Petronas Twin Towers in Malaysia, which were the tallest buildings in the world at the time. In 2004, Felix jumped off the highest bridge in the world, the Millau Viaduct in France, from an altitude of 1,125 ft. In 2007, Felix jumped to the bottom of the world's second biggest cave, called "Seating of the Spirits," located in Oman. The depth of the cave (only 395 ft.) and its tube-like shape made this challenge seem impossible. Felix, however, jumped into pitch darkness and landed unhurt six seconds later with only two seconds to open his parachute!

Before attempting the highest skydive on record, Felix had made two successful stratosphere* test jumps from 71,581 ft. and 96,650 ft. Weather conditions on October 14th, 2012 were perfect as the helium balloon and capsule* moved upwards into the sky. However, when it reached 62,000 ft., Felix reported that his visor heater wasn't working properly. The ground crew briefly considered aborting the mission, but decided to continue. It took him two and a half hours to climb to 127,851 ft. (over 24 miles) and as he prepared to jump, Kittinger told him via radio, "OK, we're getting serious now, Felix."

Along with the many dangers of skydiving, the main fear for Felix was what would happen to his body if he broke the sound barrier at 768 mph. No human had traveled faster than the speed of sound before without a vehicle. 8,000,000 people were watching the live stream on YouTube as Felix looked down at the Earth below him and said, "I'm coming home." Then he jumped. After 42 seconds of freefall, he reached a top speed of 843.6 mph. Soon after, the atmosphere became thicker and slowed him down a little. Approximately four minutes later, he opened his parachute and was safely back on the ground eleven minutes after leaving the capsule. Felix had once again succeeded, therefore proving his ability to achieve his goals. Felix broke three records and gained international fame. What will his passion make him do next?

* ascent = the act of climbing or moving upwards

* velocity = the speed of something that is moving

* stratosphere = the outer part of the air surrounding the Earth, from 32,808 ft. to 164,041 ft. above the Earth

* capsule = the part of a spacecraft in which people travel

C. Read again and write T for True, F for False or NM for Not Mentioned.

1. Joe Kittinger held three world records for 52 years. ☐

2. Felix still holds the record for the highest parachute jump from a building. ☐

3. Felix's jump into the cave lasted 8 seconds. ☐

4. Felix was forced to cancel his jump on October 14th, 2012 because of a problem with his equipment. ☐

5. Felix had no contact with the ground crew when he reached 127,851 ft. ☐

6. Felix traveled faster than the speed of sound while falling. ☐

7. The Earth's atmosphere made Felix travel more slowly. ☐

8. Felix's jump from space lasted 11 minutes. ☐

9. Felix is now planning his next breathtaking feat. ☐

D. Look at the highlighted words in the text and match them with their meanings.

1. feat ☐
2. leap ☐
3. altitude ☐
4. properly ☐
5. abort ☐
6. fame ☐
7. passion ☐

a. the height above sea level

b. correctly, right

c. a very strong interest in sth.; enthusiasm

d. an achievement

e. the success and attention you get when being famous

f. to jump

g. to stop an activity or plan before completing it

E. Discuss.

• Would you like to experience what Baumgartner went through? Why? / Why not?

Vocabulary

A. Look at the nouns below from the text. Which adjectives do they derive from?

darkness   ability   height   depth

B. Read the notes and complete the tables.

> Some nouns are formed by adding the suffix *-ness* or *-ity* to an adjective.
> e.g. sad-sadness, active-activity

Adjective	Noun
lazy	
creative	
popular	
aware	
responsible	
weak	
kind	
similar	

> Some nouns have an irregular formation.

Adjective or Verb	Noun
weigh	
	strength
dead/die	
	belief
relieve	
	anger
	thought
	growth
famous	

Listening 🔊

A. Read the questions in the quiz below and try to guess the answers.

RECORD BREAKERS !

1. What distance is the longest 24-hour bike ride without the rider's feet touching the ground?
   a. 53.1 miles   b. 553.15 miles   c. 5,533.5 miles

2. How long is the longest beard?
   a. 2.7 ft.   b. 4.7 ft.   c. 7.7 ft.

3. How many records were broken at the 2011 London Marathon?
   a. 0   b. 5   c. 35

4. In 2012 Eva and Paul Yavorzhno decided to get married underwater. But how many guests joined them underwater?
   a. 15   b. 134   c. 275

5. In 2011 Sanath Bandara, from Sri Lanka, broke the record for wearing the most T-shirts worn at once. But how many did he wear?
   a. 157   b. 257   c. 357

B. Now listen to part of a radio show and check your answers.

Speaking

Talk in pairs. Imagine your college is planning on expanding its facilities. Behind the college is an area of open ground which will be turned into one of the two options shown below. You are on the committee and have been asked to give your opinion. First discuss the advantages and disadvantages of each option using the ideas in the box and the words given. Then decide which option would appeal most to your fellow students. Use some of the phrases given.

a cafeteria with an outdoor patio

an indoor swimming pool

Talk about:
- the cost needed to build/maintain
- how appealing it is to college students
- what students can do there
- how the weather affects it
- how it can improve students' lives

pay for maintenance   (un)appealing   socialize
enjoyable   relax   energizing   beneficial
escape from routine   weather dependent   stay in shape

Opening a discussion
To begin with,...
First, we need to discuss...
Let's start by talking/thinking about...
The important thing (here) is...
The main thing we need to discuss is...

Supporting one's opinion
I believe... is a good idea because...
There are several reasons why I believe this. The first is...
... would provide students with an opportunity to...
Some students may find this... as they are (not) interested in...
The reason I think... is more appealing to students is because...
One of the advantages/disadvantages of... is...
I think... would be the most appropriate/suitable option for... as many students...

Expressing contrast
On the other hand,...
However,...
Very true, but...
You may be right, but...

Writing An essay (discussing advantages and disadvantages)

A. Discuss.
- If you were an athlete, would you like to be a professional athlete? Why?/Why not?

B. Read the writing task and underline the key words. Then read the essay and answer the questions that follow.

You have been asked to write an essay on the following topic:

What are the advantages and disadvantages of being a professional athlete?

Being a professional athlete requires a lot of effort and devotion. Many people consider it to be a dream career, while others disagree.

It is not difficult to see the benefits of being a professional athlete. To begin with, the main advantage is earning a huge income doing something you enjoy, as well as earning money from advertising products. In addition, most athletes enjoy fame and at the same time act as role models for thousands of people. Moreover, there are excellent opportunities for athletes to travel around the world as they can take part in different worldwide events and competitions.

However, there are also certain disadvantages to being a professional athlete. Firstly, there is a huge amount of stress involved, as any failure means disappointment for you, your coach, your team and your fans. Secondly, there is the lack of spare time, as athletes need to devote all their time and energy to demanding training. Besides that, extensive travel makes family life difficult. Last but not least, there is the issue of injuries. If a professional athlete gets injured, it could mean the end of his or her career.

On the whole, I believe the advantages outweigh the disadvantages. The way I see it, being a professional athlete is difficult, but rewarding. Those who have natural talent should not let it go to waste. They should turn professional.

1. How many advantages does the writer mention in the second paragraph? What are they?
2. How many disadvantages does the writer mention in the third paragraph? What are they?
3. In which paragraph does the writer express his/her opinion?

C. Look at the highlighted words/phrases in the essay and use them to complete the table below.

LINKING WORDS/PHRASES	
Listing/Adding points	_____, first of all, in the first place, _____, _____, what is more, _____, _____, furthermore, apart from that, also, _____, finally, lastly, _____
Expressing contrast	_____, but, _____, on the one hand, on the other hand
Summing up	to sum up, in conclusion, all in all, _____

D. Read the writing task below and make a list of advantages and disadvantages. Then write the essay using the TIP and the plan.

You have been asked to write an essay on the following topic:
What are the pros and cons of working out outdoors?

ADVANTAGES

DISADVANTAGES

Plan
An essay discussing advantages and disadvantages

INTRODUCTION
Introduce the subject of the essay and both sides of the topic.

MAIN PART (2 PARAGRAPHS)
Refer to the advantages/disadvantages in separate paragraphs. Cover both sides of the topic equally.

CONCLUSION
Make a general statement summing up and state your opinion.

TIP

When writing an essay discussing advantages and disadvantages,

- think about the topic carefully.
- choose two or three ideas/points (the ones that you can explain and support) for each paragraph of the main part. Don't try to deal with too many points.
- use a variety of linking words/phrases to list points, add points, express contrast, give your opinion, sum up, etc.
- write in a formal style and do not use short forms.
- avoid introducing any new ideas in the conclusion.

A. Choose a, b or c.

1. When Brian ____ a goal, he always accomplishes it.
   a. puts   b. breaks   c. sets

2. Don't ____ me for what happened. It's totally your fault.
   a. intend   b. blame   c. reveal

3. The local team's ____ made the crowd cheer.
   a. victory   b. ambition   c. intelligence

4. Climbing Mt. Everest is a dangerous and difficult ____.
   a. feat   b. passion   c. concept

5. All ____ all, we had a great time on our vacation.
   a. on   b. to   c. in

6. We were flying at a(n) ____ of about 35,000 ft. and I could see the clouds down below.
   a. depth   b. speed   c. altitude

7. Cindy's job at the hospital is pretty ____, as she sometimes has to deal with difficult patients.
   a. demanding   b. energizing   c. appealing

8. I can't stand Carl's loud and annoying ____.
   a. anger   b. response   c. laughter

9. I hate it when people make fun ____ others.
   a. of   b. with   c. on

10. Someone who is ____ doesn't know how to read or write.
    a. insecure   b. illiterate   c. immature

B. Complete the sentences with the correct form of the words in capitals.

1. Mike never says "please" or "thank you". He's very _____.   **POLITE**

2. Eating chocolate is my _____. I absolutely love it.   **WEAK**

3. Joyce didn't get the job because she was _____.   **EXPERIENCED**

4. I argued with George and now he is _____ to talk to me.   **WILLING**

5. Writing an interesting story requires _____.   **CREATIVE**

6. You should get over your _____ and go to the gym!   **LAZY**

7. I don't trust Marshall. He is completely _____.   **RELIABLE**

C. Complete with the Future will, the Future going to, the Present Simple or the Future Perfect of the verbs in parentheses.

Bill Hey, Eric. 1 _____ (you / get up) early tomorrow morning, like you said?

Eric Yeah.

Bill 2 _____ (you / wake) me up, too? I have so many things to do for my business trip! I think I 3 _____ (be) busy all day long.

Eric Don't worry. I 4 _____ (help) you. What do you want me to do?

Bill 5 _____ (you / pick up) my suit from the dry cleaner's, please?

Eric No problem. Anything else?

Bill Well, I probably 6 _____ (not finish) with my shopping by this afternoon either. 7 _____ (you / stop) by the grocery store for me?

Eric Of course. I 8 _____ (go) there anyway because I need some stuff. So, just give me the list. Listen, I 9 _____ (give) you a call as soon as I 10 _____ (finish) shopping, so that you can tell me about anything else you need. OK?

Bill Thanks, Eric.

D. Complete the sentences with the correct form of the verbs in parentheses.

1. Martin _____ (help) you if you ask him.

2. Where would you go if you _____ (can) travel anywhere in the world?

3. If you _____ (not hurry), we'll be late.

4. When people _____ (eat) unhealthy food, they put on weight easily.

5. I _____ (not go) out with William if I were you. He's boring.

6. Unless Sandra _____ (want) to get fired, she shouldn't be late for work again.

7. If Michelle had more time, she _____ (cook) more often.

8. You _____ (not succeed) unless you work hard.

9. If Jerry _____ (not live) in the countryside, we'd see him more often.

10. A "help" box _____ (appear) on the screen when you press F1.

Self-assessment

Read the following and check the appropriate boxes. For the points you are unsure of, refer back to the relevant sections in the module.

NOW I CAN...

❭ refer to the future using appropriate tenses ☐

❭ form opposites using prefixes (un-, in-, il-, ir-, im-) ☐

❭ express hypotheses about what is likely or unlikely to happen in the future ☐

❭ talk about my goals and ambitions ☐

❭ discuss the advantages and disadvantages of an issue ☐

❭ open a discussion ☐

❭ support my opinion ☐

❭ express contrast ☐

❭ use linking words/phrases to list/add points and to sum up ☐

❭ write an essay presenting advantages and disadvantages ☐

Task 5&6 p. 129

Exam Practice Modules 4-6 p. 140

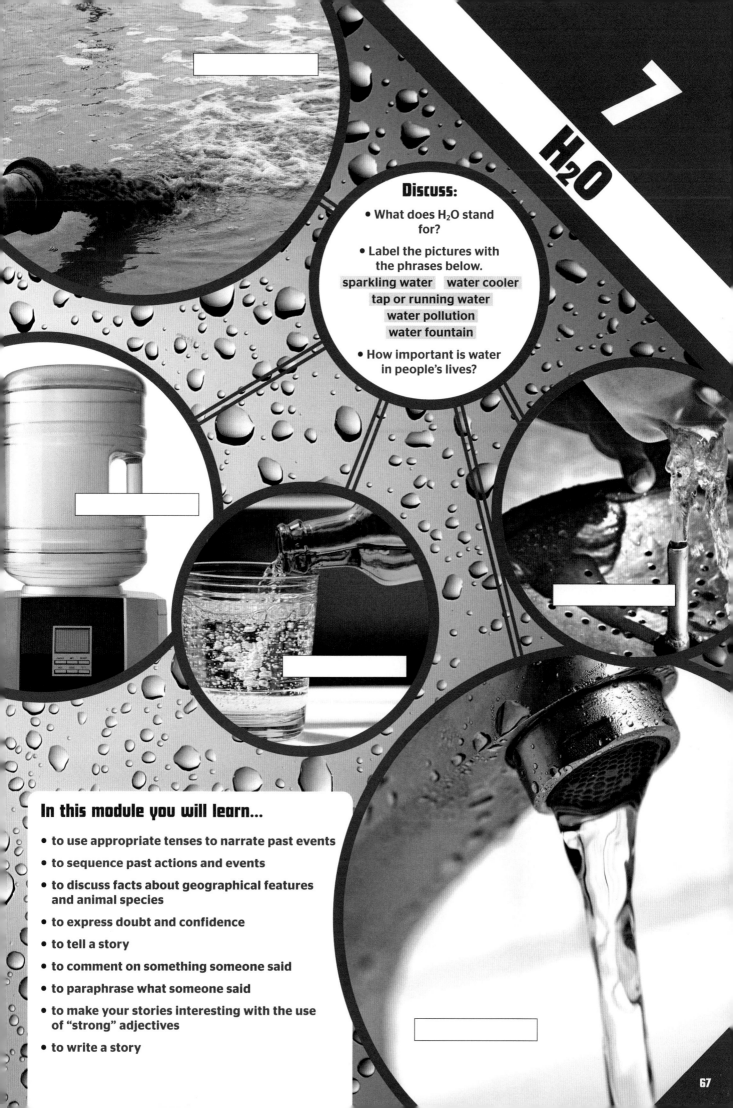

7

H₂O

Discuss:

• What does H₂O stand for?

• Label the pictures with the phrases below.

sparkling water   water cooler
tap or running water
water pollution
water fountain

• How important is water in people's lives?

In this module you will learn...

• to use appropriate tenses to narrate past events

• to sequence past actions and events

• to discuss facts about geographical features and animal species

• to express doubt and confidence

• to tell a story

• to comment on something someone said

• to paraphrase what someone said

• to make your stories interesting with the use of "strong" adjectives

• to write a story

Reading 🔊

A. Discuss.

- Do you enjoy science-fiction stories?
- Have you read any of Jules Verne's adventure novels? If so, did you like them?

Twenty Thousand Leagues Under the Sea

B. Below is an extract from an adapted version of the novel *Twenty Thousand Leagues Under the Sea*. Look at the picture. Can you guess what's happening? Read the extract and check your answers.

Twenty Thousand Leagues Under the Sea - Jules Verne

I looked out of the window of the Nautilus and saw what my companion, Ned Land, had been looking at. Before my eyes was a sea monster worthy of myth and legend. Its eight long tentacles were twice as long as its body, and its mouth was like the beak of an oversized parrot. It was swimming at great speed and staring at us with its enormous green eyes.

I overcame my horror and took out my sketch book. This was an excellent opportunity for a marine biologist. Suddenly the Nautilus stopped. A minute passed and Captain Nemo, followed by his lieutenant, entered the room. I hadn't seen him for some time. I overheard them talking about the monsters.

"Have we struck anything?" I asked.

"No, Monsieur Aronnax. I think one of the giant squid is entangled in the propeller."

"What are we going to do?"

"We are going to fight them, man to beast," he said.

"Man to beast?" I repeated.

Captain Nemo gave the order to rise to the surface. About ten men with hatchets headed towards the central staircase. I took a hatchet and my companion, Ned Land, grabbed a harpoon. As soon as one of the sailors at the top of the ladder opened the door, it was pulled off with great force. Immediately one of the tentacles of the squid slid down into the opening like a gigantic snake. With one blow of his hatchet, Nemo cut the tentacle off the squid. Then, we all rushed out.

What a scene! By the time I got outside, one of the beasts had grabbed a sailor in its tentacle and was throwing him around like a feather. He struggled, but it was no good. I shall hear his cries for the rest of my life. Captain Nemo and his lieutenant threw themselves on the beast but it shot out black liquid and we were blinded for an instant. Enough time for the monster to disappear along with the sailor. Ten or twelve squid attacked the sides of the Nautilus and we fought them as best we could. Suddenly, I turned

around and saw Ned on the floor. He had been fighting bravely until a tentacle knocked him over. A squid was about to cut him in two with its beak. Luckily, Nemo rushed to his rescue and hit the beast with his hatchet.

After a quarter of an hour of fighting, the monsters left us at last. Captain Nemo, obviously exhausted, gazed at the sea that had swallowed one of his companions and his eyes filled with tears.

C. Read the text again and answer the questions. Choose a, b, c or d.

1. Who is narrating the story?
   a. A sailor.
   b. A marine biologist.
   c. The captain of the Nautilus.
   d. The lieutenant.

2. After recovering from shock, what did the narrator want to do?
   a. speak to the captain
   b. find out why the Nautilus had stopped
   c. draw the sea monster
   d. find out what the captain and his lieutenant were talking about

3. Why did the Nautilus stop?
   a. It had hit a squid.
   b. To avoid hitting a squid.
   c. On orders from the captain.
   d. A squid had caused engine problems.

4. Why did the captain order the Nautilus to rise to the surface?
   a. So they could fight the squid.
   b. To escape from the squid.
   c. To repair the propeller.
   d. So they could get their weapons.

5. Which of the following is true?
   a. A squid attacked the men while they were rising to the surface.
   b. Captain Nemo killed a squid as soon as the door was opened.
   c. Some men grabbed weapons and went to fight the squid.
   d. A squid forced the door of the Nautilus open.

6. What happened to the sailor trapped in the squid's tentacle?
   a. He was saved by Captain Nemo.
   b. He was dragged into the sea.
   c. He was covered in black liquid.
   d. He was blinded by the squid.

D. Look at the highlighted words in the text and match them with their meanings a-j.

1. companion ☐
2. myth ☐
3. oversized ☐
4. overcome ☐
5. overhear ☐
6. grab ☐
7. struggle ☐
8. blind ☐
9. attack ☐
10. gaze ☐

a. to make it difficult or impossible for sb. to see
b. to successfully control a feeling
c. to look at sb. or sth. for a long time; to stare
d. a person that you spend a lot of time with because you are friends or are traveling together
e. to kick and fight so that you can escape from sb./sth.
f. to take or hold sth. with your hand in a sudden and violent way
g. sth. that many people believe, but which is not true
h. to hear sth. by accident or without the speaker knowing it
i. to use violence to hurt sb. or damage a place
j. bigger than usual

E. Talk in pairs. Take turns to tell the story in your own words.

F. Discuss.
- Would you like to read the rest of the story?
- What do you think happens next?

Grammar Past Perfect Simple - Past Perfect Progressive → *p. 152*

A. Read the examples and answer the questions.

> By the time I **got** outside, one of the beasts **had grabbed** a sailor in its tentacle.

1. Which action happened first and which happened next?
2. Which tenses are used?

> Ned **had been looking** out of the window of the Nautilus for a few minutes before he saw the giant squid.

3. How long had Ned been looking out of the window?
4. When is the Past Perfect Progressive used and how is it formed?

B. Complete the text with the Past Simple, the Past Perfect Simple or the Past Perfect Progressive of the verbs in parentheses.

Fresh ice 1 _____ (form) around the Nautilus all morning. We were stuck and the situation was getting worse. It was becoming obvious that we could go no further south. I 2 _____ (talk) to the other sailors for most of the morning, but nobody 3 _____ (have) any idea about how to escape. I 4 _____ (decide) to go and see Captain Nemo on the platform. He 5 _____ (observe) our situation for some time and when I 6 _____ (speak) to him, he 7 _____ (already / decide) how to solve the problem. He 8 _____ (suggest) something which I 9 _____ (not think) of. "We will sail under the ice to the South Pole," he said.

I 10 _____ (think) about the idea for a moment, and 11 _____ (realize) that we might have to stay underwater for several days. It would be extremely dangerous.

Vocabulary

A. Read the words below. Can you think of any well-known examples of these geographical features?

ocean   river   lake   mountain (mount / Mt.)   island   volcano

B. Complete the names below with the geographical features in the box.

| rainforest   falls   canal   canyon   bay   sea   gulf   desert |

Panama _____

Amazon _____

San Francisco _____

Grand _____

Angel _____

Red _____

_____ of Mexico

Gobi _____

Grammar Articles → p. 152

A. Read the examples below and circle the correct words to complete the rules in the box underneath.

- **The** Caspian Sea is **a** lake, not **a** sea.
- Suddenly, **the** sharks attacked **the** boat and **the** passengers got really scared.
- There's **a** national park in California, U.S.A. which is called Sequoia National Park. **The** park is famous for its giant sequoia trees.

- We use **a(n) / the** before a singular countable noun when we refer to it in a general sense or when it is mentioned for the first time.

- We use **a(n) / the** before a noun which is something unique, is used in a specific sense or has been mentioned before.

- Before a noun which represents a species, we can use *a(n)*, *the* or the plural form.
  A penguin can't fly.
  The penguin can't fly.
  Penguins can't fly.
- **No article** is used before uncountable nouns and plural countable nouns which refer to something in a general sense.
  Water is something we shouldn't waste.
  Volcanoes exist on Earth but also on other planets like Mars.

B. Complete the texts with *a(n)*, *the* or -.

1.

Have you ever seen **1** _____ rhinoceros? I saw one up close when I was in **2** _____ South Africa last year, and they are one of **3** _____ most amazing animals in **4** _____ world. In **5** _____ Africa, there are two species of **6** _____ rhinos. **7** _____ white rhino is **8** _____ largest and most numerous rhinoceros species that exists. **9** _____ black rhino is smaller and it is **10** _____ endangered species because people hunt it. **11** _____ hunting is illegal nowadays, however there are still **12** _____ people who hunt **13** _____ rhinos.

2.

14 _____ golden toad, also known as **15** _____ Monteverde toad, used to live in **16** _____ rainforest of **17** _____ Costa Rica. It was **18** _____ common species in **19** _____ past, but in 1988 only 10 were found. Sadly, **20** _____ research team which was sent in 1989 could only find one. It was declared extinct in 2007 and **21** _____ biologists say **22** _____ main cause was pollution and **23** _____ disease.

Listening 🔊

A. Discuss.

• Have you ever watched a documentary about underwater life? Was it interesting?

B. Read the statements below. Which one do you think is false? Listen to a TV documentary and check your answers.

1. A green sea turtle travels thousands of miles to find the beach it was born on.

2. An anglerfish lives in the deepest part of the ocean.

3. A blue whale has a heart the size of a car.

C. Listen again and write T for Turtles, A for Anglerfish or W for Whales.

1. They spend their lives in complete darkness. ☐

2. They are fast swimmers for their size. ☐

3. They are in danger of becoming extinct. ☐

4. They are in danger from the day they are born. ☐

5. They have a clever way of finding food. ☐

Pronunciation 🔊

A. Listen to the following extracts from the listening activity above. *The* is not pronounced the same in all cases. Can you see why?

*"We're exploring **the** seas and oceans of **the** world and discovering why **the** Earth is known as **the** blue planet."*

*"Here I am on Ascension Island, right in **the** middle of **the** Atlantic Ocean."*

B. Read the sentences below and try to pronounce *the* correctly. Listen and compare your answers.

1. The island of Sicily is the largest island in the Mediterranean Sea.

2. The Grand Canyon is in the U.S.A.

3. The ocean contains 97% of the Earth's water.

4. The underwater mountain range Mid-Oceanic Ridge has peaks higher than those in the Alps.

Speaking

Talk in pairs. Discuss whether the statements below are true or false. Use some of the phrases in the box. Then check your answers with your teacher.

TRUE or FALSE?

1. The animal with the most species on the planet is the beetle. ◯

2. Koalas never drink water. ◯

3. There are no animals living in Antarctica. ◯

4. The Arctic is considered a desert. ◯

5. The cheetah is the fastest animal on the planet. ◯

6. The octopus smells with its tentacles. ◯

7. Most of the world's islands are found in the Pacific Ocean. ◯

8. Tigers have never lived in Africa. ◯

Expressing doubt
I'm not really sure, but… may/might/could…
Oh, I don't know. I suppose/guess…
I think…, but I can't be certain.
I can't say for sure, but maybe/perhaps…
It seems unbelievable, but my guess is that…
I could be wrong, but I believe…
I'm not completely confident, but…

Expressing confidence
I'm certain/sure…
I'm absolutely certain…
I'm positive…
I'm (very/fairly) confident that…
I know for a fact that…
I have no doubt that…

Q&A: H₂O

A. Look at questions 1-4 below. Do you know or can you guess the answers?

B. Read the text and match the questions 1-4 with the answers a-d.

1 ☐ A friend of mine says he uses up 2,000 gallons of water a day just from his diet. Is this possible? *Bob, Toronto*

2 ☐ Is it true that half of the world's population doesn't have access to clean running water? *Liz, Cardiff*

3 ☐ I've heard that drinking eight glasses of water a day is good for our health. Would it do me any good if I drank double that amount? *Cliff, Boston*

4 ☐ With 72% of the Earth's surface covered in water, why do people keep talking about a water shortage? *Sandy, Perth*

a Actually, the total amount of water on the Earth is a huge 326,000,000,000,000,000,000 (326 million trillion) gallons! Did you know that the same water that exists on our planet today has been around for millions of years? All this water is always in motion – evaporating from oceans, traveling through the air, raining on the land and running through rivers, even through our bodies. The supply of fresh water is limited to just 3% of the total amount and there are fears that it won't be enough to keep the world population alive. After all, the human population has increased in size and the fresh water supply has decreased because of pollution.

b Many of us have never bothered to link the food on our plate with the 70% of our planet's fresh water used in agriculture. For instance, we think that a cup of instant coffee requires the use of just a cup of water. However, it takes 37 gallons of water to produce a teaspoon of coffee beans. And if you add some toast with a slice of cheese along with your coffee, then you can add another 13 gallons to the total amount of water required for your food supply. Add all this up and that's just 50 gallons of water for a simple breakfast. A day's supply of food for an average family of four requires 6,800 gallons of water. This amount doesn't even include the amount of water they use when taking showers, flushing toilets, doing the laundry or washing the dishes!

c Most of us take it for granted that we can turn on the faucet and have a cool glass of water whenever we want. According to the United Nations, however, half of the global population can't do this. In many places, families rely on the young female members, who are forced to stop school just to collect water for their family. They walk for approximately three hours a day to the nearest swamp or river to collect water that has been sitting in the open and is full of germs. The World Health Organization (WHO) says that 3.4 million people die yearly from water-related diseases. More specifically, every twenty seconds a child dies from drinking dirty water. Every week, 42,000 people die from diseases caused by unsafe water.

d Water is a source of life, but sometimes you can get too much of a good thing. A person who has drunk more water than they need can suffer from water intoxication. People have even died in water drinking competitions when they consumed too much too quickly because of imbalances created in their body. Other people at risk of water intoxication are athletes such as marathon runners. The symptoms of water intoxication include nausea, headaches and vomiting as well as muscle weakness.

C. Read again and match the numbers 1-8 to what they refer to.

1. 72 percent
2. 50 percent
3. 42 thousand
4. 6,800 gallons
5. 3.4 million

6. eight glasses
7. 3 percent of 326 million trillion gallons
8. 37 gallons

a. fresh water on the planet ☐
b. amount of water one should drink daily ☐
c. water needed to produce a teaspoon of coffee ☐
d. deaths from dirty water every year ☐
e. the percentage of people without running water ☐
f. amount of water on the surface of the planet ☐
g. daily water needed to prepare the food for a family of four ☐
h. deaths from dirty water every week ☐

D. Find words/phrases in the text and match them with the meanings below.

1. when there is not enough of sth. that is needed (questions)
2. moving (answer a)
3. an amount of sth. that is available to be used (answer a)
4. to make a connection between two things (answer b)
5. the science or practice of farming (answer b)
6. land that is very wet or covered with water (answer c)
7. very small living things that cause disease (answer c)
8. to eat or drink sth. (answer d)

E. Discuss.

• Do you know of any other amazing facts about water?

SAVE WATER

Please turn OFF the faucet after use.

Vocabulary

A. Find the following verbs in the text in the reading activity. Which prepositions are they followed by?

link   rely   **die**   suffer

B. Look at the verbs in the box. Which prepositions are they followed by? Complete the table.

depend   cope   benefit   deal   rescue
recover   insist   spend   escape   cooperate
communicate   congratulate

with

on

from

Listening 🔊

A. Listen to a radio interview about World Water Day. Which of the following topics are mentioned?

the first World Water Day ☐
the official website ☐
World Water Day events ☐
water footprint ☐
the countries facing water shortage ☐
the goals involved ☐

B. Listen again and write T for True or F for False.

1. World Water Day is on a different date every year. ☐
2. World Water Day raises awareness about how people can access clean water. ☐
3. Walk for Water is an event mostly for women and children. ☐
4. During Walk for Water participants carry water. ☐
5. To produce a pint of milk, 12,000 gallons of water are needed. ☐

Speaking

Work in small groups. Make up a story using as many of the prompts given as possible. Discuss how you each think the story should develop. Use some of the phrases given below. After you have finalized your story, tell it to the class.

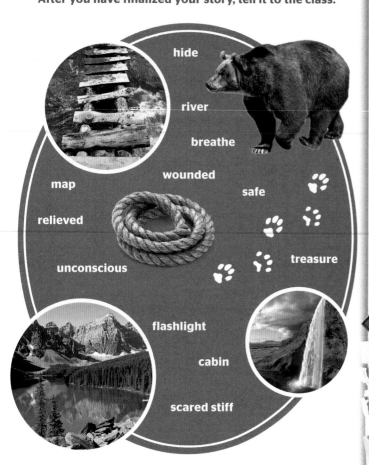

hide
river
breathe
wounded
safe
map
relieved
unconscious
treasure
flashlight
cabin
scared stiff

- When you want to make a comment or add something to an ongoing conversation, it's polite to acknowledge what someone has just said before stating your own idea.
- Paraphrasing involves saying someone else's ideas in your own words.
- A useful way of bringing new ideas into a conversation is by asking questions.

TIP

Commenting
That's interesting. I think that...
That sounds like a good idea. And then we could have...
OK. I would add...
Can I add something here? Maybe the... could...
Hmmm. I hadn't thought of that.
What do you think about...?
What about...?
I have a better idea. What if...?

Paraphrasing (rephrasing the other person's idea)
So, you think that we should...
In other words...
I understand. You're saying that...
I get it. He/She...
So, what you're saying is...
Let me see if I understand you correctly...

Writing A story (II)

A. Read the writing task on the right and the story that follows. Has the writer included the two ideas specified?

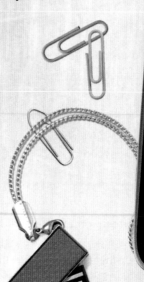

speakloud.com

We are looking for stories for our new short story section. Your story must begin with this sentence:

I couldn't believe my eyes when I saw the enormous waves.

Your story must include:
- a fishing boat
- a flashlight

I couldn't believe my eyes when I saw the enormous waves. The weather was supposed to be marvelous. That's why Jack and I had decided to go fishing. However, the gentle breeze started getting stronger and stronger until our fishing boat was rocking on the rough water. We were terrified!

Suddenly, a wave hit us hard and I almost fell overboard. Our boat started filling with water and I knew we had to act fast. I yelled to Jack, "Get into the lifeboat! We're going down!" We got in just in time to see our boat sink.

The wind died down several hours later. We were both seasick and freezing, but relieved. "What now?" I thought to myself. I looked through the safety equipment and found a pair of binoculars. I immediately started searching for other boats on the water. Hours later, I felt miserable. Nobody was looking for us.

Just when I thought we were out of luck, a tiny dot appeared on the horizon. It was a boat. We were rowing towards it, waving at the same time, when we realized that it was probably too dark for anyone to see us. "Let's use our flashlight!" Jack shouted and started signaling in the boat's direction.

Fortunately, it worked! It was too good to be true! We were absolutely thrilled. The boat soon spotted us and, within minutes, we were safely on our way home.

B. Read the story again and answer the questions.

1. What tenses has the writer used throughout the story to narrate what happened?

2. Has the writer used linking words/phrases to indicate the sequence of events? Which ones?

3. Find examples of the following features which make the story interesting: direct speech, exclamations, adverbs and adverbial phrases, adjectives describing feelings.

C. Read the story again and find words that mean:

1. very big (para. 1): _____

2. very nice (para. 1): _____

3. very scared (para. 1): _____

4. very cold (para. 3): _____

5. very unhappy (para. 3): _____

6. very small (para. 4): _____

7. very excited (para. 5): _____

E. Read the writing task below and write the story.

You have seen this announcement in an international magazine.

speakloud

We are looking for stories for our new short story section.
Your story must begin with this sentence:

After walking around for a few hours, I realized I was lost.

Your story must include:
- **a key**
- **a forest**

D. Read the note. Replace the "strong" adjectives in the sentences 1-7 below with an appropriate adverb and the "weak" adjectives in the box.

To add emphasis, use the following adverbs before "weak" or "strong" adjectives.

ADVERBS BEFORE "WEAK" ADJECTIVES

| really, very extremely, incredibly terribly, a little | good angry funny tired | etc. |

ADVERBS BEFORE "STRONG" ADJECTIVES

| really, completely absolutely, totally | fantastic furious hilarious exhausted | etc. |

*I'm **very/really** tired.*
*I'm **absolutely/really** exhausted.*

| surprised | interesting | hungry | dirty | hot |
| beautiful | angry | | | |

1. I was **furious** with myself when I lost my cell phone.

2. It's **boiling** outside. We should go for a swim.

3. I watched a **fascinating** documentary about dolphins last night.

4. My cousin Stephanie has **gorgeous** blue eyes.

5. I was **astonished** to hear that Frank got fired.

6. Your hands are **filthy**. You'd better wash them before dinner!

7. I haven't had anything for breakfast and I'm **starving**.

TIP

When writing a story:

- follow the plan on page 133.

- use the given sentence without changing it and remember to include any other points/ideas required.

- try to keep the plot simple and divide your story into paragraphs.

- use past tenses and time linkers to indicate the sequence of events (see page 25).

- try to make it interesting for the reader by using:

  - Direct Speech, questions and exclamation marks

  - adverbs/adverbial phrases (*e.g. suddenly, fortunately, to my surprise*)

  - a variety of adjectives (e.g. *awful* instead of *bad*)

  - expressions or idioms like:
    It was too good to be true.
    The next thing I knew,...
    There was no hope left.
    Without thinking,...
    Within minutes,...
    I was in/out of luck.
    I nearly jumped out of my skin.
    I went red as a beet.

A. Circle the correct words.

1. Gloria **gazed / struggled** out the window at the beautiful coast.

2. Many people feel **disease / nausea** when they travel by ship.

3. I hate being sick. It makes me feel **miserable / gorgeous**.

4. When he realized he was late, he **bothered / grabbed** his coat and rushed out the door.

5. You shouldn't **increase / consume** too much caffeine. It's not good for you.

6. The airplane looked like a tiny **bay / dot** as it flew across the sky.

7. Mark hit his head and fell down **hilarious / unconscious**.

B. Complete the sentences with the correct preposition.

1. Susan is a good friend, who I can rely _____ for whatever I need.

2. The firefighter rescued the baby _____ the burning building.

3. Kevin finally recovered fully _____ his illness.

4. If we all cooperate _____ each other, we will quickly solve the problem.

5. I don't know if I'll go out tonight. It depends _____ how much studying I'll have.

6. How much did you spend _____ your new car?

7. Eric couldn't cope _____ the stress at his job so he quit.

8. My sister insisted _____ lending me the money.

C. Complete the sentences with the Past Simple, the Past Perfect Simple or the Past Perfect Progressive of the verbs in parentheses.

1. By the time we _____ (reach) the park, it _____ (already / start) raining.

2. Joey _____ (study) all afternoon and was glad when Gus _____ (call) him.

3. We _____ (row) the lifeboat for a couple hours when we finally _____ (see) a ship in the distance.

4. On the first day of our trip to Melbourne, we _____ (get) lost in the city because we _____ (not take) a map with us.

5. When I _____ (arrive) at the airport, my sister's flight _____ (not land) yet.

6. The children _____ (be) exhausted because they _____ (play) on the beach for hours.

7. The explorers _____ (find) the treasure after they _____ (search) for it for over three days.

8. Amy _____ (talk) on the phone with Tanya for an hour by the time she _____ (hang) up. They _____ (not speak) to each other for a long time and they _____ (have) lots of news to catch up on.

D. Complete the sentences with a(n), the or -.

1. _____ Amazon Rainforest has many _____ rivers, _____ lakes and _____ waterfalls. _____ Amazon River is _____ second longest river in _____ world.

2. _____ Ibiza is _____ island off _____ coast of _____ Spain and is part of _____ Balearic Islands.

3. It's been _____ long time since I last spoke _____ Italian. You see, there aren't many _____ Italians living in _____ area where I live.

4. _____ Hyde Park is one of _____ biggest parks in _____ London. Millions of _____ tourists visit _____ park every year.

5. _____ Siberian tiger is _____ endangered species. There are around 400-500 _____ Siberian tigers left in _____ wild.

6. Drive down this road for about half _____ hour and you'll find _____ Grand Hotel on _____ right-hand side of _____ road.

E. Read and choose a or b.

1. **A:** I'm sorry, but we seem to have made a mistake. The room is $100 more expensive.
   B: ____

| a. | It was too good to be true. |
| b. | I took it for granted. |

2. **A:** Do you understand what I mean?
   B: Yeah, ____

| a. | I'm positive. |
| b. | I get it. |

3. **A:** What did you do when you saw the toad in your car?
   B: ____

| a. | I nearly jumped out of my skin! |
| b. | I went red as a beet! |

4. **A:** What? You lost control of the car?
   B: Yep. ____, I had crashed into a tree!

| a. | The next thing I knew |
| b. | For an instant |

Self-assessment

Read the following and check the appropriate boxes. For the points you are unsure of, refer back to the relevant sections in the module.

NOW I CAN...

- ▶ use appropriate tenses to narrate past events ☐
- ▶ sequence past actions and events ☐
- ▶ discuss facts about geographical features and animal species ☐
- ▶ express doubt and confidence ☐
- ▶ tell a story ☐
- ▶ comment on something someone said ☐
- ▶ paraphrase what someone said ☐
- ▶ make my stories interesting with the use of "strong" adjectives ☐
- ▶ write a story ☐

eco-tourism

eco-bags

GO GREEN

GREEN BAG

Discuss:

• How important are environmental issues for you?

• Look at the pictures. How green is your lifestyle?

• What do you do to protect the environment?

• Would you like to become greener?

eco-transportation

eco-house

eco-activism

In this module you will learn...

• to talk about environmental issues

• to emphasize an action using the Passive Voice

• to distinguish between verbs easily confused

• to state accepted facts

• to discuss healthy eating habits

• to compare situations

• to express and support an opinion

• to form well-organized paragraphs

• to write an essay expressing an opinion

eco-products

ORGANIC

100% RECYCLED

Reading 🔊

A. Discuss.

• Do you face any of the following problems in the area where you live? How serious are they?

air pollution water pollution water shortage
destruction of forests too much trash traffic congestion

B. Read the title of the text. What do you think the Green Wall of China is? Read the text and find out.

The Green Wall of China

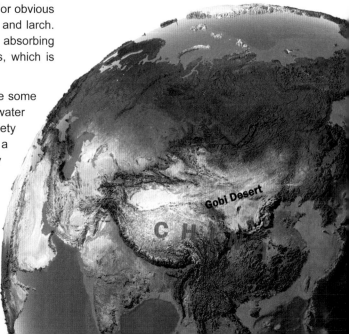

In Ancient China, several walls were being built as early as the 7th century BCE to protect the north of the empire from enemy attacks and intruders. Throughout the ages these walls were joined together, were made bigger and stronger, and became known as The Great Wall of China. Today, China has to deal with a different kind of intruder, the Gobi Desert. This time, the wall they have decided to build is made of trees instead of stone.

Every year 1,400mi² of China's grasslands are taken over by the Gobi Desert. It is a serious environmental problem which results in the loss of valuable agricultural land in the region and also in the increase of devastating sandstorms that seriously affect Beijing.

In 1978, China introduced the Green Wall project. This involves a series of human-planted strips of forest which are designed to be 2,800 miles long on the completion of the wall by around 2050. The idea was to increase the number of forests in China from 5% to 15%, and block the expanding desert as well as the dust carried by the wind. The Green Wall has become the largest tree-planting project the world has ever seen. In 2009 alone, China planted 22,700mi² of forest creating the largest artificial forest in the world.

Trees are being planted by farmers, but ordinary people have gotten involved too, planting 56 billion trees in the past decade. Aerial seeding over wide areas has also been used to speed up the process. For obvious reasons, fast-growing trees have been chosen, such as poplar and larch. Chinese forestry scientists say that these trees are better at absorbing carbon dioxide and producing oxygen than slow-growing trees, which is great news for reducing global warming.

However, over the years the Green Wall project has had to face some problems as well as criticism. The forests use up a lot of groundwater in areas where water is scarce. Also, because there is little variety in the trees that are planted, the areas that are created aren't a suitable habitat for animals and other plants which are normally found in forests. It is also believed that completing the project simply isn't possible, and, at the current rate, it would take 300 years to reclaim the land that has become desert.

Will the Gobi Desert be held back by the Green Wall? Only time will tell. Whatever the outcome, it seems like a step in the right direction.

C. Read again and answer the questions.

1. Why was a wall built in China in the past?
2. How much land becomes desert yearly?
3. What happens because of the expanding desert?
4. How much of China was forestland in 1978?
5. When do the Chinese expect to finish the Green Wall?
6. Why do the Chinese also use aerial seeding?
7. Why did they choose to plant larch and poplar trees?
8. What is the main disadvantage of artificial forests in areas where there isn't a lot of water?
9. Why don't artificial forests make a good place for animals to live?

Gobi Desert

D. Look at the highlighted words in the text and choose the correct meaning, a or b.

1. devastating
   a. well-known
   b. damaging

2. expanding
   a. damaging
   b. growing

3. artificial
   a. man-made
   b. natural

4. scarce
   a. rare
   b. rich

5. outcome
   a. problem
   b. result

E. Discuss.

• Do you think the Green Wall of China is a good idea?

• Can you think of any similar projects in your country?

Vocabulary

Match the verbs in the box with the groups of nouns. Can you add any more words to each group?

> make   build   invent   produce
> create   discover   develop

1. _____
   → a machine
   → a road
   → a bridge
   → an airport

2. _____
   → skills and talent
   → new technology
   → an idea

3. _____
   → cars
   → a movie
   → a cake

4. _____
   → a web page
   → problems
   → a dish
   → jobs

5. _____
   → cars
   → electricity or power
   → oranges

6. _____
   → a machine
   → the telephone

7. _____
   → an island/planet
   → oil
   → the truth

Grammar Passive Voice I → *p. 153*

A. Look at the examples and answer the questions that follow.

> The artificial forest **is designed** to be 2,800 miles long.
>
> The project **was given** the name "The Green Wall of China".

1. Why has the writer used the Passive Voice?
   a. to emphasize the person who does the action
   b. to emphasize the action itself

2. How is the Passive Voice formed?
   a. subject + verb *to be* + past participle
   b. subject + *is* or *was* + Past Simple

B. Read the table below and find more examples of the Passive Voice in the text in the reading activity.

Active Voice	Passive Voice
Present Simple	
They plant trees.	Trees are planted.
Past Simple	
They planted trees.	Trees were planted.
Present Perfect Simple	
They have planted trees.	Trees have been planted.
Past Perfect Simple	
They had planted trees.	Trees had been planted.
Future *will*	
They will plant trees.	Trees will be planted.
Modal verbs	
They may plant trees.	Trees may be planted.

> When we want to mention who or what is responsible for the action, we use the agent (*by* + noun or pronoun).
>
> *These trees were planted **by schoolchildren** from Beijing.*

C. Read the text and circle the correct verb form.

After the success of last year's *Plant a Tree Day*, the local Department of Parks and Recreation **1 has decided / has been decided** to organize a bigger event this year. Last year, 5,000 trees **2 planted / were planted** in parks all around the city. This year we **3 want / are wanted** to try and reach 10,000. All the local schools and colleges **4 have asked / have been asked** to get involved. All equipment **5 will provide / will be provided** by the Department of Parks and Recreation and volunteers of any age **6 can join / can be joined** in the fun. It's an enjoyable event and volunteers **7 asked / are asked** to bring picnic lunches as well. In the end, all volunteers involved **8 will give / will be given** a T-shirt to remember this special day.

Vocabulary

Match the definitions a-g below with the words/phrases.

a. a mixture of smoke and fog caused by exhaust fumes and factory gases

b. rain containing acids which are harmful to trees and forests, as well as buildings and monuments

c. materials containing poisonous chemicals which are no longer used and are pumped into rivers, lakes and oceans

d. substances such as coal and oil that were formed over millions of years from the remains of animals and plants, and are burned for energy

e. a layer of oil on the surface of the water which comes from leaking ships or sinking tankers and is a large threat to marine animals

f. the process of cutting down or burning trees in a large area for agricultural, commercial, housing or firewood use

g. power that is produced using the energy from the sun, wind, water, etc.

acid rain **1** ☐

toxic waste **2** ☐

smog **3** ☐

oil spill **4** ☐

alternative energy **5** ☐

fossil fuels **6** ☐

deforestation **7** ☐

Grammar Passive Voice II → *p. 153*

A. Read the examples in the Passive Voice below and answer the questions.

Active Voice	Passive Voice
• The Department of Parks and Recreation are _____ in the region.	• Trees **are being planted** in the region by the Department of Parks and Recreation.
• The last time I was on the island, they were _____ on the top of some hills.	• The last time I was on the island, wind turbines **were being built** on the top of some hills.

1. How would the examples be written in the Active Voice? Complete the table.

2. How do we form the Present Progressive and Past Progressive in the Passive Voice?

B. Read the example. What is impossible? Who believes so?

> **It is believed** that completing the project simply isn't possible.

Now read the table below and come up with your own examples.

Active Voice	Passive Voice
Verbs *believe, say, think, know, consider,* etc.	
They say the factory causes a lot of pollution.	**It is said that the factory causes** a lot of pollution. **The factory is said to cause** a lot of pollution.

C. Rewrite the following sentences in the Passive Voice starting with the words given.

1. They were giving out flyers for Earth Day at the supermarket.

Flyers for Earth Day _____

2. They say that the oil spill near the island is a huge disaster.

The oil spill near the island _____

3. They are making a documentary at our college at the moment.

A documentary _____

4. Everyone knows that car exhaust fumes pollute the air.

It _____

5. Scientists believe that many famous monuments are in danger because of acid rain.

Many famous monuments _____

_____

Listening 🔊

A. Discuss.

• What do you think a wind farm is?

B. Listen to an interview with a woman, Emily Taylor, from the Environmental Protection Agency and write T for True or F for False.

1. More electricity will come from fossil fuels than the wind farm. ☐
2. Some of the wind turbines will be built on farms. ☐
3. It is possible to have wind turbines and farm animals in the same field. ☐
4. Cars kill more birds than wind turbines every year. ☐
5. After research, Emily Taylor realized that the wind farm would be unpopular with most people. ☐
6. Emily Taylor believes house prices will change because of the wind farm. ☐

Speaking

A. Discuss.

• What do you think are the most important environmental issues our planet is facing today?
• Do you think enough is being done by governments and people about these issues?

B. Talk in groups. Look at the headlines, discuss the problems and say what you think should/can/has to be done. Use some of the words/phrases in the boxes.

use cars less
carpool
public transportation
alternative transportation
ban cars
promote electric cars
take stricter measures
pay fines
move factories away
close down factories
clean up
government pass laws
environmental organizations
raise environmental awareness
reuse and recycle
build more recycling plants
plant more trees
protect existing forests
reduce carbon footprint
save energy
use alternative energy sources

Stating accepted facts
Everyone knows that...
It is a fact that...
It is generally believed that...
It's common knowledge that...

SEVERE SMOG COVERS CITY

Paper factory pollutes river

OIL SPILL SPREADS AND HITS COAST

SCIENTISTS WARN: FOSSIL FUELS AND DEFORESTATION ARE INCREASING GLOBAL WARMING

OUR TRASH IS JUST TOO MUCH

66 *It is a fact that smog is a problem many cities are facing nowadays. Air pollution is a serious health hazard to the local population. That's why something has to be done not only by the government but also by the people. What do you think?*

I couldn't agree more. I think people should be encouraged to... 99

Reading 🔊

A. Discuss.

• What do you know about vegetarian diets?

• Do you think vegetarians are healthier than people who eat meat?

B. Read the text quickly and decide which food expert's point of view is for the issue or against the issue.

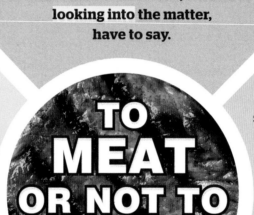

More and more people are not only cutting down on meat but are also turning to vegetarianism for health reasons. However, are vegetarians healthier than meat eaters? Is meat bad for our health or is it nutritious? Here is what two experts, Brian Wilton and Amanda Simmons, who have been looking into the matter, have to say.

TO MEAT OR NOT TO MEAT

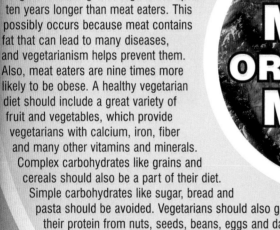

The human body needs a variety of nutrients to function properly, which doesn't necessarily mean that you have to include meat in your diet. You can be a vegetarian and also be healthy at the same time. Studies have shown that vegetarians along with vegans live up to ten years longer than meat eaters. This possibly occurs because meat contains fat that can lead to many diseases, and vegetarianism helps prevent them. Also, meat eaters are nine times more likely to be obese. A healthy vegetarian diet should include a great variety of fruit and vegetables, which provide vegetarians with calcium, iron, fiber and many other vitamins and minerals. Complex carbohydrates like grains and cereals should also be a part of their diet. Simple carbohydrates like sugar, bread and pasta should be avoided. Vegetarians should also get their protein from nuts, seeds, beans, eggs and dairy products. It is no surprise that many vegetarians have healthy cholesterol levels, low blood pressure and a lower risk of having heart disease or diabetes. It is a common myth that vegetarians end up not getting enough iron or other vitamins. If they have a balanced diet and get nutrients from different sources, this is not a problem.

**Brian Wilton,
Nutritional Consultant**

Many vegetarians argue that their diet makes them healthier than non-vegetarians. However, cutting all types of meat out of your diet is risky. Studies have repeatedly shown that vegetarians who fail to have a balanced diet can exclude many essential vitamins or nutrients from their diet. This, in the long run, can easily lead to malnutrition. Meat is the best source of protein, a substance which protects our immune system and builds our muscle mass. Red meat is a good source of iron and vitamin B. So, vegetarians need to do some very careful planning and replace meat with other kinds of food which will give them these nutrients. This, however, is not very easy. For example, protein which you get from beans or dairy products isn't the same type of protein you get from meat. I'm not saying that I don't see the benefits of a vegetarian diet or that we should eat red meat every day. Don't get me wrong. I would like to point out that if we want to be healthy, we should stick to a balanced diet which includes lots of fruit and vegetables, dairy products and a little bit of meat.

**Amanda Simmons,
Member of Dietetic Association**

C. Read again and answer the questions.

1. According to Brian Wilton, what can vegetarianism help prevent?

2. What does Brian Wilton say about carbohydrates?

3. According to the two experts, which foods are rich in protein?

4. What does Brian Wilton say about the belief that vegetarians end up not getting enough iron or other vitamins?

5. According to Amanda Simmons, what are the risks of being a vegetarian?

6. According to Amanda Simmons, why is meat good for us?

7. According to Amanda Simmons, what kind of diet is recommended?

D. Look at the highlighted phrasal verbs in the text and match them with their meanings.

1. cut down on sth. ☐
2. look into sth. ☐
3. end up (doing sth.) ☐
4. cut sth. out ☐
5. point out ☐
6. stick to sth. ☐

a. to be in a particular situation, especially when you didn't plan it

b. to try to find out the truth about sth.

c. to continue doing sth., even when it is difficult

d. to consume less of sth.

e. to tell sb. sth. and make them notice it

f. to stop eating sth.

E. Discuss.

• Are you a vegetarian? If not, would you consider becoming one? Why? / Why not?

Vocabulary

Look at the groups of words below. How many other words can you add to each group?

spinach
cauliflower
apricots
grapefruit
FRUIT pears
eggplant
VEGETABLES
watermelon
pumpkin
cheese
DAIRY milk
rice
GRAINS
oatmeal
yogurt
butter
noodles
bread
PROTEIN FOODS shrimp
lamb
lentils
peanuts

Listening 🔊

You will hear people talking in six different situations.
For questions 1-6, choose a, b or c.

1. What is Jason avoiding eating at the moment?
   a. carbohydrates
   b. protein
   c. vegetables

2. What advice does the doctor give the man?
   a. stick to his diet
   b. eat more meat
   c. cut down on calcium

3. What meal does the man eat on the plane?
   a. beef
   b. fish
   c. vegetarian

4. What does the woman on the TV cooking show wish she had?
   a. some watermelon
   b. some apricots
   c. some strawberries

5. What is the man talking about?
   a. safe ways to lose weight
   b. the reasons why people become obese
   c. the health hazards of obesity

6. What doesn't the woman want?
   a. eggplant
   b. shrimps
   c. mushrooms

Speaking

A. Talk in pairs. Look at the pictures below and compare them, discussing the similarities and differences between them. Talk about the ideas given using the words/phrases in the box.

traditional restaurant

food stand

IDEAS:	
• location and atmosphere	outdoors / indoors
	affected by weather conditions
• service	air conditioning
• type of food	heating
• health and safety	peaceful / noisy
• cost	informal environment
	(in)convenient
Comparing two pictures	staff
	street vendor
• In the first picture we can see... whereas in the second picture...	snack
	fast food and beverages
• ... is... while... is...	lack of / wide variety
• Both options offer...	three-course meal
	preparation time
• The (main) similarity/ difference is that...	better quality ingredients
	risk of food poisoning
• The... at... are usually... than...	affordable
	(in)expensive

TIP Do not describe the pictures in detail. Compare them keeping the ideas given in mind.

B. Discuss.
• Which of the two places would you prefer to eat at? Why?

Writing An essay expressing an opinion

A. Discuss.
• Do you know what organic food is?
• Do you think that organic food is more nutritious?
• Do you believe that it is safer for the environment?

B. Read the writing task and underline the key words. Then answer the question.

Your teacher has asked you to write an essay on the following topic:

Many people think that it is better to eat organic food. What is your opinion?

What are you asked to do?

a. discuss the advantages and disadvantages of eating organic food
b. present your ideas and arguments and give your opinion
c. express your opinion and give advice

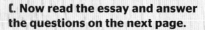

C. Now read the essay and answer the questions on the next page.

It is a fact that more and more people nowadays are choosing organic food over conventionally-grown food. The reason for this is that organic food is believed to have more benefits.

First of all, consuming organic food is considered to be safer and better than non-organic food. This is because conventional farming uses man-made chemicals, such as pesticides to kill insects, as well as various fertilizers to help crops grow faster. It is a fact that many of these are highly toxic and put human health in danger. In organic farming, on the other hand, natural substances or methods are used. As a result, organic food is healthier for us because it is almost chemical free.

Another reason why people choose to eat organic food is to protect the environment. Organic farming uses more environmentally-friendly ways to grow crops and as a result is kinder to our natural world. Conventional farming is harmful to the environment. Pesticides and fertilizers from farmlands pollute and destroy the soil and land as well as habitats. Furthermore, they wash into rivers and lakes and pollute waterways.

In my opinion, more people should consider the benefits of organic food and start including it in their diet. Choosing to consume organic food is better for our health and can help protect the environment.

1. What is the function of the sentences underlined in the essay?

    a. to introduce the main idea of the paragraph

    b. to summarize what the writer has said in the previous paragraph

2. What does the writer do in paragraph 2?

    a. describes the nutritional value of organic food

    b. explains the reasons why organic food is healthier

3. What does the writer do in paragraph 3?

    a. explains how organic farming helps protect the environment

    b. gives examples of how people can protect the environment

D. Read the note and the paragraph below about carbonated drinks. Then choose the most suitable topic sentence from the sentences (a-c), giving reasons for your choice.

Topic sentences
The sentence that introduces the central idea of a paragraph is called a topic sentence. This is usually the first sentence in the paragraph. The other sentences develop the idea expressed in the topic sentence by expanding on it, giving examples or explaining it.

_____ The reason for this is that carbonated drinks contain a lot of sugar, which means a lot of calories, and hardly any nutrients. As a result, they can make you put on weight without realizing it. Apart from obesity, both diet and regular carbonated drinks have been linked to other diseases like high blood pressure and cancer. In addition, carbonated drinks can damage your teeth from a very young age because of the acids they contain.

a. For these reasons, carbonated drinks are bad for us and should be avoided.

b. Carbonated drinks may be tasty, but at the same time they are harmful to our health.

c. There is no doubt that carbonated drinks are very popular with young people.

E. Read the writing task and complete the notes below.

Your teacher has asked you to write an essay on the following topic:

People should avoid eating junk food. Do you agree?

> **People should avoid eating junk food.**
>
> I agree. ☐   I disagree. ☐
>
> **Reason 1:** _____
>
> _____
>
> **Reason 2:** _____
>
> _____

F. Now use your ideas to write the essay. Make sure you read the TIP and plan below.

> **TIP**
>
> When writing an essay expressing an opinion:
>
> - choose a few ideas/points/arguments (the ones you have the most to say about). Don't try to deal with too many points.
> - use topic sentences to express the central idea of each paragraph.
> - develop the paragraphs by expanding on the idea in the topic sentence. Justify your ideas and, when possible, use examples to illustrate them.
> - use a variety of linking words/phrases to list points, add more points and express your opinion.
> - write in a formal style and do not use short forms.
> - avoid introducing any new ideas in the conclusion.

Plan

An essay expressing an opinion

INTRODUCTION
- **Briefly introduce the topic you are going to discuss.**
- **Say how you feel about it.**

MAIN PART (2 PARAGRAPHS)
- **Choose two main aspects of the issue and write one paragraph on each.**
- **Explain your ideas/points and give examples if possible.**

CONCLUSION
- **Sum up by stating your overall opinion.**

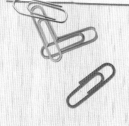

A. Choose a, b or c.

1. Mark is going to a special camp for ____ people because he needs to lose weight.
   a. obese   **b.** expanding   **c.** artificial
2. Animals become endangered or extinct because of the destruction of their natural ____.
   a. habitats   **b.** threats   **c.** nutrients
3. Car exhaust ____ are seriously polluting our city.
   a. fumes   **b.** smog   **c.** waste
4. Brown bread is more ____ than white. So I don't eat white bread anymore.
   a. organic   **b.** carbonated   **c.** nutritious
5. If you leave your car here for longer than you should, you will have to pay a ____.
   a. rate   **b.** loss   **c.** fine
6. Peter ____ a web page on how to save energy.
   a. built   **b.** created   **c.** produced
7. We have a variety of digital cameras to choose from at ____ prices.
   a. valuable   **b.** balanced   **c.** affordable
8. Fiber is a ____ that is found in plants.
   a. substance   **b.** calorie   **c.** beverage
9. You should try to ____ things instead of throwing everything away.
   a. spread   **b.** reuse   **c.** absorb
10. **A:** Would you like some ice cream?
    B: No, thanks. I'm following a special diet that ____ dairy products.
    a. excludes   **b.** prevents   **c.** leaks

B. Complete the sentences with the correct preposition.

1. After discussing where to go for about an hour, we ended _____ staying home.
2. If you want to lose weight, you should stick _____ this diet.
3. The doctor told Frank to cut _____ on fat if he wanted to avoid heart disease.
4. Natalie has completely cut meat _____ of her diet, because she wants to become a vegetarian.
5. The nutritional consultant pointed _____ the advantages of eating lots of green vegetables.
6. The authorities are looking _____ the problem of traffic congestion.
7. You have to speed _____ if you want to finish your work before 5 o'clock.
8. I think they should close _____ the factory on the outskirts of our town because it is causing a great deal of pollution.

C. Rewrite the sentences using the Passive Voice. Start with the words given.

1. People shouldn't throw garbage in the park.
   Garbage _____
2. They say that the lake is polluted.
   It is _____
3. They are building a new airport near our town.
   A new airport _____
4. Alexander Graham Bell invented the telephone.
   The telephone _____
5. Extreme weather conditions have caused damage to the building.
   Damage _____
6. Everybody knows that Carrie cooks delicious vegetarian meals.
   Carrie _____
7. They will serve a three-course meal for dinner.
   A _____
8. The government may ban cars from the downtown area.
   Cars _____

D. Circle the correct words.

1. People of all ages **can take / can be taken** part in Plant a Tree Day.
2. Solar energy **produces / is produced** with the help of the sun.
3. The nutritional consultant **recommended / was recommended** a balanced diet for Melissa.
4. It **is believed / is believed to** that people should try to reduce their carbon footprint.
5. The winners of the contest **will give / will be given** a book as a prize.
6. Wind turbines **were building / were being built** on the top of those hills the last time we were here.
7. The chef **has decided / has been decided** to include vegan meals on the menu.
8. The food from that stand **made / was made** me sick.

Self-assessment
Read the following and check the appropriate boxes. For the points you are unsure of, refer back to the relevant sections in the module.

NOW I CAN...
- talk about environmental issues ☐
- emphasize an action using the Passive Voice ☐
- state accepted facts ☐
- discuss healthy eating habits ☐
- compare situations ☐
- express and support an opinion ☐
- form well-organized paragraphs ☐
- write an essay expressing an opinion ☐

Task 7&8 p. 130

Discuss:

- When was the last time you went shopping? What did you buy? How long did it take you to decide?

- If you had to buy a T-shirt, which of the following would influence your choice? Put them in order, from the most to the least important.

color ☐   price ☐   quality ☐
brand ☐   design or slogan ☐
how it looks on you ☐
how much you need it ☐

Hey, you... Follow me!

Collegiate TRA.REG. CHAMPION EST. 37

LIFE is simple

I HATE T-SHIRT SLOGANS

In this module you will learn...

- to talk about your shopping habits
- to express preference
- to change the meaning of a sentence through word stress
- to understand online advertisements and product reviews
- to form opposites of words
- to talk about books
- to write a book review

Reading 🔊

A. Discuss.

- Do you find it difficult to make decisions?
- What was the last major decision you had to make?

B. Read the text quickly. What is the purpose of the text?

a. to advise people on how to make more rational decisions

b. to analyze the pros and cons of rational decision-making

c. to warn people of the dangers of risky decision-making

d. to inform people about what affects decision-making

We like to believe that before we make a decision, most of the time, we take all the facts into consideration and take our time to think about all the options carefully. However, this just isn't the case. In fact, experts believe that only 5% of our decisions are based on a rational thought process. So, what factors influence our decision-making process?

We often leave decision-making to our instincts. Scientists have proved that if we had the choice, we'd prefer to avoid pain or misery rather than gain something. In fact, we're twice as happy when we try to avoid a bad situation than when we experience a good one. This is why when companies send spam e-mail, they use phrases like "How to avoid...", "Don't miss out!", "What never to eat when...", etc. because people are more likely to open them.

There are also physical factors that affect our decision-making. Psychologist John Bargh conducted an experiment where people were asked to give their impression of a fictional person, while holding a cold or a hot cup of coffee. Those holding the hot cup believed the person to be warmer and more sociable than those holding the cold cup. So, when temperatures rise, the more likely we are to trust strangers.

Stress is another factor which affects our decisions, but we can't measure this very easily, especially as different situations are more or less stressful for different people. Researchers have found, though, that women tend to be more conservative about decisions when stressed, whereas men tend to make riskier choices.

It may come as a surprise but every day from the minute we get up, we have to make countless decisions, like what to wear, what coffee to have, which elevator to take and so on. Each choice, no matter how unimportant, makes our brain a little bit more tired, and without realizing it, this affects our decision-making. This means we are much more likely to make decisions that we regret at the end of the day. That's why you often see important people like presidents wearing the same three suits all the time. This is because they want to limit the small choices and spend more brain power on the bigger ones.

When it comes to decision-making, most people would rather have a wide range of options to choose from. Again, however, research indicates that this does not necessarily lead to wiser decisions. In an experiment, one group of people had to pick from a selection of 30 chocolate bars and another group from a selection of 6. Initially, those who chose from the larger selection liked the idea of having variety, but ended up being unhappy with their choice and regretted it more than those who chose from 6. Living in the modern world, we are bombarded with options and choices that we think will make us happier. The question is, do they?

C. Read again and write T for True, F for False or NM for Not Mentioned.

1. Experts say most of our decisions are incorrect. ☐

2. According to the text, it's more important for people to be happy than to avoid being unhappy. ☐

3. When people are warm, they consider other people to be friendly. ☐

4. Stress doesn't affect decision-making as much as we previously thought. ☐

5. Men are less careful than women with their decisions when they are under stress. ☐

6. It's better to make important decisions earlier in the day. ☐

7. Important people try to reduce the number of unimportant decisions. ☐

8. According to the text, people are less satisfied when they have more to choose from. ☐

D. Find words in the text that mean the same as the following.

1. great suffering, unhappiness (para. 2)

2. not real (para. 3)

3. to be likely to do sth. (para. 4)

4. not liking changes or new ideas (para. 4)

5. very many (para. 5)

6. to choose sth. (para. 6)

7. at the beginning (para. 6)

E. Discuss.

- Do you agree with the information presented in this text?
- Do you think you will change the way you make decisions from now on?

Grammar Infinitives, -ing form → p. 153

A. Read the examples and match them with the uses of the full and bare infinitives.

1. I've learned **to think** carefully before making a decision ☐
2. You should **install** this program **to stop** receiving spam e-mail. ☐☐
3. It's stressful **to make** a decision when there isn't much time. ☐
4. Advertisements make us **buy** things we don't really need. ☐
5. I'm too tired **to discuss** how **to solve** the problem right now. ☐☐

The full infinitive (to + base form) is used:

a. to express purpose.
b. after certain verbs (want, would like, hope, decide, learn, etc.).
c. after too and enough.
d. after it + be + adjective.
e. after question words (who, what, how, etc.).

The bare infinitive (base form without to) is used:

f. after most modal verbs (can, could, must, may, etc.).
g. after the verbs let and make in the Active Voice.

B. Read the examples and match them with the uses of the -ing form.

1. How about **helping** me choose which shoes to buy? ☐
2. Thank you for **taking** me to the airport. ☐
3. **Making** important decisions is part of the job. ☐
4. Does Steve enjoy **living** by himself? ☐

The -ing form is used:

a. as a subject.
b. after certain verbs (consider, finish, avoid, imagine, etc.).
c. after certain expressions (what about, it's no use, it's worth, etc.).
d. after prepositions (for, of, in, etc.).

C. Read the examples and decide what they mean. Choose a or b.

1. I should **remember / not forget** to turn off the computer before I leave. ☐
2. I'll **always remember / never forget** choosing my first car. ☐

a. remember / not forget sth. that has already happened
b. remember / not forget sth. that you are supposed to do

D. Complete the text below with the correct form of the verbs in parentheses.

I wish I could **1** _____ (go) back in time and change a decision I made. It was the night before my big job interview and I was out with friends. We decided **2** _____ (go) to a new restaurant. Instead of **3** _____ (have) a light meal as my friends advised me, I ordered too much. As a result, I was up all night with a terrible stomachache. I wasn't sure what **4** _____ (do) the next morning. I considered **5** _____ (cancel) the interview, but I was worried it would **6** _____ (look) bad. That was another bad decision I made. **7** _____ (go) to an interview and trying **8** _____ (make) a good impression while feeling terrible isn't a good idea. I was too sick **9** _____ (finish) the interview, and there was no point in **10** _____ (stay) till the end, so I made up an excuse and left early. I had made a fool of myself!

89

Vocabulary

Read the dialogues and find phrases which mean the following:

1. It's not available for sale at the moment. _____

2. I'd like my money back. _____

3. It's very expensive. _____

4. It's not worth that much. They're cheating us out of our money. _____

5. I don't have much money available to spend at this period of time. _____

6. It doesn't matter how much it costs. _____

7. It's very cheap. _____

8. I have no money. _____

9. I don't have enough money. _____

10. I can give you some money. _____

11. I'm just looking around. _____

Salesperson Can I help you?	
Woman Thank you, but **I'm just browsing**.	

Brian Check out this video game. I've been looking for it for a long time!

Bill Great. Now you can buy it!

Brian I can't. **I'm a little short of cash**.

Bill **I can spare some cash**, if that's the problem!

Terry You should go to the Street Beat Store. I went yesterday and all the T-shirts are on sale. I bought three for $20.

Brad **That's a steal**! I need some too, but **I'm broke**. I'll go next week when I get paid.

Mary Look at that dress!

Tina It's nice. How much does it cost?

Mary $150.

Tina What? **It costs a fortune**! Are you going to get it?

Mary Well, I'm definitely going to try it on. **Money is no object** if I like it.

Tina Do as you please, but **it's a rip-off**. There's a store downtown with beautiful dresses for half the price.

Anne Hello, **could I have a refund** for this cell phone? I don't particularly like it.

Salesperson You haven't opened the box so, yes, you can get a refund or another model.

Anne How much is this model here?

Salesperson I'm afraid **that's currently out of stock**, but I have newer models for just $30 extra.

Anne **I'm on a tight budget this month**, so I'd prefer the refund.

Grammar Prefer, would prefer, would rather → *p. 154*

A. Read the examples and answer the questions.

a. I **prefer** the white sneakers.

b. I **prefer** wearing casual clothes **to** wearing formal clothes.

c. Sue **prefers to** shop online **rather than** shop in stores.

d. I'd **prefer to** buy a new smartphone **rather than** (buy) a tablet.

e. I'd **rather** buy the white sneakers.

f. We'd **rather not** spend any more money.

g. I'd **rather** shop online **than** (shop) in stores.

1. Which examples show a general preference?

2. Which examples show a preference in a particular situation?

B. Rewrite the sentences starting with the words given.

1. I don't want to talk to Mike right now.

   I'd rather _____

2. I'd rather have some tea than coffee.

   I'd prefer _____

3. Most people don't like reading in the evenings; they'd rather watch TV.

   Most people prefer _____

4. I think Kevin likes swimming more than playing hockey.

   I think Kevin prefers _____

5. We'd prefer to live in the countryside rather than in the city.

   We'd rather _____

Intonation 🔊

A. Listen and repeat. Notice the stressed words and how the focus of the sentence changes, affecting the meaning.

I prefer the **red** T-shirt. (not any other color)

I prefer the red **T-shirt**. (not any other item of clothing)

I prefer the red T-shirt. (not anyone else, just me)

> A simple sentence can have many different meanings based on the word(s) we stress.

B. Say the sentence below aloud stressing different words each time. How many different meanings did you get?

I'd rather buy a house in the countryside.

C. Listen to the sentence spoken with different words stressed each time. Consider the meaning and match each sentence to the correct answer.

Sentence 1 ☐   **a.** Nobody else, just me.

Sentence 2 ☐   **b.** Not somewhere else.

Sentence 3 ☐   **c.** Not a farm or anything else.

Sentence 4 ☐   **d.** Not rent one.

Listening 🔊

You will hear people talking in five different situations. For questions 1-5, choose the picture which answers the question correctly.

> **TIP**
> • Before you start, look at the three pictures carefully to get a general idea of what you are going to hear.
> • Listen carefully and focus on the question. All three pictures may be referred to in the dialogue. However, only one of them correctly answers the question.

1. Which item does the man decide to buy?

2. What time does the store close today?

3. How much did the woman spend?

4. What special offer can you get on DVDs today?

5. What would the husband rather do than go shopping?

Speaking

A. Discuss.

• Do you consider shopping a chore or an enjoyable activity?

• Where do you prefer to go shopping? Why?

• What do you think of online shopping?

• Do you consider yourself to be a shopaholic? Why? / Why not?

• Do you shop around before you decide what to buy? Why? / Why not?

B. Talk in pairs. Imagine that you are roommates and are talking about what to buy for your new apartment. Look at the items in the catalogue and decide. You have only $100 to spend. Use phrases from the vocabulary activity and the box below.

THIS WEEK'S AMAZING OFFERS!

game console ~~$199~~ $99

beanbag ~~$65~~ $50

giant clock ONLY $10

vacuum cleaner ~~$239~~ $79

storage boxes $7 each 5 for $30

rug $30

> **Expressing preference**
> I prefer... because...
> I like... more than...
> I'd rather/prefer (not)...
> My first choice would be...
> I definitely think we should...
> I believe... is (not) worth it...
> If it were up to me, I'd choose...

> 66 *I definitely think we should get a... because we need it.*
> *Have you looked at the price? It's a rip-off!*
> *Oh, you're right and we're both on a tight budget.*
> *I'd rather...* 99

Reading 🔊

A. Discuss.

- Do you read reviews of products online? Why? / Why not?
- Do you think they are useful?

B. Look at the products below. Would you like to buy any of them? Read the reviews and see if they change your mind.

http://www.giftsforlaughs.com/reviews/

Canned Unicorn Meat
$12.99 - FREE SHIPPING In stock

REVIEWS
★★★★☆

This isn't as good as fresh unicorn meat, but who can be bothered to get their bow and arrow and hunt unicorns these days? I just love the taste of unicorn and I usually have a few cans at work for lunch. But seriously, this was a really cool gag gift, which my sister found very amusing. It has realistic product and nutritional information on the label, and when you open the can, a really cute stuffed animal pops out. A harmless joke you can play on your friends. Definitely worth it!

Scottish accent mouth spray
$7.99 - Shipping: $3 per item Only 7 in stock

REVIEWS
★☆☆☆☆

I was dissatisfied with this product. Don't get me wrong. I wasn't expecting to magically have a Scottish accent when I used the spray. I realized it was a joke, but the ad was misleading. It was supposed to be minty fresh, but when I tried it out with my friends, it had a disgusting taste that made me feel sick. What's more, it was kind of overpriced for a ten-minute laugh. I wouldn't recommend it.

Inflatable banana case
$2.99 - FREE SHIPPING In stock

REVIEWS
★★★★☆

I bought this for my daughter because she's careless with her backpack and dislikes it when her banana gets bruised. To be honest, I thought it would be totally useless, but got it anyway as it was so cheap. What can I say? She absolutely adored it, and it really works. It also has a handy clip to attach it to a bag. In fact, I had to order a second one for myself. My colleagues burst out laughing when they saw it at the office, but now they want one too. The only problem is that I have to choose my bananas carefully at the supermarket, because not all of them fit in the product.

USB Typewriter
$39.99 - FREE SHIPPING Currently out of stock

REVIEWS
★★★☆☆

I'm really into modern gadgets, and I don't go anywhere without my tablet. But there is something about pressing the keys of a good old-fashioned typewriter that is really satisfying. So, I was so happy when I came across this product because it combines the two. I thought setting up the device would be tricky, but all you do is plug it in and you're ready. The only complaint I have is that there was a misunderstanding and I was sent the wrong color, but I couldn't be bothered to send it back. For retro typewriter fans, it's a must!

PURCHASE THE BEST GADGETS HERE

C. Read the reviews again and the statements below. Which review(s) do they refer to? Write U for Unicorn Meat, A for Accent Spray, B for Banana Case or T for Typewriter.

TIP

• When matching questions with short texts, scan each text and look for the specific information mentioned in each question.

• Find the part of the text which correctly answers the question.

• Be careful! Don't choose a text just because the vocabulary or phrasing in the text is similar to that of the question.

1. The reviewer pretends that he has used the product when he hasn't. ☐

2. The reviewer wasn't sent what he/she ordered. ☐

3. This product doesn't contain what is described on the packaging. ☐ ☐

4. The product was so good, the reviewer bought two. ☐

5. The reviewer found the product surprisingly easy to use. ☐

6. The reviewer thought the product wasn't worth the money. ☐

7. The reviewer gave the product to someone else. ☐ ☐

8. You are charged for delivery. ☐

9. This product sometimes has a slight drawback. ☐

10. You can't buy this product at the moment. ☐

D. Discuss.

• Have you ever come across any funny or strange online advertisements? What were they about?

Vocabulary

A. Read the note and complete the table using the words in the box.

> • The prefix **dis-** is used before adjectives, nouns and verbs to give them the opposite meaning (e.g. like-dislike).
>
> • The prefix **mis-** is used before verbs, and means to do wrongly or badly (understand-misunderstand).
>
> • The suffix **-less** is used after a noun to form an adjective which means *without* that quality or characteristic (e.g. care-careless).

satisfied lead harm wire spell honest place respect hope appear inform approve worth behave end

dis-	mis-	-less
dissatisfied	mislead	harmless

B. Complete the sentences below with the correct form of some of the words from the table above.

1. I want to buy a _____ mouse. How much do they cost?

2. Some students feel that teachers _____ them.

3. I'm sorry but you've _____ my name. It's with one "s," not two.

4. Have you seen my keys? I seem to have _____ them.

5. Danny wants to become an actor, but his parents _____.

6. This bus journey seems _____. When do we arrive?

Listening 🔊

A. Listen to a conversation between a man and a customer service representative. Was the representative's call successful?

B. Listen again and write T for True or F for False.

1. The man doesn't want to have a contract with Globofone anymore. ☐

2. The man has found a cheaper alternative to Globofone. ☐

3. The woman offers the man a free smartphone. ☐

4. The woman gets the man's name wrong more than once. ☐

5. The helpline is usually closed when the man calls. ☐

6. Globofone are making improvements to their signal at the moment. ☐

7. The man doesn't mind people calling him about special offers. ☐

C. Discuss.

• Have you ever bought a product or used a service which you ended up being dissatisfied with? What was it?

• What did you do about it? Did you make a complaint?

Speaking

A. Discuss the following. Use the words in the box.

- What type of books do you like reading?
- Do you have a favorite author? If yes, who is it?
- What's the most interesting book you have ever read? Why did you like it?

• fiction (e.g. sci-fi, thriller, crime, mystery, fantasy trilogy)	plot
• non-fiction (e.g. biography, travel, history, cookbook, journal)	chapter
• short stories collection	author
• poetry	characters
• classic	hero
• graphic novel	heroine

B. Talk in pairs. Read the blurbs from five different books and talk about each of them. Then decide which two books you would definitely be interested in reading, giving reasons.

MUST-READ BOOKS

Steve Jobs *Walter Isaacson* (biography)

Based on more than forty interviews with Jobs, as well as interviews with more than a hundred family members, friends and colleagues, Walter Isaacson has written an in-depth biography of a man whose personality and passion for perfection changed the world of personal computing, animated movies and digital publishing.

A Brief History of Time
Stephen Hawking
(popular science)

If you've always wanted to understand how the universe started but were afraid you'd get lost in very technical, scientific language, then this book is for you. Hawking has the ability to explain very complicated ideas in simple, everyday language.

A Night to Remember
Walter Lord (non-fiction)

This book gives a fascinating account of the first and last voyage of the Titanic. It describes the behavior of the passengers and crew, and the sacrifices many had to make. Women and children rushed to the lifeboats, but while the enormous ship sank, the band played on.

Pay it Forward
Catherine Ryan Hyde (fiction)

This is the story of how a boy tried to change the world using the goodness of human nature. Trevor McKinney, a twelve-year-old from a small California town, accepts his teacher's challenge to come up with an idea to change the world for the better. His idea "pay it forward" is very simple but has long-lasting effects.

Safari Jema *Teresa O'Kane* (travel memoir)

Award-winning writer Teresa O'Kane describes her ten-month adventure during which she and her husband travel from Casablanca to Cape Town. Her book contains vivid descriptions of their various experiences as well as the breathtaking landscapes and historic locations. It also provides the reader with information about African culture.

fascinating   enjoyable   amusing
a page-turner   a good read   (un)original
(un)appealing   gripping   dull

... sounds kind of... so I (don't) think I'd be interested...
... seems to be...
... is not the type of book I'd like to read.
I'd rather/prefer... because...
I don't think I'd like... as I'm not really into...
I think... would be fascinating to read because...
I would definitely read... because...
I'm (not) really into...
I can't stand...

Writing A book review

A. Discuss.

- How do you choose which books to read?
- Do you ever read book reviews in newspapers or magazines?

B. Read the review below. Would you be interested in reading this book? Why? / Why not?

Book review
by Neal Peansman

Agatha Christie's timeless novel, *Death on the Nile* was first published in 1937. It is a crime novel in which the fictional famous detective, Hercule Poirot, tries to solve another murder.

The story is set in Egypt and on the River Nile where, while on a cruise boat, Poirot meets Linnet Doyle and her husband, Simon. All is not as it seems between the newlyweds, and when Linnet is found murdered, Poirot is asked to find the killer. It seems like a simple case, but everything becomes complicated as more passengers are somehow connected with the victim. Poirot, therefore, has to question all the suspects on the boat and put all the pieces together to solve the mystery.

Agatha Christie does a great job of keeping the reader interested throughout the book. Her style never fails to surprise the reader who can almost never predict what will happen next. The ongoing suspense of this whodunit is one of the features that make this book a real page-turner.

This book will especially appeal to readers who like a plot full of twists and turns, suspense and puzzles. If you are a crime novel fan, don't forget to put it on your list of books to read!

C. Read the review again and answer the questions below.

In which paragraph does the writer:

a. give his/her overall opinion of the book? ☐
b. tell us who the author is? ☐
c. present the plot of the story? ☐
d. comment on the interesting features of the book? ☐
e. tell us where the story takes place? ☐

D. Complete the sentences with the words/phrases in the box.

> award-winning   is set   bestseller
> appeals to all ages   a good read   vivid   heroine
> autobiography   dull

1. Lauraine Snelling is a(n) _____ author.
2. The _____ description of the characters brings them to life.
3. This novel has been an international _____ for over a decade.
4. Unfortunately, the book turned out to be kind of _____.
5. This is a timeless classic that _____.
6. *What About Cimmaron*? is _____, especially for teenagers.
7. The story _____ in a small Italian town.
8. Helen Keller's _____ is definitely worth reading.
9. The _____ of the novel is a teenage girl named Amanda.

E. Think of a book you have recently read and know well and complete the outline below.

INTRODUCTION

TITLE: _____

AUTHOR: _____

TYPE: _____

PUBLISHED IN: _____

MAIN PART

SET IN: _____

NOTES FOR PLOT: _____

_____

_____

INTERESTING FEATURES: _____

_____

CONCLUSION

OPINION: _____

F. Use your ideas from the outline above to write a book review. Make sure you read the TIP below and the plan on page 134.

> **TIP**
>
> When writing a book review:
> - remember to use the Present Simple to describe the plot. Don't include too many details and don't reveal the ending.
> - use a variety of adjectives to make it more interesting.

A. Circle the correct words.

1. The novel I read was **gripping / dull**. I found it hard to put down.

2. By the sound of his **label / accent**, I think that he's Australian.

3. The **hero / author** is signing copies of his book at the bookstore down the street.

4. I can't lend you any money because I'm **broke / conservative**.

5. Penny bought two pairs of sneakers because they were on **budget / sale**.

6. When I fell down, everyone **popped / burst** out laughing.

7. **Pick / Pretend** a number from 1 to 100.

8. My brother has a very **timeless / vivid** imagination. You should hear his stories!

B. Complete with the correct form of the words in capitals.

1. I can't find my gloves anywhere. I must have _____ them.   **PLACE**

2. There are _____ reasons why you shouldn't quit your job.   **COUNT**

3. I was _____ with the service at that restaurant so I am not going to eat there again.   **SATISFY**

4. My mother always told me never to _____ older people.   **RESPECT**

5. I have lots of jewelry, but it's mostly _____ junk.   **WORTH**

6. This article is _____. You can't lose 10 pounds in three days!   **LEAD**

7. If Tommy continues to _____, he won't get any ice cream after dinner.   **BEHAVE**

C. Complete with the correct form of the verbs in parentheses.

1. It's no use _____ (call) Stan. He has a class now. Remember _____ (call) him later.

2. _____ (help) endangered species is something my uncle has been doing for years. This year he's made plans _____ (help) out at a bird sanctuary.

3. My brother promised _____ (lend) me his car this weekend. To be honest, I was afraid _____ (ask) him because he usually refuses _____ (let) me _____ (borrow) it.

4. Chuck is thinking of _____ (move) to another city. However, he hasn't decided where _____ (go) yet.

5. Pat believes she isn't doing enough _____ (keep) in shape. So she is considering _____ (exercise) more often.

D. Rewrite the sentences starting with the words given.

1. I'd rather have a sandwich than a proper meal.
   I'd prefer _____

2. I think it's a good idea to go shopping together.
   How about _____?

3. Susan doesn't want to wear the yellow skirt.
   Susan would rather _____

4. Most people don't like working out indoors; they'd rather go jogging.
   Most people prefer _____

5. The doctor said that I should stay in bed for a few days.
   The doctor advised _____

E. Match with the responses a-h. There are two extra responses which you do not need to use.

1. I like this book, but I'm a little short of cash. ☐
2. I'd prefer to buy the hat rather than the shirt. ☐
3. Is there something I can help you with? ☐
4. Could I try this on in purple? ☐
5. This scarf is absolutely gorgeous, but it costs a fortune! ☐
6. They say "The Storm" is a fascinating read. ☐

> **a.** I know. It's a rip-off.
> **b.** Yes, it was better than I expected. You should get it.
> **c.** Thanks, but I'm just browsing.
> **d.** Don't worry. I can spare some.
> **e.** Get both. Money is no object.
> **f.** I'm sorry, but it's currently out of stock.
> **g.** Well, I just can't be bothered.
> **h.** Great! It's a steal!

Self-assessment

Read the following and check the appropriate boxes. For the points you are unsure of, refer back to the relevant sections in the module.

NOW I CAN...

▶ talk about my shopping habits ☐
▶ express preference ☐
▶ change the meaning of a sentence through word stress ☐
▶ understand online advertisements and product reviews ☐
▶ form opposites of words ☐
▶ talk about books ☐
▶ write a book review ☐

Exam Practice Modules 7-9 p. 142

Discuss:

• What's the most popular form of entertainment with people your age?

• Read the sentences in the box. Do the idioms in bold have a positive or negative meaning?

• What do you do in your spare time? How do you feel about your spare-time activities? Use the idioms.

• We **had a whale of a time** at the concert on Saturday night.

• It rained all day on our trip, which was **a bit of a downer**.

• It **makes my day** when I find a good bargain at the mall.

• Kelly **gets a kick out of** beating her brother at video games.

• I was **bored stiff** on the flight because I didn't have a book to read.

• We were **thrilled to pieces** when our team won the game.

• It really **winds me up** when my friends want to stay in and watch DVDs instead of going out.

• Roger really **gets on my nerves** whenever we order a pizza and he doesn't pay his share.

In this module you will learn...

• to talk about various forms of entertainment and spare-time activities

• to report statements, questions, commands and requests

• prepositional phrases with "in" and "out of"

• to talk about staying in shape

• collocations with "lose" and "miss"

• to write an article describing an event

Reading 🔊

A. Discuss.

- What do you consider to be an extreme sport?
- What is the most extreme activity you have tried?

B. Read the text quickly without paying attention to the missing sentences and choose the best description of the writer's opinion.

a. Pogo has transformed into something else since I was young.

b. I wish pogo sticks were more like the ones of the past.

c. I never want to try pogo jumping again after my experience.

d. Pogo jumping is an activity everyone should take up.

XPOGO! *by Gary Adams*

IT'S POGO, BUT NOT AS YOU KNOW IT.

My editor asked me to go to Pittsburgh and cover Pogopalooza, the annual pogo world championships. **1** I tried to do some research about the event on the train, but I couldn't help thinking about my first pogo stick and how much fun it was jumping down the street with my friends! However, I wasn't really prepared for what I was about to witness.

As soon as I arrived at Pogopalooza, I was blown away. I saw someone leap over a car on a pogo stick, then another pogoer did a backflip. My mouth fell open. This wasn't a kid's game; it was an extreme sport! A crowd had gathered around one pogoer who was just jumping up and down. "I can do that!" I shouted. **2** He wasn't even slightly out of breath! He was trying to break the record for the most jumps, and he was only halfway there. Later in the day, they held a pogo high jump contest, where pogoers were jumping over 7 feet. An event organizer informed me that the world record was 9 feet 6 inches. **3** I had to learn more.

Luckily, one of the pioneers of Xpogo, MIT-trained physicist Bruce Middleton, was at this year's event and he gave me information about the evolution of the pogo stick. The original pogo stick, which I used to play with, had springs and you could reach a height of about 6-9 inches. Middleton explained that he had reinvented the pogo stick by using elastic bands. The new pogo stick is called the Flybar and on it you can reach heights of 7 feet. **4** The latest models, like the Vurtego, use air pressure to propel the jumper and they are setting new world records all the time.

After a while, I asked one of the pogoers if I could give it a shot. I told him that it looked like fun. "Are you sure?" he asked, looking me up and down, which made me kind of nervous. **5** Then I thought, what could go wrong? So, I put on a helmet and some knee pads and started jumping. I was amazed at how high I could jump. It all came back to me very quickly. I was having a whale of a time, but I stopped before I fell and made a fool of myself. **6** After a few tricks, he did three backflips in a row and then jumped down a whole flight of steps, making me look like an amateur.

As soon as I got home, I searched the garage for my old pogo stick. I took one look at it, threw it in the trash and went online to order myself something a little more extreme.

C. Read the text again. Complete the gaps 1-6 with the sentences a-g below. There is one extra sentence which you do not need to use.

a. The first pogoer to do a somersault used one of these.

b. How was this possible?

c. In particular, one pogoer who was only eleven years old.

d. Then I handed the stick over to the professional.

e. Then I noticed an electronic scoreboard showing his jumps, 104,454 and counting.

f. I was a big pogo fan in my youth so I jumped at the chance.

g. Perhaps I was a little out of shape.

D. Look at the sentences below from the text and match the phrases in bold with their meanings.

1. I **jumped at the chance**.
2. I **couldn't help** thinking about my first pogo stick.
3. I was **blown away**.
4. I asked one of the pogoers if I could **give it a shot**.
5. "Are you sure?" he asked, **looking me up and down**.
6. It all **came back to me** very quickly.

a. to try
b. to remember sth.
c. to be unable to change your behavior or feelings
d. to accept sth. quickly and in an enthusiastic way
e. to be impressed
f. to examine sb. closely, judging their appearance or character

E. Discuss.

• Would you like to try Xpogo? Why? / Why not?

• How have toys/sports changed since you were young?

Vocabulary

Look at the prepositional phrases in the table and circle the correct words in the sentences 1-8.

IN	OUT OF	IN / OUT OF
case (of)	work	danger
general	breath	control
particular	the question	sight
charge of	one's mind	trouble
person	date	use
need	the ordinary	shape
a row	(one's) reach	order

1. We waved until the car was in / out of sight.
2. You can't use the elevator. It's out of **order / control**.
3. I'd like to speak to whoever is in **charge of / person** the project.
4. I have only $20 left, so going away this weekend is out of the **ordinary / question**.
5. Keep chemicals out of children's **reach / danger**.
6. The police are once again in **trouble / control** of the situation.
7. This map is out of **use / date**. We should get a newer one.
8. I love extreme sports, skydiving in **general / particular**.

Grammar Reported Speech: Statements → *p. 154*

A. Read the examples below and complete the speech bubbles with the speakers' exact words. Then answer the questions.

I told him that it looked like fun.

> It _____ like fun!

Middleton explained that he had reinvented the pogo stick by using elastic bands.

> I _____ the pogo stick by using elastic bands.

1. When do we use Reported Speech?

2. Which words change in Reported Speech?

3. What's the difference between *say* and *tell*?

He said he could do three backflips in a row and that he would show me.

> _____ do three backflips in a row. _____ show _____.

A pogoer told me that I was going to love Xpogo.

> _____ going to love Xpogo!

Apart from *say* and *tell*, other verbs can also be used to introduce reported statements: *explain, inform, add,* etc.

B. Complete the sentences using Reported Speech.

1. "I may play tennis next Saturday," Tony said.

Tony said _____

2. "I haven't seen that movie yet," Sally said to me.

Sally told _____

3. "I don't know what time I will be home this evening," Diana told us.

Diana informed us _____

4. "Lucy is thinking of taking up Xpogo," John said to Lee.

John told _____

Vocabulary

Read the dialogue. What do the phrases in bold mean?

A: Let's **grab a bite to eat** before we go to Science class.

B: No, I'm really overweight and **I can't take it anymore**.

A: You should increase the amount of exercise you get. Come to the gym with me.

B: **It had crossed my mind**, but the last time I lifted weights, I pulled a muscle in my back.

A: That's because you didn't warm up. You need to do gentle stretching exercises first so that you don't injure your muscles.

B: No, **I'll pass**. I don't think I'm a gym person. I don't enjoy weight training or running on the treadmill.

A: How about aerobics or zumba? Zumba's fun and good exercise, too. **You kill two birds with one stone**. They have classes **every other day**.

B: Sounds too good to be true. I **ran into** Sandra the other day and she told me her zumba class is a pretty tough workout.

A: It's so much fun you don't realize you're exercising. And you don't need to be a dancer to take it up. You'll get the hang of the moves after a few times.

B: Sounds like **a piece of cake**.

A: Yeah, maybe too much cake's the reason you need to go to the gym in the first place.

Grammar Reported Speech: Questions-Commands-Requests → *p. 155*

A. Read the examples below and complete the speech bubbles with the speakers' exact words. Then complete the rules.

*I asked Rita **if she had been** to the new gym.*

> _____ to the new gym, Rita?

*Karen asked me **why I wanted** to take up tennis.*

> _____ to take up tennis?

Reported questions

- They are usually introduced with the verbs: _____, *wonder, want to know*.
- If a direct question begins with a question word, the reported question begins with _____.
- If a direct question does not begin with a question word, the reported question begins with _____ or *whether*.
- The verb in a reported question is in the _____ form.

B. Read the examples below and complete the speech bubbles with the speakers' exact words. Then complete the rules.

*The receptionist at the gym **asked me to sign** at the bottom of the page.*

> _____ at the bottom of the page, please.

*The coach **told Doug not to be** late for practice again.*

> Doug, _____ late for practice again!

Reported commands and requests

- Commands are usually introduced with the verbs *tell* and *order* and requests with the verb _____.
- The imperative changes to: _____ **+ base form**
- The negative imperative changes to: _____ **+ base form**

C. Complete the sentences using Reported Speech.

1. "Show me your ID card," the police officer said to me.

The police officer ordered me _____.

2. "Who did you play soccer with?" Fred asked Keith.

Fred asked Keith _____.

3. "Don't jump on the treadmill!" Sally said to the child.

Sally told the child _____.

4. "Please stretch your arms," the gym instructor said to us.

The gym instructor asked us _____.

5. "Should I take up karate?" Debbie thought.

Debbie wondered _____.

6. "Are there any exercise bikes at the gym?" Gary asked.

Gary wanted to know _____.

Listening 🔊

You will hear people talking in five different situations. For questions 1-5, choose the picture which answers the question correctly.

1. Where might Jenny be now?

2. What is the hourly rate for a tennis instructor?

  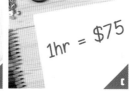

3. How often should Linda go to the gym?

4. What is the woman trying to persuade the man to take up?

5. What happened to Derek?

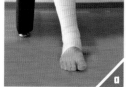  

Speaking

Talk in pairs. Act out the following conversations.

Student A: You go to a martial arts class for the first time and you meet an old friend (Student B) from school. Catch up on your news.

Student B: You meet an old friend (Student A) from school at a martial arts class you go to, but you don't recognize him/her at first.

Student A: You are at a coffee shop having coffee with Student B. You recently joined the gym. Report a conversation you had with the gym instructor.

Student B: You are at a coffee shop with Student A. Listen to his/her news and ask him/her any questions.

Student A: You want to become more active but aren't sure what to do. You don't particularly like the idea of joining a gym. Talk to Student B about it.

Student B: You have recently joined the local gym. Advise Student A to do the same. Explain to him/her what you do there and what else the gym offers.

Student A: You are running in the park and you injure your leg. You can't walk.

Student B: You see Student A in the park. Offer him/her help and advice.

Student A: You want to take up swimming at the sports center but need some information. Talk to the receptionist (Student B).

Student B: You are a receptionist at a sports center. Student A wants to take up swimming but needs some information. Help him/her out.

Reading

A. Discuss.

- Do you like playing video games? Why? / Why not?
- Are they a popular form of entertainment in your country?

B. Read the first part of the text quickly. What is the purpose of it?

a. to summarize a story

b. to lead the reader step by step through a process

c. to advertise a game

http://www.willswalkthruz.org

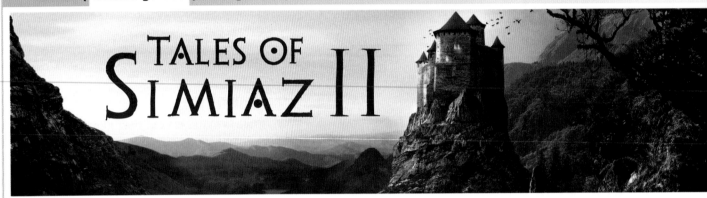

Will's Ultimate Walkthrough Site

Games | **Games guides** | Web games | News | Videos | Reviews

TALES OF SIMIAZ II

Level 9: Castle Idnárpila

This next level is pretty easy compared to the previous levels, so you don't need to be an expert gamer. It's a short part of the quest, but only if you know where to go. If you start wandering around the castle, you could be there for hours.

Follow the trail along the coast until you reach the castle. Approach from the south, dismount your horse and proceed cautiously towards the castle. First, you need to reach the closest tower, but do not attempt to climb the steps. It's a trap. As soon as you're halfway up, soldiers come from in front and behind and surround you. There's no escape. So, your best option is to get across the river and climb up the rocks to the tower. However, don't make the mistake of entering the water because there are piranhas in the river. They won't kill you, but they will reduce your strength and you need all of it to climb to the tower.

Take your time as you're climbing up. However, you may attract the attention of the guard. He won't attack you, but he will go and get more guards, so you'd better be quick after that. You have no time to lose!

Once at the tower, don't enter it. Grab onto the ledge of the bridge and move across. You need to be careful with the controls, and you need good reflexes at this stage. Make sure you don't fall into the water. Once on the other side of the bridge, be careful. There are four guards in the windmill. Climb to the top of the windmill without attracting their attention. There, you will find the emerald key, which you will need for the next level.

next level walkthrough >

Comments:

Joe44: Hi, Will. I love this game. The sequel is so much better than the original. I hope they turn it into a multiplayer online game in the future. Great job on the walkthrough BTW. I was really struggling with level 7 until I found your site. I was trying to kill that dragon with my bow and arrow, but there was no way. I would never have thought about using my sword. Awesome! But now, I can't get past level 9. I've found a good place to jump over the river, so no problem there. But every time I enter the tower, I wake up the guard and I lose a life. Any suggestions? I've heard there are some good cheats for this game, but I try to avoid using them generally. It ruins the game for me. Get back to me whenever you can.

C. Read again and answer the questions.

1. What could make level 9 take a long time to complete?
2. What happens if you climb the steps to the tower?
3. Why is it difficult to climb to the tower if you fall in the river?
4. What might happen while you're climbing to the tower?
5. What skill do you need to be able to cross the bridge?
6. What should you do when you reach the windmill?
7. What was Joe44's problem with level 7?
8. What is Joe44 doing wrong in level 9?

D. Look at the highlighted words in the text and match them with their meanings.

1. quest ☐   5. surround ☐
2. wander ☐   6. reflexes ☐
3. dismount ☐   7. sequel ☐
4. trap ☐   8. dragon ☐

a. a plan designed to trick or catch sb.

b. a large imaginary animal with wings and a long tail that breathes out fire

c. the ability to react quickly

d. a long search

e. a book, movie, video game, etc. that continues the story of an earlier one

f. to get off

g. to be all around sb./sth.

h. to walk slowly around an area usually without purpose

E. Discuss.

• Would you like to play this video game? Why? / Why not?

• What are some popular video games that you or people you know play?

Vocabulary

A. Read the sentences below from the text. Do you know any other collocations with the verb *lose*? Do you know any collocations with the verb *miss*?

You have no time to lose!

But every time I enter the tower, I wake up the guard and I lose a life.

B. Complete with the verbs *lose* or *miss* to form collocations.

1. _____ a class
2. _____ a game/race, etc.
3. _____ contact
4. _____ a plane/train, etc.
5. _____ one's job
6. _____ a meeting / an appointment
7. _____ one's temper/patience
8. _____ money
9. _____ a meal
10. _____ interest in

Listening 🔊

A. You will listen to an interview with a video game designer. Which of the following do you think will be mentioned? Listen and check your answers.

actors ☐   game controllers ☐
scriptwriters ☐   artists ☐
sound ☐   game types ☐
drawings ☐   walkthroughs ☐
game testers ☐   movies ☐

B. Listen again and complete the sentences.

1. The first thing game designers create is a _____.

2. It is becoming common for video games to be based on _____.

3. It takes _____ to make a character that you can move around.

4. For a successful video game, you need to have a good script as well as good quality _____ and _____.

5. Computer _____ and _____ make the game work.

6. Before marketing and advertising, the game goes through the _____ stage.

Speaking

A. Discuss.

- How often do you go out with friends?
- Where do you usually go?
- What kind of events do you enjoy attending?

B. Talk in pairs. Read the three posters advertising events below and decide which one you'd most like to attend, giving reasons. Talk about the ideas given using the words/phrases in the box.

Sounds of Africa Concert

Friday, June 17th

groups and singers from all over the continent

doors open: 8 p.m.

Tickets: $20
(Students: $10)

Traditional African dishes available

Charity fancy-dress bike ride

This year's theme: "insects"

Take part in our fund-raiser on **Saturday June 18th**

Give disabled people a chance for a healthy life

All ages welcome
Entry fee $10

Donations also accepted
Meeting point: Woburn Park 8 a.m.

Local Art Exhibition
June 18th–19th

Painting | Drawing | Sculpture

FREE admission!

Come buy and support local artists

Refreshments available

Open: 10 a.m.–10 p.m.
Venue: City Hall

IDEAS:

- venue
- when it is best to go
- the age group it is for
- what you can do there
- the cost
- whether or not it is worth going

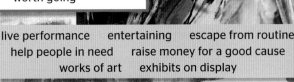

live performance   entertaining   escape from routine
help people in need   raise money for a good cause
works of art   exhibits on display

Writing An article describing an event

A. Look at the webpage below. What is this event about?

www.lightupthenight.net

About | Course Details | Equipment | Charity | Register

Rollerblading night!
Join us and light up the night!

Date: Saturday, May 10th
Meeting point: 526 Englinton Avenue
Starting time: 8 p.m., as the sun is setting!
Distance: 10 miles
Fee: $15

All donations welcome.
Funds raised will go to the Children's Hospital.

B. Read the article below. The paragraphs are jumbled up. Put them in the correct order by writing 1-5 in the boxes.

Light the night on skates!

 a

In the end, there were refreshments and snacks waiting for us at the finish line. I had the opportunity to meet other skaters and we were all thrilled to hear that we had managed to raise $25,000! Not bad, huh?

 b

During the event, everything went according to plan. It wasn't a competition or a race, so the main goal was to enjoy the ride. Apart from avoiding straying from the chosen route, the organizers encouraged us to "let loose and improvise" and so we did. We rolled down streets and sidewalks, circled around a large fountain, zigzagged through the park and some of the more experienced also did a few tricks like slaloming and crisscrossing. It was awesome!

c

Last Saturday, on May 10th, people had the chance to participate in the annual charity event *Rollerblading Night* that takes place in our city. Skaters over the age of 18 helped raise money for the local Children's Hospital, and I can proudly say that this year I was one of them.

 d

Overall, attending this event was an exciting and fun experience and I would recommend it to anyone who enjoys rollerblading. I am looking forward to participating again next year and inviting my friends to join as well.

 e

I reached the meeting point at 7:45 p.m. with my rollerblades and helmet light. All the participants had gathered and the organizers were handing out name tags and bright neon yellow T-shirts. We were also given glow-in-the-dark accessories, like wristbands and flashing necklaces. Then, the organizers informed us about the rules and assured us that the chosen route was safe. Our mission was to "light the night" and have fun, while at the same time rollerblade for a good cause.

C. Read the article again. What does the writer do to attract the reader's attention?

D. Read the writing task below and complete the outline.

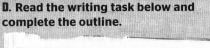

Write an article for cityevents.com!
Tell us about an event (celebration, festival, ceremony, fund-raiser) that takes place or took place in your city. Give information about it, describing what happens/happened and give your opinion. The most interesting articles will be published in the next issue.

TITLE

What is a catchy title for your article?

_____

INTRODUCTION

What's the name of the event?

_____

When and where does/did it take place?

_____

Who takes/took part in it?

_____

What kind of event is/was it?

_____

Have you ever taken part in this event?

_____

MAIN PART

What are/were the preparations for the event?

_____

What kind of activities take/took place during the event?

_____

What happens/happened after the event?

_____

CONCLUSION

What is your overall opinion of the event? Do/Did you like it?

_____

E. Use your ideas from the outline above to write an article describing an event. Make sure you read the TIP below and the plan on page 134.

the plan on page 134

> **TIP**
> - An article is usually written for a newspaper, magazine or website. Use different techniques to make it more interesting. Have a catchy title, include exclamation marks, ask questions, and use a variety of words and expressions.
> - Use the Present Simple when describing an event which takes place regularly.
> - Use past tenses when describing an event which took place in the past and that you know about or attended.
> - Organize the article in paragraphs.

10 REVIEW

A. Choose a, b or c.

1. A: Should I give this to Mr. Knowles?
B: No thanks. I want to give it to him in ____.
   a. charge   **b.** person   **c.** particular

2. The little girl wandered off the ____ and got lost.
   a. trail   **b.** trap   **c.** treadmill

3. We are looking for a bigger ____ for the event, because there will be over 100 people.
   a. venue   **b.** exhibit   **c.** admission

4. Taylor lost his ____ in the end and shouted at everybody.
   a. contact   **b.** life   **c.** temper

5. We decided to make a ____ to the charity.
   a. donation   **b.** fee   **c.** fund

6. The performers did many entertaining ____ on stage.
   a. skates   **b.** tricks   **c.** reflexes

7. I was thrilled to ____ when I won the competition.
   a. nerves   **b.** kicks   **c.** pieces

B. Circle the correct words.

1. I am not coming with you! It is out of **the question / control**!

2. I got up late and **lost / missed** my dentist appointment.

3. As he **proceeded / approached** the door, the sound got louder.

4. I like reading **tails / tales** of mystery and suspense.

5. It was time for dinner but the children were nowhere **in / out of** sight.

6. I can do three somersaults in a **row / sequel**.

7. He took up volleyball but eventually he **missed / lost** interest in it.

C. Rewrite the sentences using Reported Speech.

1. "I won't tell anyone your secret," Chuck said to Kate.

2. "I don't think Belinda knows where the city hall is," Beth informed us.

3. "I have never tried martial arts before," Jeff told the instructor.

4. "Is Peter coming to the barbecue this weekend?" Dean wondered.

5. "Don't forget to bring my necklace!" Lindsay said to Mary.

6. "Why did you leave so early yesterday?" Todd asked me.

7. "You shouldn't judge a person by their appearance," my parents said to me.

D. Rewrite the sentences from Reported Speech to Direct Speech.

1. I told Jill that I didn't know anything about the meeting.

2. The gym instructor told me to run on the treadmill for 30 minutes.

3. Jack asked me how long it had taken me to get to level 10.

4. Kelly wanted to know if we were attending the fund-raiser the following day.

E. Complete the dialogue with the phrases a-g. There are two extra phrases which you will not need to use.

a. Let's go grab a bite to eat now.
b. It's a piece of cake.
c. You kill two birds with one stone.
d. Are you out of your mind?
e. I'll pass!
f. It crossed my mind, but I thought why not give it a shot!
g. I had a whale of a time.

A: Oh, dear. I think I pulled a muscle yesterday.
B: What were you doing?
A: Well, in my youth, I could do some amazing backflips! So yesterday I tried doing one.
B: 1 ____ You are too out of shape to do something like that anymore!
A: 2 ____ And you know what? I managed to do a backflip! I just think that I didn't warm up well enough and now my back hurts.
B: You're lucky you didn't get injured. You could have broken something.
A: Oh, come on! I can show you how it's done.
B: No, thanks. **3** ____ I barely remember how to do a somersault!
A: Trust me. I can show you how to do a backflip step by step. **4** ____
B: Not today. **5** ____ I'm starving!

Self-assessment

Read the following and check the appropriate boxes. For the points you are unsure of, refer back to the relevant sections in the module.

now I can...

▶ talk about various forms of entertainment and spare-time activities	☐
▶ report statements, questions, commands and requests	☐
▶ use prepositional phrases with "in" and "out of"	☐
▶ talk about staying in shape	☐
▶ use collocations with "lose" and "miss"	☐
▶ write an article describing an event	☐

Task 9&10 p. 131

106

Night

Discuss:

- Can you find the following things in the picture?
  - Polaris (The North Star)
  - Ursa Major (The big dipper)
  - Orion
  - a comet
  - a satellite

- Are you a night owl or an early bird?

In this module you will learn...

- to talk about sleeping habits and problems

- to express contrast by using clauses of concession

- to express purpose, reason and result

- phrases that help you emphasize what you are saying

- to indicate that you are following what someone is saying

- to form adjectives (ending in *-able, -al, -ive, -ous, -ful, -ing*) from nouns or verbs

- to analyze problems concerning your city and propose solutions

- to brainstorm ideas using a mind map

- to write a letter (to the editor) expressing an opinion

Reading 🔊

A. Discuss.
- Do you enjoy sleeping?
- Do you think you get enough sleep?
- Do you often wake up feeling tired?

B. Read the problems 1-3 below quickly and match them with the advice a-c.

Solving your sleep problems

with Dr. Penny Fischer

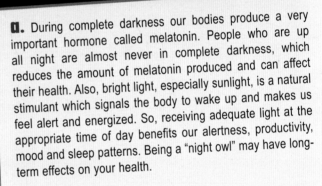

1

I really struggle to get to sleep at night and when I manage to fall asleep, I wake up after a short while. Despite being exhausted all the time, I rarely sleep for more than 3 hours. Recently I've been suffering from headaches, too, which make it hard to concentrate in class. I'm anxious about falling behind at college. I've heard that exercising helps, but I'm neither into sports nor have much energy. Can you help?

Amy, 22

2

My sleep problem is really getting me down; I'm constantly exhausted even though I sleep a lot at night and take naps during the day. My sleepiness is uncontrollable and I fall asleep at inappropriate times, such as during meals and conversations. It's really embarrassing and also dangerous. I have given up driving because last week I fell asleep behind the wheel. Also, I sometimes lose control of my muscles when I laugh a lot. What's wrong with me?

Peter, 27

3

My sleep "problem" is a little unusual. I don't have any trouble sleeping and I almost never feel tired. However, I sleep during the day and I'm up all night. Even though it's not a problem for me, my friends and family consider it unhealthy. I prefer the night to the daytime; it's quieter and, as a writer, I'm able to get more work done. It's when my best ideas come to me and I can concentrate better. During the day, I get distracted too easily. Is this habit bad for my health?

Jamie, 35

a. During complete darkness our bodies produce a very important hormone called melatonin. People who are up all night are almost never in complete darkness, which reduces the amount of melatonin produced and can affect their health. Also, bright light, especially sunlight, is a natural stimulant which signals the body to wake up and makes us feel alert and energized. So, receiving adequate light at the appropriate time of day benefits our alertness, productivity, mood and sleep patterns. Being a "night owl" may have long-term effects on your health.

b. It sounds like you are suffering from insomnia, a common sleep disorder, especially in adult women. In order to figure out what is causing your lack of sleep, try keeping a sleep diary that includes what you ate or drank before bedtime, what activities you did during the day, how you were feeling and how you sleep each night. I recommend consulting a physician or specialist who will advise you how to treat your condition. Also, although you're feeling tired, it's a good idea to take a walk every day as exercise really helps.

c. All the symptoms you describe lead me to believe you have narcolepsy, a sleep disorder that makes you extremely sleepy during the day. It is caused when the part of the brain that controls sleeping and waking is not functioning properly. Your feelings are very natural as these "sleep attacks" can be both frightening and embarrassing. It is common for people with narcolepsy to lose control of their muscles when they are experiencing strong emotions. I recommend consulting a doctor so as to get more information about the condition. Although narcolepsy cannot be cured, most of the symptoms can be controlled with medical treatment, as well as lifestyle adjustments like avoiding caffeine, scheduling meals and sleep and including exercise in your routine.

C. Read again and answer the questions.

1. Why is Amy having problems paying attention at college?

2. Why doesn't Amy want to exercise?

3. Why does Dr. Fischer advise keeping a sleep diary?

4. Why does Peter say that his problem is embarrassing?

5. Why does Peter say that his problem is dangerous?

6. What causes narcolepsy?

7. What can help reduce the symptoms of narcolepsy?

8. Why does Jamie prefer the night time?

9. Why is complete darkness important for our health?

10. How does bright light affect us?

D. Find words/phrases in the text that mean the same as the following.

1. to fail to keep level with others who are doing the same activity (problem 1)

2. to make sb. feel unhappy or depressed (problem 2)

3. driving a car (problem 2)

4. unable to concentrate on sth. (problem 3)

5. able to think clearly and quickly (advice a)

6. enough (advice a)

7. to understand and find the answer (advice b)

8. to ask for information or advice from sb. who has knowledge about the subject (advice b)

9. to make an illness or medical condition go away (advice c)

E. Discuss.

• Do you think the people were given good advice?

• Do you know of any other remedies for insomnia or narcolepsy?

Grammar Clauses of concession and purpose
→ *p. 155*

A. Read the examples and complete the rule.

> Although I don't work on Saturdays, I always get up at 8 in the morning.
>
> Despite setting my alarm, I still didn't get up on time.

Clauses of concession
Use *although, even though, in spite of* and *despite* to express an idea which is in contrast with the idea expressed in the main clause.

• **although / even though** + _____ + verb

• **in spite of / despite** + noun or _____

B. Look at the examples and underline the phrases which are used to express purpose.

> I went to bed early so that I would feel fresh and alert in the morning.
>
> Ronald drank two cups of coffee in order to stay awake and finish his assignment.

Clauses of purpose
• **to / in order (not) to / so as (not) to** + base form

• **so that** + subject + *can/could/will/would/may/might* + base form

C. Read the text and circle the correct words.

I'm in a bad mood today as I had a terrible night's sleep last night. I didn't go to bed early 1 **so as to / so that** watch a movie I really wanted to see. I ended up going to bed at 1 a.m. 2 **in spite of / even though** I had to be up early for work. Anyway, I set my alarm for 6 a.m. 3 **in order to / so that** have some breakfast before I left, but something went wrong and it went off at 4 a.m. I reset it and went to the kitchen 4 **so as / to** get a glass of water, but accidentally dropped it on the floor. 5 **Even though / In spite of** the light was on, I didn't see a piece of glass, stepped on it and cut my foot. I was in terrible pain. My roommate was still asleep 6 **despite / although** all the noise, so I went to his room and woke him up 7 **so that / so as to** he could help me. 8 **In order to / Although** he wasn't very happy, he helped me bandage my foot and clean up the mess. When it was time for me to go to bed again, I couldn't sleep. I need sleep!

110a

Vocabulary

A. Complete the sentences with the correct form of the words in the boxes.

affect   effect

1. Smoking has a negative _____ on our health.
2. Research has shown that certain colors _____ our mood and behavior.

advise   consult   recommend

3. Which hotel would you _____?
4. The doctor _____ me to take up a healthier lifestyle.
5. If I were you, I would _____ a lawyer about the matter.

sleep   sleep in   sleepy   asleep

6. My brother was so tired he fell _____ on the couch.
7. I'm so _____ I can barely keep my eyes open.
8. It's Saturday tomorrow so let's _____.
9. Tina was _____ peacefully so we tried not to wake her up.

treat   cure   recover

10. I thought I was completely _____, but I've started coughing again.
11. My dad had a heart attack, but doctors say he will fully _____ from it.
12. Some sleep problems are _____ with sleeping pills.

mood   feelings   emotion

13. Mr. Benson doesn't seem to be in a good _____ today.
14. I didn't want to hurt her _____, so I didn't say what I was thinking.
15. Greg was furious but he didn't let his face show any _____.

B. Read the sentences and match the phrasal verbs with "up" with the definitions.

1. You're doing great! **Keep up** the good work. ☐
2. Could you please **turn up** the heater? I'm freezing. ☐
3. The meeting was canceled because not many people **turned up**. ☐
4. Mom, please let me **stay up** a little bit more. I want to see the end of the movie. ☐
5. My grandmother **brought up** seven children. ☐
6. I couldn't hear him well so I **hung up** and dialed again. ☐
7. I was too tired to go out, so I just **made up** an excuse about my kid being sick. ☐
8. They **called** us **up** in the middle of the night to tell us the news. ☐
9. I **give up**! What's the answer? ☐

a. to go to bed later than usual
b. to increase the power being produced
c. to look after a child until it is an adult
d. to invent sth., such as a story
e. to end a telephone conversation
f. to continue doing sth.
g. to telephone sb.
h. to stop trying to do sth.
i. to appear or arrive

Grammar All / Both / Neither / None / Either, Both... and... / Neither... nor... / Either... or... → p. 156

A. Read the examples below and complete the rules.

- **Both** children woke up from nightmares, but **neither** of them could remember their dreams in the morning.
- **All** the students thought they did well on the exam, but **none** of them passed.
- **A:** Would you like tea or coffee?
  B: Either. I don't mind.

both, either and _____	_____ and *neither*
are used for two people, things, ideas, etc.	are used in affirmative sentences and give them a negative meaning.

_____ and *none*	_____
are used for more than two people, things, ideas, etc.	means one or the other (it doesn't matter which of the two).

B. Read the examples below and match them with their meanings.

We can visit **both** Oxford **and** Cambridge while we're in England. ☐

We can visit **either** Oxford **or** Cambridge while we're in England, whichever you prefer. ☐

We can visit **neither** Oxford **nor** Cambridge while we're in England. We won't have time. ☐

a. We can't visit the two cities.
b. We can visit one of the two cities.
c. We can visit the two cities.

110

C. Complete the dialogues with all, both, and, neither, nor, none or either.

1. A: Have you tried any of Olivia's cakes?

   B: Yes, I've tried _____ her lemon cake _____ her chocolate cake. To be honest, _____ of them was very nice. I think yours are better.

2. A: Did you like the exhibition?

   B: Yeah, _____ the paintings were beautiful, but _____ of them were very cheap, so I didn't buy anything.

3. A: What should we do tomorrow?

   B: We can _____ go for a walk in the forest or go fishing at the lake. What do you think?

4. A: What did your parents study at college?

   B: _____ my father _____ my mother went to college. They found jobs straight out of high school.

5. A: Stress can affect _____ your mental and physical health, so you should do something to reduce it. Exercising helps a lot. Do you go to the gym or play any sports?

   B: Unfortunately, Dr. Jones, I do _____ of them. I work too much.

   A: Well, you need to start looking after yourself.

Pronunciation ◀))

A. Listen and repeat. Which letters are silent?

nightmare   exhausted

B. Read the words and underline the silent letters. Then listen and check your answers.

although	wheel	muscle	answer
assignment	doubt	extremely	writer	knowledge
receipt	thought	half	honest

Listening ◀))

A. Listen to four people describing dreams they had. Match the speakers with the statements a-f. There are two extra statements which you do not need to use.

Joey ☐

Tonia ☐

Ryan ☐

Kylie ☐

   a. I tried something new because of my dream.

   b. My friends have had a similar dream to mine.

   c. Someone ended my dream for me.

   d. It was the first nightmare I've ever had.

   e. I've had this dream before.

   f. I know why I had this dream.

B. Listen again and write T for True or F for False.

1. Joey had his dream while he was in school. ☐
2. In his dream, Joey was worried about classes and exams. ☐
3. In her dream, Tonia discovered something she had never seen before. ☐
4. Tonia rode a horse in her dream. ☐
5. A friend told Ryan to get out of the airport. ☐
6. Although Ryan was hiding, the men found him. ☐
7. Kylie's friends saw the snake first. ☐
8. Kylie was physically disabled in her dream. ☐

Speaking

Talk in pairs.

Student A: Think of a dream you've recently had and describe it to Student B. Use the questions below as a guide and the phrases to emphasize and make your description more dramatic.

- Who was in the dream?
- What happened?
- How did it make you feel?
- Did you want the dream to end or not?
- Have you had this dream before?

Emphasizing

I was pretty/so/totally/completely...!

It was so/such a... that...

You won't believe what happened next!

The next thing I knew...

I'm serious!

Student B: Listen to Student A describing a dream he/she had. Respond to what he/she is saying to show that you are following.

Showing that you are following

Really?

No!

No way!

Yes?

That's incredible!

Uh-huh.

Then what?

Oh!

I see.

Reading 🔊

A. What do you know about the northern lights? Can you answer the questions below?

1. What is another name for the northern lights?
2. Where can you see this phenomenon?
3. What causes it?
4. When's the best time to see it?

B. Read the text quickly and check your answers in activity A.

11:55 AM

Northern Lights, a spectacular display *by Peter Gray*

It had always been a dream of mine to have first-hand experience of the *aurora borealis*, more commonly known as *the northern lights*. I had been in the Arctic Circle more than once (in Sweden, Norway and Canada), but unfortunately hadn't yet witnessed the remarkable display.

That is why I decided to find an expert to help me "hunt" the northern lights. "Aurora hunters" are specialized in leading groups of people interested in seeing the northern lights. I contacted Ray Owens, who is constantly in search of the perfect conditions in order to view this unpredictable display. Being a professional light chaser, he has devoted the past 5 years to finding the most impressive views of the aurora borealis.

Since ancient times, people have created many legends centered on this phenomenon in an effort to explain why it occurs. For example, the Finnish name for the northern lights is "Revontulet," which means "fox fires." In an old Finnish fable, the northern lights were caused by a fox sweeping its tail across the snow and spraying it up into the sky.

However, the glow coming from the northern lights, which causes the mysterious display of colors, is actually particles that are released from the Sun's surface and are attracted to the magnetic pull of the north and south poles. This process releases energy and electric power is generated, causing explosions of colorful light to cover the sky.

I took the trip in early March, since the period from September to April is considered best to view the spectacle. The journey that I had always dreamed of making began in Trondheim, Norway. I met up with my guide, Ray, and from there we took a train to Bodo, while admiring the scenery along the way.

Next was a ferry ride across the Vestfjord to the Lofoten Islands, which also gave us the opportunity to admire the beautiful fjords. That night we stayed in a glass igloo but unfortunately we didn't see the natural display of light we were so much anticipating.

Then we were off to Tromsø, which is considered one of the best places to observe this phenomenon. We ate, rested and then later in the evening, we headed towards Tomak Valley, where the dry and cold climate is perfect for viewing the northern lights. We traveled through the valley on our snowmobiles and after a while we reached our destination for the night, a Sami* tent. There, we were treated to a traditional Sami meal which included reindeer meat and berries.

That is when the moment I had been waiting for finally arrived! The northern lights appeared! We stared in awe at the astonishing display. I observed as the beams of light flickered overhead and the curtains of red and green light brightened the dark sky. It was an incredible experience that was worth waiting for and one that I will never forget.

*Indigenous people who live in the Arctic area of Sápmi, which includes parts of northern Norway, Sweden, Finland and Russia.

C. Read the text again and find evidence to prove the following.

1. The writer had the chance to see the northern lights before but didn't.
2. The writer didn't go on the trip alone.
3. Humans weren't always able to explain this natural phenomenon.
4. The writer used different modes of transportation during his trip.
5. The writer stayed at different types of accommodations during his trip.
6. The writer failed to see the northern lights at least once during his trip.
7. The writer had the opportunity to experience a different culture.
8. The writer was fascinated by what he saw.

D. Look at the highlighted words in the text and match them with their meanings.

1. first-hand ☐
2. view ☐
3. sweep ☐
4. generate ☐
5. spectacle ☐
6. anticipate ☐
7. awe ☐
8. flicker ☐

a. to shine or burn with a light that keeps going on and off quickly
b. a very impressive event or sight
c. to expect sth.
d. to move sth. over a surface touching it lightly
e. to look at or watch sth.
f. gained by doing sth. yourself
g. a feeling of great respect, admiration and slight fear
h. to produce

E. Discuss.

• Would you go on a trip to see the northern lights? Why? / Why not?
• What other types of natural phenomena would you like to experience?

Vocabulary

A. Read the note, look at the adjectives below from the text and write how they are formed, as in the example.

> A lot of adjectives are formed by adding a suffix to a verb or noun.

1. remarkable __*remark + able*__
2. professional _____
3. impressive _____
4. mysterious _____
5. colorful _____
6. astonishing _____

B. Form adjectives to complete the table. Use the words in the box and a suitable suffix. Make any necessary changes.

environment	predict	challenge	suit
adventure	culture	luxury	delight	attract
	power	thrill	create	

-ous / -ious	-al	-ful

-able	-ive	-ing

Listening 🔊

A. Before you listen, try to answer the questions below. Then listen to a scientist speaking at a planetarium and check your answers.

1. How old is the universe?
2. How old is the Earth?
3. How many stars can you see on a clear night?
4. How many moons does Jupiter have?
5. How many more years will the Earth be able to support life?

B. Listen again and write T for True or F for False.

1. The Sun is older than the Earth. ☐
2. Seeing the light from the stars doesn't mean they are still there. ☐
3. The moon is the largest natural satellite in the solar system. ☐
4. Uranus is the planet with the most moons. ☐
5. The moon is getting closer to the Earth. ☐

Speaking

A. Talk in small groups. Read through the survey below, discuss the problems and choose the ones that apply to your town/city.

City Survey

City: _____   Population: _____

What are the most serious problems your city is facing today?

☐ not clean enough
☐ not green enough
☐ poor condition of roads
☐ too much traffic
☐ limited public transportation system
☐ schools in bad condition
☐ not enough facilities and services (e.g. banks, hospitals, stores, restaurants, sports centers, libraries, parking lots)
☐ high crime rate
☐ high unemployment rate
☐ few job opportunities

Other: _____
       _____

Analyzing problems

In my opinion, the major problem in our city is...
The main problem we need to solve is...
As I see it, the most important issue is...
I think that... is causing the most problems in our city.
Our main concern should be...

Expressing reason and result

The reason for this is (that)...	Therefore...
This is because...	As a consequence...
This is due to the fact that...	... which means that...
For this reason,...	... which makes it more...
As a result...	

B. Talk in small groups. Imagine you are all on the town/city council. Discuss how you could change and improve your town/city for the better. Use the ideas in the box.

have more garbage trucks/collectors
place more recycling bins / garbage cans around the city
have stricter measures / higher fines
get residents involved in cleaning, planting trees, painting, etc.
turn vacant lots into parks
give funds for maintenance costs
create traffic priority lanes for buses
increase bus and subway lines
create bicycle lanes
increase the number of patrol officers on streets
have better lighting on roads
create neighborhood watch groups
organize courses at community centers
organize careers guidance seminars
organize fund-raisers
create jobs e.g. open malls

Writing A letter (to the editor) expressing an opinion

A. Discuss.

• Why do you think people write letters to the editors of newspapers and magazines?

• Have you ever read any of these letters?

• Would you consider writing a letter to the editor of a newspaper? Why? / Why not?

B. Read the extract from a newspaper article below and the letter to the editor on the next page. Do you agree with the writer or not?

In a press conference yesterday, Mayor Barnes announced a series of measures aiming to save energy and cut down on town expenses. One controversial measure involves switching off a number of street lights from midnight to 5 a.m. Although the mayor claims that it will not affect the residents' daily life, many people are not happy with this decision. They fear an increase in road accidents as well as in crime due to inadequate lighting. Speaking to us, long-time resident and father of a family of four, Tony Cooper said, "This is outrageous! If the mayor goes ahead with these plans, our safety and the safety of our children will be at risk. We need to stop this nonsense at all costs!"

Dear Sir/Madam,

I am a concerned resident, and I am writing in response to your article about the mayor's plans to switch off the street lights after midnight in order to save energy and money.

First of all, I would like to point out that recent studies have shown that inadequate lighting at night leads to more road accidents. Already certain areas in our town lack sufficient lighting, which makes them particularly dangerous for drivers and pedestrians. If this spreads to other areas, it will only make an existing problem worse.

Moreover, our town will become less safe. With this measure, the mayor is simply making it easier for criminals to commit crimes such as vandalism and burglaries. Surely, a more suitable solution to the problem can be found. For example, why don't we consider installing energy-efficient lighting, which saves both energy and money in the long run?

In conclusion, I must agree with Tony Cooper when he says that we need to stop these plans at all costs. If we do not take action, our lives will be threatened in more ways than one! The safety of the town and its residents should be our number one priority.

Yours truly,

M. Cunningham

Melanie Cunningham

C. Read the following sentences and check the ones that apply to the letter above.

The writer:

1. uses an appropriate greeting and signature ending.
2. explains why she is writing the letter in the first paragraph.
3. complains in a rude manner.
4. justifies her opinion and gives examples.
5. uses rhetorical questions for emphasis.
6. uses linking words/phrases.
7. writes in a formal style.
8. makes suggestions.
9. refers to specific points made in the newspaper article.

D. Read the writing task below and discuss the questions that follow in pairs or groups. Then complete the mind map.

You read this article in a local newspaper. Write a letter to the editor expressing your views on the issue.

Yesterday Mayor Donaldson announced plans to build a modern shopping mall in Clifton Park. He says it will serve the needs of the residents and also attract shoppers from neighboring towns. Many people are not happy with this decision. One resident, Diane Crane, told us, "We don't need a mall in our town! So many trees will be cut down if the mayor goes ahead with his plans. Clifton Park gives us the oxygen we breathe and it's where our children play. We need to save it at all costs!"

idea

1. How will the residents benefit from the shopping mall?
2. What are the drawbacks of building the shopping mall in the park?
3. In your opinion, what should be done?

benefits ← MALL → drawbacks

E. Write a letter to the editor of the local newspaper, using some of your ideas from activity D. Use the TIP below and the plan on page 135.

TIP

When writing a letter (to the editor of a newspaper, etc.) expressing your opinion:

- use the appropriate layout and style (formal) (see page 137).
- group related ideas together in paragraphs.
- refer to specific points made in the newspaper article.
- state your opinion clearly.
- use rhetorical questions for emphasis.
- do not be aggressive or use offensive language.
- use linking words/phrases.

A. Circle the correct words.

1. I find it hard to work at home as I easily get **delightful / distracted**.

2. A fever, a runny nose and a sore throat are all common **symptoms / treatments** of the flu.

3. Sunlight can **effect / affect** the quality of our sleep.

4. Your cough can be **recovered / treated** with this medicine.

5. We waited for Mr. Harrison for an hour and in the end he didn't even **keep / turn** up.

6. Drivers should always be careful of **criminals / pedestrians** crossing the road.

7. I didn't **concentrate / anticipate** such a difficult day today!

8. Diane is feeling **depressed / alert** because she lost her job.

9. You're very close to the finish line! Don't **give up / make up** now!

10. Keeping our customers happy is our number one **consequence / priority**.

B. Complete the sentences with the correct form of the words in capitals.

1. That man is _____. Nobody knows anything about him. **MYSTERY**

2. The weather in London is very _____. In the morning it may rain and by noon it may be sunny. **PREDICT**

3. This toy isn't _____ for children that are younger than three years old. **SUIT**

4. Traveling to different countries can be an interesting _____ experience. **CULTURE**

5. Last year, we stayed at a very _____ hotel in the Bahamas. **LUXURY**

6. A doctor's job is very demanding and _____. **CHALLENGE**

7. A(n) _____ amount of protein in your diet could cause health problems. **ADEQUATE**

8. The northern lights are a very _____ display. **IMPRESS**

C. Choose a, b or c.

1. The boys continued playing outside ____ it was raining.
   a. despite   **b.** although   **c.** even

2. John went to the planetarium in ____ to attend a talk about the solar system.
   a. order   **b.** so   **c.** spite

3. ____ the cold, Lucy went jogging.
   a. In spite   **b.** Although   **c.** Despite

4. ____ I was very sleepy, I couldn't sleep.
   a. Even though   **b.** In order to   **c.** Despite

5. I didn't tell Mark the truth ____ not to hurt his feelings.
   a. so that   **b.** so as   **c.** to

6. He worked all night, in ____ of being tired.
   a. order   **b.** spite   **c.** despite

7. We took our muddy boots off before entering the house ____ we wouldn't make a mess.
   a. so as   **b.** in order to   **c.** so that

D. Complete the sentences with all, both, neither, nor, none, either, or.

1. _____ Larry and Harry are doctors and they work at the local hospital.

2. _____ my sister _____ my brother have ever been to Germany, but they are going to go next month.

3. I am going to cook _____ spaghetti _____ soup, but I'm not sure which yet.

4. I searched _____ of the books in your bookcase, but _____ of them appealed to me.

5. I have two formal dresses, but I don't want to wear _____ of them to the wedding.

6. _____ my parents are from Ireland, but _____ of them has visited Ireland for years.

E. Rewrite the sentences using the words given.

1. In spite of being angry at her son, Becky didn't yell at him.   **although**

   _____

2. Paul went to bed early so that he wouldn't be sleepy the next day.   **order**

   _____

3. Even though Dan was feeling sick, he continued working.   **spite**

   _____

4. Janice and Gloria hate Japanese food, so I don't think that they will come to the restaurant with us.   **neither**

   _____

5. We can go to the park or to the beach, whatever you prefer.   **either**

   _____

Self-assessment

Read the following and check the appropriate boxes. For the points you are unsure of, refer back to the relevant sections in the module.

now I can...

- talk about sleeping habits and problems ☐
- express contrast by using clauses of concession ☐
- express purpose, reason and result ☐
- use phrases that help me emphasize what I'm saying ☐
- indicate that I'm following what someone is saying ☐
- form adjectives (ending in -able, -al, -ive, -ous, -ful, -ing) from nouns or verbs ☐
- analyze problems concerning my city and propose solutions ☐
- write a letter (to the editor) expressing my opinion ☐

Discuss:

• Read the sentences in the box. Do you understand what the phrases in bold mean?

• Do you leave things to chance?

In this module you will learn...

• to talk about imaginary and hypothetical situations in the past

• to express wishes and regret about something in the past

• phrases to show you are sympathetic and encouraging

• to discuss problems and ask for and give advice

• how to edit your own work

• to write an informal e-mail giving advice

• I didn't arrange to see Karen. We just met **by chance**.
• Tonight's your **last chance** to see the performance. Are you coming?
• There is a **slim chance** that I will pass my physics exam. I didn't study much.
• He's crashed my car already! I'm not giving him a **second chance**.
• There's a possibility of rain at the flower show today, but I'll **take my chances**.
• He'll eat your pizza too, **given half the chance**.
• The Bears **don't stand a chance** against the Vikings today.
• I **leave nothing to chance**. I plan everything down to the last detail.
• **A:** Maybe your brother will lend you his car.
  B: Fat chance!

Reading 🔊

A. Read the quote below and discuss the questions.

"Chance favors the prepared mind"
Louis Pasteur

- What do you think it means?
- Can you think of any things that happened by accident, that turned out to be beneficial?

B. Look at the four items pictured. How do you think they were discovered? Read the text and find out.

Oops! *Accidental discoveries*

Nice idea!
Post-it®

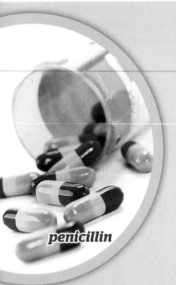
penicillin

In 1928 a Scottish scientist was doing experiments on the influenza virus, commonly referred to as "the flu," at a hospital in London. His name was Alexander Fleming, and he had a reputation for being a careless lab technician. After a two-week vacation, he returned to find some mold growing on one of his culture plates which he had left uncovered. After closer inspection, he realized that the mold produced a substance which was preventing the growth of the bacteria on the plate. He had discovered the first antibiotic, which was later found to be effective against a wide range of harmful bacteria. He named it "penicillin," which means "paintbrush" in Latin, because of the shape of the cells. If Fleming hadn't made that accidental discovery, medicine wouldn't have progressed the way it did.

Dr. Spencer Silver was working as a scientist for 3M in the U.S.A. in 1968. He was trying to create super-strong glue, but instead he created something weak. It was useless for most purposes, and for years he tried to promote his discovery but nobody was interested. It later became known as a "solution without a problem." Then, in 1974, a colleague of his named Art Fry came up with the idea to use it on his bookmark, so he could stick it into his book and remove it as many times as he liked. This led to the idea of using the glue on small pieces of paper for note-taking, and the Post-it® note was born. But why yellow? Well, the lab next door to where they were working only had yellow scrap paper, and that's what they used to make their samples.

On August 24, 1853, a hotel chef named George Crum had to deal with a particularly irritating customer. The customer had sent back his fried potatoes numerous times, because they were too thick and soggy. Crum was so annoyed he decided to slice the fries very thinly, cook them till they were crispy, and add a lot of salt. He expected the customer to find them disgusting, but on the contrary, the customer was thrilled. A new snack had been invented. The chips became popular and were given the name "Saratoga chips," after the city where the hotel was located. If that customer hadn't been so picky, the chef wouldn't have invented this tasty snack.

potato chips

It's difficult for us to imagine life without electricity or the Internet, but what about life without matches? In 1826, making fires became a lot easier thanks to an English chemist named John Walker. Walker noticed a dried lump at the end of a stick he had used to stir a mixture of chemicals. He tried to scrape it off and it produced sparks and a flame. He went on to invent the first friction match. He called them "Friction Lights" and sold them at his pharmacy. If only he had patented his idea, but he chose not to because he considered it to be a benefit to mankind. Of course, this didn't stop others from copying his idea and making a profit.

matches

C. Read again and write P for penicillin, PC for potato chips, PN for Post-it® notes or M for matches.

1. The person who discovered this didn't believe that it would get a positive response. ☐

2. If someone had been more careful, this wouldn't have been discovered. ☐

3. It took a long time to find a use for this discovery. ☐

4. The person who discovered this missed out on a chance to make money. ☐

5. This discovery is not known by its original name. ☐

6. This discovery was named after a place. ☐

7. It needed someone else to point out the usefulness of this discovery. ☐

D. Look at the highlighted words in the text and match them with their meanings.

1. reputation ☐
2. lab ☐
3. irritating ☐
4. numerous ☐
5. soggy ☐
6. picky ☐
7. remove ☐
8. mankind ☐
9. profit ☐

a. many; existing in large numbers
b. all humans as a group
c. liking specific things and difficult to please
d. a room used for scientific research, experiments, etc.
e. to take sth. away from somewhere
f. annoying
g. the opinion that people have about sb./sth. based on past behavior and/or events
h. unpleasantly wet and soft
i. money gained in business

E. Discuss.
- Which of the four discoveries do you find the most surprising? Why?
- Which of the four do you think changed the world?

Vocabulary

A. Read the sentences below and look at the words in bold. What do you notice?

a. **Slice** the apple very thinly.
b. Put each **slice** next to each other on the pie.

> Some words can be both verbs and nouns. Their meanings could be very similar (e.g. help) or different (e.g. watch).

B. Complete the sentences with the correct form of the words in the box. Use the same word for each pair of sentences.

stick	experiment	match	benefit
	stay	support	

1. a. I had a lot of problems in my first year at college, but my friends _____ me a lot.
   b. The organization gives a lot of _____ to the city's homeless people.

2. a. I don't think this dress _____ my shoes.
   b. Do you have any _____ to light a fire?

3. a. Many people are against doing _____ on animals.
   b. I enjoy _____ with different ingredients when cooking.

4. a. Did you enjoy your _____ in Geneva?
   b. Jean _____ in Warsaw for two weeks.

5. a. Get a _____ and try to get the ball down from the tree.
   b. I used some glue to _____ the pieces of the broken vase together.

6. a. How does mankind _____ from this invention?
   b. Tourism has brought many _____ to our city.

Grammar Conditional Sentences Type 3
→ *p. 156*

A. Read the example and answer the questions.

> Perhaps **if I had gone** to college, **I would have become** a scientist.

1. Did this person go to college?
2. Did this person become a scientist?
3. How does this person feel about it?

B. Read and complete the rule below.

> **Conditional Sentences Type 3** are used for unreal situations in the past or to express regret about something that happened or didn't happen.
>
> If + Past Perfect → would/could/might + _____ + past participle

C. Complete the dialogues with the correct form of the words in parentheses.

1. **A:** Is Dennis there?
   B: No, you just missed him. If you _____ (call) five minutes ago, you _____ (be) able to speak to him.

2. **A:** If you _____ (not yell) at your brother in front of everybody, he _____ (not get) angry at you.
   B: Well, if he _____ (be) more careful, he _____ (not crash) my motorcycle into the tree!
   A: It wasn't his fault. The accident _____ (not happen) if the road _____ (not be) so slippery.

3. **A:** How's life in the city? Exciting?
   B: Sure, but I _____ (not leave) my home town if I _____ (know) how expensive it is here in the city.

Vocabulary

Read the sentences and match the phrases in bold with their definitions.

1. I **have no time for** disorganized and lazy people in my life. ☐
2. I'm living in a friend's basement **for the time being**, until I find my own place. ☐
3. I got an F on the test. I wish I could **turn back time** and take it again. ☐
4. We ate our breakfast **in no time** and left for work. ☐
5. We **have some time to kill** before our train arrives, so let's go look at those magazines. ☐
6. Will the train from Birmingham arrive **on time**? ☐
7. The store was closing but we managed to find what we wanted **in time**. ☐
8. Julia likes to visit her grandparents in Arlington **from time to time**. ☐
9. This is a place of work, so I'd prefer it if you chat with your friends **in your own time**. ☐
10. Many people believe Pelé was the greatest soccer player **of all time**. ☐

a. to go back in time
b. sometimes
c. just for now
d. during your spare time
e. very soon, very quickly
f. to have nothing to do
g. at the correct time
h. not late; early enough
i. to disapprove of or dislike sth./sb.
j. that has ever existed

Grammar Wishes and Unreal Past → *p. 156*

A. Read the speech bubbles and answer the questions that follow.

> I wish I could travel around the world.
> If only traveling around the world was easy and inexpensive.
> SANDRA

1. Can Sandra travel around the world?
2. Does Sandra believe that traveling around the world is easy and inexpensive?
3. Do the sentences refer to the present/future or the past?
4. Would Sandra like the situation to be different?

> I'm late again! I wish I had set my alarm for 6 a.m.
> If only I had gotten up earlier!
> ALEX

1. Did Alex set his alarm for 6 a.m.?
2. Did Alex get up early?
3. Do the sentences refer to the present/future or the past?
4. How does Alex feel about the situation?

B. Read the rules below and match the speech bubbles above with the uses of *wish / if only*.

We use wish / if only + Past Simple:
to make a wish about a present or future situation which we would like to be different.

We use wish / if only + Past Perfect Simple:
to express regret or sorrow about something that happened or didn't happen in the past.

C. Read the following situations and write sentences starting with the words given.

1. I have to get up early every morning and I don't like that.
   I wish _____

2. I'd love to be able to buy that car but I can't.
   If only _____

3. We should have asked Tony for his phone number when we saw him.
   I wish _____

4. I lied to my best friend and that was a mistake.
   If only _____

5. Unfortunately, last weekend I was sick and I couldn't go to the barbecue.
   I wish _____

6. Debbie doesn't exercise as much as she used to and she's worried about it.
   Debbie wishes _____

7. Yesterday, my sister borrowed my cell phone and lost it.
   If only _____

Listening 🔊

You will hear people talking in six different situations. For questions 1-6, choose a, b or c.

1. What does the woman say?
   a. Working abroad is a great experience.
   b. She wishes she could change her job.
   c. She's glad she didn't accept the job offer abroad.

2. Why isn't the man playing tennis today?
   a. It's raining.
   b. He can't find anyone to play with.
   c. There are no free courts.

3. What is true about the woman?
   a. She thought she'd lost her purse.
   b. She wishes she hadn't bought the dress.
   c. She regrets going to the mall.

4. Why did Kevin miss the train?
   a. There was a problem with his ticket.
   b. He didn't get to the station in time.
   c. He wasn't concentrating on what he was doing.

5. What does Danny wish he had done?
   a. Stayed at a hotel.
   b. Bought a new tent.
   c. Stayed at the campground.

6. What does Jenny regret doing?
   a. Going to the job interview.
   b. Listening to her sister.
   c. Being unprepared.

Speaking

A. Look at the picture and discuss the questions.

- What do you think has happened?
- How do you think the man feels?
- What do you think he's thinking?

66 *If only my team had won.* **99**

B. Talk in pairs.

Student A: Think of things that you wish were different in your life and discuss what you could do about them.

Student B: Listen to Student A, be sympathetic towards him/her and try to encourage him/her to do sth. Use some of the phrases in the box.

Being sympathetic and encouraging
I'm sorry to hear that.
What a shame!
What a pity!
I know the feeling.
It's better than nothing.
Better luck next time.
It's never too late.
You win some, you lose some.
Look on the bright side.
Better late than never.

66 *If only I had studied computer programming! I regret not doing it.*
Yeah, what a shame. You'd be able to find a job easily.
I wish I could turn back time and do things differently.
It's never too late. Why don't you sign up for a course? **99**

Reading 🔊

A. Discuss.

- Do you have a favorite number?
- Do you use significant numbers for PINs or passwords?

B. Read the text quickly and choose the best title.

a. **A coincidence that changed my life forever**

b. **I never want to see that number again**

c. **Why did I choose that number?**

Coincidences happen all the time, but last week something happened that really blew my mind.

I'm from Chicago, but I do a lot of business in Baltimore. That's where it all started, on the night before an important business lunch. I usually sleep like a log, but I was tossing and turning in bed for no apparent reason. I must have fallen asleep at around 2 o'clock because the last time I looked, it was 1:45. The following morning, I woke up very late, got ready in a flash and rushed out of the hotel room. As I slammed the door, I noticed the number. Room 145. "That's odd," I thought.

I asked the hotel receptionist about the best way to get to the downtown area. He explained where the bus stop was and told me any bus that says "downtown" would take me to my destination. As soon as I got to the bus stop, I saw a bus coming and the number sent a shiver down my spine. It was 145; however, it didn't say "downtown." It came to a stop right in front of me and the doors opened. I don't know what came over me, but I just got on.

The bus was empty and I went to the back and sat down. "What am I doing?" I thought to myself. I was just about to get off when I saw an envelope on a seat and picked it up. It wasn't sealed so I looked inside and my jaw dropped. It was full of money. I started counting - 140 dollars. "Almost," I thought. "That would have been strange." Then, I noticed something on the floor. A five-dollar bill had fallen out. Things were starting to get spooky.

There was an address on the envelope; Bellmore Street and you can guess which number. I had to go there, I didn't have a choice. So, I waited for the bus driver to stop and asked him how to get to Bellmore Street. "Is this some sort of joke?" he asked as he pointed at a street sign. We were on Bellmore Street, so I got off. The day was getting weirder and weirder.

I searched for the number and was soon knocking on the door. My heart was in my mouth when an old lady answered. She looked at me, and then at the envelope and simply said "Oh, thanks," and closed the door. And that was it.

I stood there for a while. I couldn't make heads or tails of it, but then I remembered I had a business lunch to go to. "What time is it?" I thought, but hesitated before I looked at my watch. I gave a sigh of relief when I saw it was 12:45. But as I was walking towards the bus stop, I realized something. My watch was still set to Chicago time, which is an hour behind! The actual time was...

C. Read again and answer the questions. Choose a, b, c or d.

1. Why couldn't the writer sleep very well?
   a. He was worried about something.
   b. He went to bed too early.
   c. The bed wasn't comfortable.
   d. He doesn't know why.

2. Which bus did the writer take?
   a. The 145 bus that was going downtown.
   b. A bus that wasn't going downtown.
   c. The first bus that stopped and was going towards his destination.
   d. A bus that the receptionist told him to take.

3. How did the writer feel when he got on the bus?
   a. He was sure he was doing the right thing.
   b. He was confident he was going in the right direction.
   c. He was anxious he was going to get lost.
   d. He was worried he had made a mistake.

4. Why did the writer say: *"Almost," I thought. "That would have been strange."*
   a. He was surprised to find so much money.
   b. He expected to find a different amount.
   c. He realized he had made a mistake while counting.
   d. He was happy that he had noticed the envelope before getting off.

5. Why did the bus driver stop at Bellmore Street?
   a. Because that's where the next stop was.
   b. Because the writer asked him to stop there.
   c. Because that was the address on the envelope.
   d. Because the driver wanted to play a joke on the writer.

6. How did the old lady feel when she saw the writer?
   a. She was thrilled to get her money back.
   b. She felt nervous when she saw the writer.
   c. She didn't show any emotion.
   d. She was angry that the writer had her money.

7. What was the actual time in Baltimore when the writer looked at his watch?
   a. 11:45 a.m.
   b. 12:45 p.m.
   c. 1:45 p.m.
   d. 2:45 p.m.

D. Discuss.

- What's the most amazing coincidence that has happened to you?
- How do coincidences make you feel?

Vocabulary

A. Look at the highlighted idioms in the text in the reading activity and guess what they mean.

B. Read the sentences and match the idioms in bold with their meanings a-f.

1. We were enjoying a picnic in the park, when **out of the blue** it started pouring. ☐

2. Our neighbor is **a pain in the neck** sometimes, because he plays loud music at night. ☐

3. When our team won the championship, we felt **on top of the world**! ☐

4. **A:** How did you find out about my decision?
   B: Your sister **spilled the beans**. ☐

5. **A:** Does the name Amy Jones **ring a bell**? ☐
   B: No, I don't think so. Does she work here?

6. Tell me exactly what happened, Greg. I'm **all ears**. ☐

a. annoying	**d.** to tell a secret
b. to sound familiar	**e.** eager to listen
c. suddenly; unexpectedly	**f.** very happy

Listening 🔊

A. Discuss.

- What do you think it's like to be an identical twin?
- Scientists believe that identical twins can both feel things at the same time, even when they are not in the same place. Do you believe this?

B. Listen to a radio show about identical twins and write T for True or F for False.

Story 1

1. Two twin boys from Finland died during a blizzard. ☐

2. The brothers were riding their bikes when they got hit by the same truck. ☐

Story 2

3. The twins had the same name. ☐
4. According to research, the adopted brothers aren't typical twins. ☐

Story 3

5. Ashley and Angie found out they were pregnant on the same day. ☐
6. Ashley and Angie gave birth to twins. ☐

Speaking

Talk in pairs.

I can't pay my credit card bill.

depressed broke get a part-time job borrow cancel card throw money around put money aside	have an argument gossip behind my back feel rejected jealous work out your differences make new friends cheer up ignore

Student A: Choose one of the pictures and imagine you have the problem shown. Explain the problem to Student B and ask him/her for advice. Use the words/phrases in the boxes.

Asking for advice

I need your advice because...
What should I do? Any ideas?
I know I shouldn't have done that, but what do I do now?
What would you do if you were in my position?
How should I deal with the situation?

Student B: Listen to Student A's problem, be sympathetic and give him/her advice. Use the words/phrases in the boxes.

Giving advice

I think you should / had better...
If I were you, I'd...
If I were in your shoes, I'd...
Why don't you...?
It would be a good idea to...

Writing An informal e-mail (III)

A. Read the writing task below. Which of the functions listed do you think the receiver of the e-mail should include in the reply?

Below is part of an e-mail you have received from a friend. Read it and write a reply.

We were supposed to go out yesterday, but Alice canceled on me, saying that she had to study. So, I ended up going to the movies by myself and guess what! By chance I saw her hanging out at the mall with a group of friends from college! I couldn't believe it! She didn't see me, and I didn't talk to her, but why would she lie to me? She hasn't called me up and I haven't called her either. To be honest, I don't know what to say when I face her. I feel so lonely.

1. expressing enthusiasm ☐
2. giving advice ☐
3. expressing sympathy ☐
4. expressing regret ☐
5. complaining ☐
6. requesting information ☐
7. apologizing ☐
8. making suggestions ☐

B. Read the e-mail Lisa has written in response ignoring the mistakes underlined. Which of the functions (1-8) from activity A are expressed in her e-mail? What other advice would you give Emily?

Dear Emily,

I'm very sorry to hear about what happened
with Alice? I'm sure there's some reasonable
explanation for her behavior, so don't be too upset.
I hope my advice will help you deal about your
problem.

First of all, you should talk to her soon as possible.
If I were you, I will tell her that her behavior
disappointed me. It is important to be honest with
your friends about how you feel because hiding
your feelings can only cause bigger problems.
The way I see it, Alice probably changed her mind
about studying, decided to go out to clear her head
a little and ran into her friends. I don't think she
planned anything behind your back. Things aren't
always as they seem, so maybe you shouldn't jump
to concluzions.

There's one more thing I'd like to point out. Have
you ever thought of expanding your circle of
friends? You won't feel so lonely and you'll be
able to go out with other people apart from Alice.
Why you don't arrange to go out with Alice and
her friends? That way you'll get to know them.
I'm not saying it'll be easy, but friendships are the
important part of life.
Make sure you right back and let me know how
everything turns out.

Best wishes,
Lisa

C. Read the e-mail again paying attention to the mistakes which have been marked using the correction code below. Correct the mistakes.

CORRECTION CODE
WW: wrong word
WO: word order
Pr: preposition
T: tense
A: article
Sp: spelling
P: punctuation
∧: something missing

14

D. Read the writing task below. What advice would you give your friend?

Below is part of an e-mail you have received from a friend. Read it and write a reply.

Remember how I helped Tony get a job at the
company where I work? Well, I think I'm regretting
it now. Many of our other colleagues have started
complaining that he is being lazy and that they
have to finish his work for him. I've been helping
him out, too, but lately I've noticed that he wastes
his time doing other things, like chatting on the Net
or talking on the phone. If our boss finds out, we
could both get in trouble. How should I handle it
without getting into an argument? Should I continue
helping him out until he realizes his mistake on his
own?

E. Write your reply. Use the plan on page 135.

The End

Produced & Released by
PIONEER

A. Choose a, b or c.

1. The scientists are in the ____. They are conducting an experiment.

    a. inspection   **b.** lab   **c.** cell

2. She got out of the car and ____ the door shut.

    a. slammed   **b.** knocked   **c.** removed

3. Go on. I'm listening. I'm all ____.

    a. tails   **b.** heads   **c.** ears

4. I don't know how to ____ this situation! Any ideas?

    a. handle   **b.** expand   **c.** hesitate

5. My nephew can be a real pain in the ____ sometimes.

    a. jaw   **b.** neck   **c.** heart

6. I'm ____ the world, because I just found out that I got a promotion!

    a. all around   **b.** on top of   **c.** out of

7. There is now only a ____ chance of Rogers winning the race. He's way behind.

    a. last   **b.** half   **c.** slim

8. Miss Bond has a ____ for being a strict teacher.

    a. coincidence   **b.** position   **c.** reputation

B. Circle the correct words.

1. The show was amazing. It blew my **head / mind**.

2. I told Kevin to keep it a secret, but he **spilled / sliced** the beans.

3. Don't jump to **differences / conclusions** if you don't know exactly what happened.

4. I shouldn't have reacted like that. I don't know what came **to / over** me.

5. If you need help, call me. I'll be there **on time / in no time**.

6. I don't trust Penny. She is always talking about other people **below / behind** their backs.

7. I'd lost contact with Jerry for years, and yesterday, **out of the blue / in a flash**, he e-mailed me.

C. Complete the sentences with the correct form of the verbs in parentheses to form Conditional Sentences Type 3.

1. I _____ (not come) by if I _____ (know) that you had so much work to do.

2. We _____ (go) out to eat if you _____ (tell) me that you didn't want to cook.

3. If Brian _____ (follow) his diet, he _____ (not put) on weight.

4. If Kate _____ (ask) her colleague for help, she _____ (finish) her project by now.

5. If I _____ (not travel) to Brazil, I _____ (not meet) my wife.

D. Read the situations below and write sentences using *wish* or *if only*.

1. My sister rarely helps with the housework. I hate that.

_____

2. I wasn't careful while playing basketball and I sprained my ankle.

_____

3. I stayed up late last night and now I feel exhausted.

_____

E. Complete the dialogue with the phrases a-g. There are two extra phrases which you will not need to use.

> **a.** I know the feeling
> **b.** For the time being
> **c.** If I were you
> **d.** If only I could turn back time
> **e.** It rings a bell
> **f.** I have some time to kill
> **g.** I'll take my chances

A: What's the matter, Tina? You look upset.

B: Well, I had an argument with a friend, and now she isn't talking to me.

A: Why did you argue?

B: I just wanted to give her some advice because she has been throwing money around lately, but she got mad.

A: **1** ____. Last week, the same thing happened with my brother and me. It's impossible for him to put money aside.

B: What should I do?

A: **2** ____, I'd leave her alone for a few days until she calms down. She'll realize that you didn't mean to hurt her feelings.

B: OK. **3** ____, I'll wait.

A: Do you have any plans right now?

B: I have a class in a couple of hours but until then **4** ____.

A: Let's go for a coffee then, so that you can cheer up a little. Do you know the coffee shop "Coffee Break"?

B: **5** ____. Is that the one on Rainbow Road?

A: Yes.

B: OK, let's go!

Self-assessment

Read the following and check the appropriate boxes. For the points you are unsure of, refer back to the relevant sections in the module.

NOW I CAN...

> ❭ talk about imaginary and hypothetical situations in the past ☐

> ❭ express wishes and regret about something in the past ☐

> ❭ use phrases to show sympathy and to be encouraging ☐

> ❭ discuss problems and ask for and give advice ☐

> ❭ edit my own work ☐

> ❭ write an informal e-mail giving advice ☐

Task 11&12 p. 132

Exam Practice Modules 10-12 p. 144

A. How much do you know about bar graphs? Look at the bar graph below and answer the questions.

CAR ACCIDENTS
according to gender in South Dakota, U.S.A. (2010-2012)

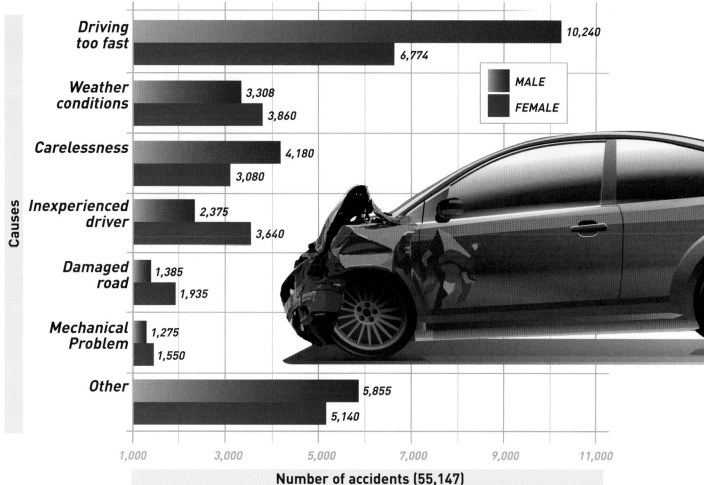

Causes

| Driving too fast | MALE 10,240 / FEMALE 6,774 |

Driving too fast — 10,240 / 6,774
Weather conditions — 3,308 / 3,860
Carelessness — 4,180 / 3,080
Inexperienced driver — 2,375 / 3,640
Damaged road — 1,385 / 1,935
Mechanical Problem — 1,275 / 1,550
Other — 5,855 / 5,140

Key: MALE / FEMALE

x-axis: 1,000 3,000 5,000 7,000 9,000 11,000

Number of accidents (55,147)

1. What is the subject the bar graph presents?
2. What data is presented on the x-axis (horizontally)?
3. What data is presented on the y-axis (vertically)?
4. How many bars are there per category?
5. What data does the key provide?

B. Look at the bar graph again. Are the statements below True or False?

1. Driving too fast caused the most accidents. ☐
2. More accidents were caused by damaged roads than by weather conditions. ☐
3. More accidents were caused by inexperienced women drivers than by inexperienced men drivers. ☐

C. Talk in pairs. Discuss the data in the bar graph above using some of the phrases in the box.

> This bar graph shows that...
> Fewer/More women drivers... than men...
> Not many accidents...
> The most/least common cause of accidents was...
> The fewest/most accidents were caused by...
> Another interesting fact is that...
> It suggests that men/women are more likely to...

D. Discuss.

- Which piece of information in the bar graph was the most interesting or surprising for you? Why?
- What are the main causes of car accidents in your country?
- In your country, who drives more carefully, men or women? Why do you think this is so?
- Do you think bar graphs are a good way of presenting data? Why? / Why not?
- Where have you seen a bar graph before?
- Do you think bar graphs are useful for project work or presentations? Why? / Why not?

Task
modules 3&4

A. Listen to a travel agent talking about 3 tours in Croatia and answer the questions. Write Tour 1, 2 or 3.

1. On which tour can you learn about wildlife?
2. According to the travel agent, which tour is more appropriate for younger people?
3. If you want to buy something, which tour is the best?
4. On which tour can you see ancient architecture?
5. Which tour includes a cruise?
6. On which tour will there be guides to show visitors around?

B. Work in pairs to design a tour of the Netherlands. First, look at the information below, discuss the different places and decide on the tour you would like to create. Then design it in detail. Your tour must consist of 4-5 places. Use some of the phrases in the box.

Consider the following:
- What kind of travelers would enjoy the tour?
- What will travelers see and do during the tour?
- How long will the tour last?
- What will you name the tour?

Amsterdam – Home to many world-class museums, such as the Van Gogh and Rijksmuseum. Regular outdoor music and theater events during the summer. Great for walking along the canals, or renting a bicycle to admire the fascinating architecture and historic buildings. Excellent restaurants, coffee shops and stores.

Texel – Peaceful island with beautiful beaches, parks and wildlife. Attractive little villages. Excellent for cycling, walking, windsurfing and surfing.

Biesbosch – One of the Netherlands' larger national parks, near Dordrecht. Take a relaxing boat trip around the large river network to see many different species of birds.

Utrecht – Lively student town with a beautiful traditional old downtown area. Lots of lively coffee shops and restaurants, as well as plenty of stores. Home to a large movie festival every September. Close to several interesting castles such as Nijenrode Castle in Breukelen.

Hoge Veluwe National Park – Large sandy area with lakes and small forests. Ideal for cycling, horseback riding and guided walks. Home to lots of wildlife. Excellent museum with Van Gogh and Picasso paintings.

Schouwen-Duiveland - Windy island popular for windsurfing and surfing. Nice, long beaches good for walking. Quiet and peaceful destination away from urban areas.

Gouda – Historic town with attractive architecture. Interesting cheese museum and excellent cheese market every week during the summer. Beautiful 15th-century city hall.

Rotterdam – Busy city with rich history and the largest port in Europe. Excellent art museums and large cultural area with theaters, concert halls and galleries. Regular music and art festivals throughout the year.

Map labels
TEXEL
Deb Burg
Zwolle
Harlem
Amsterdam
Utrecht
Gouda
Hoge Veluwe National Park
Rotterdam
Schouwen-Duiveland
Biesbosch
THE NETHERLANDS
Eindhoven
Maastricht

I think the tour should include...
We can also include a visit to...
I believe travelers may find this... because...
This might be too... for...
This type of tour would be more suitable for...
I definitely think that... would be more fun for travelers...
This tour would appeal to...
This would be more popular with...
Travelers will be able to...
... is famous for... so travelers will have the opportunity to...
I don't think the tour should last longer than...

C. Talk with another pair.

Pair 1: Imagine you are interested in going on a tour of the Netherlands. Ask the travel agents (Pair 2) about the tour they offer.

Pair 2: Imagine you are travel agents and the customers (Pair 1) are interested in going on a tour of the Netherlands. Describe the tour you have designed and try to persuade them that it's ideal for them. Use some of the phrases in the box.

Our tour is ideal for... who are interested in...
I definitely recommend this tour because...
I wouldn't recommend this tour to... because...
If you're looking for... then this tour is for you.
You will be able to enjoy...
It's a great way to...
You are given the opportunity to...
Apart from..., it also includes...
It's perfect for...
One of the highlights of the tour is...

A. Below is part of an article on how students can improve their vocabulary. Read the text and answer the questions.

A WORLD OF WORDS

Remembering vocabulary is very important when learning a foreign language. When studying, for example, students can learn about 10-20 new words in one hour. However, studies have shown that students can benefit greatly from reading extra material like magazines, newspapers or books, just by being exposed to the new vocabulary in a text. When learners see a word about 6-10 times in a text, they will eventually remember it and in this way further expand their vocabulary.

The good thing is that the more vocabulary students remember, the better they understand a language. This can lead to even better and quicker vocabulary learning. However, reading books is not enough to expand a student's vocabulary. Below we will look into various techniques that students can use to practice and remember vocabulary in the classroom, when they are studying and in their spare time.

1. Do you agree with this article? Why? / Why not?

2. Do you read books in English? If yes, what do you do when you come across a word that you don't understand? Has reading books in English helped you expand your vocabulary?

3. What other ways/techniques do you use to learn/remember vocabulary?

B. Talk in pairs and discuss the different techniques you use when learning a foreign language. Look at the mind map below and try to complete it by brainstorming ideas. Try to think of the different things you do when trying to develop your listening, reading, writing and speaking skills in class and outside the class.

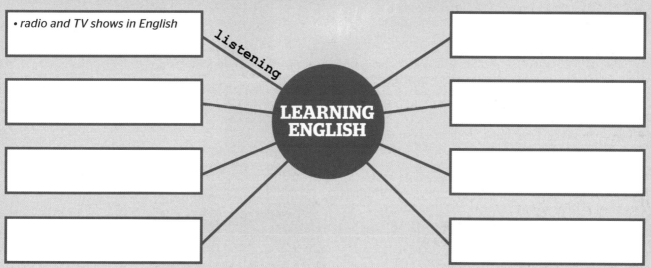

- radio and TV shows in English

listening

LEARNING ENGLISH

C. Compare your ideas with those of another pair. Discuss any ideas you hadn't thought of and say how useful they could be.

D. Report your findings to the class and make a list of guidelines on how you can improve and enhance your language learning skills.

A. Look at the chart below. What kind of information does it give you? Do any of the amounts on the chart surprise you?

Average daily water use

Bath	28-36 gallons (full tub)
Shower	2.5 gallons per minute *(7-8 gallons per minute)**
Brushing teeth	1 gallon per minute
Toilet flush	1.6 gallons per flush *(3-6 gallons per flush)**
Dishwasher	4-10 gallons per load *(15 gallons per load)**
Dishwashing by hand	2.2 gallons per minute
Washing machine	18-25 gallons per load *(40-55 gallons per load)**
Outdoor watering	5 gallons per minute *(10 gallons per minute)**
Car wash	5 gallons per minute *(10 gallons per minute)**

* non water-saving devices and appliances

B. Look at the chart again and answer the questions.

1. Which activity saves more water, showering or taking a bath? What does it depend on?
2. Does dishwashing by hand save more water than using a dishwasher?
3. Which activity do you think consumes more water for a household?
4. Do you think that water-saving devices and appliances make a big difference in the amount of water a household consumes?

C. Read the statements below and decide if they are true or false. Then listen to part of a talk on saving water and check your answers. 🔊

1. Fixing a leaky toilet can save up to 200 gallons of water a month. ☐
2. Fixing a faucet that leaks 20 drops a minute can save over 700 gallons of water a year. ☐
3. Turning off the faucet while brushing your teeth can save up to 500 gallons of water a month. ☐
4. Taking a 5-minute shower saves over 350 gallons of water each week. ☐
5. Using a dishwasher always saves more water than washing the dishes by hand. ☐
6. To save water you should fill up your washing machine. ☐

D. Talk in pairs. The average person uses about 80-100 gallons of water daily. Look at the chart above again and discuss how much water you use as an individual and what kind of chores/activities make you consume more water. Do you need to make changes to save water? Discuss and decide how.

E. What did you learn about yourself? What changes are you going to make to save more water? Report to the class.

A. Listen to a radio advertisement and complete the flyer below.

LUMSDEN COLLEGE
CHARITY CAR WASH

Location: 1 _____ **Date:** 2 _____

Time: 8 a.m. - 8 p.m.

Prices:
Exterior: $10
Interior: 3 $ _____
Interior and Exterior: 4 $ _____

Help us raise $1,000 for the
5 _____

B. Talk in small groups. Imagine you and your classmates want to organize an event to raise money for the homeless in your town/city. Discuss the fund-raisers below and decide which of them would be the most suitable to raise the largest amount of money. Give reasons for your decision.

a bake sale

a flea market

a concert

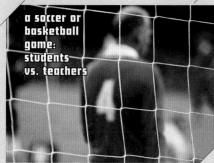
a soccer or basketball game: students vs. teachers

a car wash

a charity run

C. Talk in small groups. Discuss the fund-raiser you have chosen and decide what needs to be done to organize it. Think about the ideas below.

Think about:
- how to advertise the event
- how to make tickets, flyers, posters, etc.
- the venue
- who will help out and how
- the prices
- the things needed (food, books, clothes, sponges, buckets, etc.)

D. Present your fund-raiser to the class. When all of them have been presented, vote for the best one.

DONATIONS PLEASE HELP

A. Look at the statement below and read the two arguments that follow. Which person is FOR and which person is AGAINST the statement?

"The Internet is making us stupid."

Our brain is affected by the way we use it, and these days with the Internet, we use it more and more to follow many ideas at once, usually only reading a few lines of information on any site. We log onto several sites at the same time and move quickly between them. As a result, we don't concentrate in depth anymore, and fewer people read whole books from the beginning to end. What's more, we don't learn much from it anymore. The Internet is full of sites with gossip and silly videos which easily distract people. To me, it's clear that the Internet is making us stupid.

Jeremy, 25

People have always tried to blame new technology for making people stupid. In the past, it was the radio or television and today it's the Internet. However, I think it is clear that, as humans, we are becoming more intelligent and achieving more incredible things. More people have access to information than ever before and everyone can learn whatever they want online. So, as a society, we are becoming smarter. Sure, there is a lot of useless information on the Internet, but it is like food; you can eat all kinds of healthy food that are good for you, or you can eat junk.

Heather, 24

B. Read again and write T for True, F for False or NM for Not Mentioned.

According to Jeremy:
1. We give our attention to many things at the same time. ☐
2. The Internet is making us lazy. ☐
3. The Internet has many low quality sites that do not educate us. ☐

According to Heather:
4. People have a habit of suggesting that new technology is a bad thing. ☐
5. The Internet is better than it used to be. ☐
6. All of the information online is useful in some way. ☐

C. Discuss.

What is your opinion of the above statement? Are you for or against it? Why?

D. Work in groups. Read the statement below. Group A should think of arguments FOR the statement and Group B should think of arguments AGAINST it. Think about the ideas given and also add your own. Make sure you support your arguments by giving persuasive reasons. Discuss your ideas with your group, keeping any necessary notes.

"Social media bring us closer together."

Think about:
- the different types of social media
- how people use them
- how people used to communicate before social media

E. Debate with the other group and try to win them over to your point of view. Use some of the phrases below.

First of all,...
To begin with,...
Secondly,...
In addition,...
Furthermore,...
Moreover,...
What is more,...
Finally,...
Last but not least,...
To sum up,...

In our opinion/view,...
We believe/think,...
The way we see it,...
We would like to point out that...
The main advantage/disadvantage of... is...

One of the best/worst things about social media is...
We all know for a fact that...
As a consequence,...
We agree, but think about...
You have a point, but...
Very true, but that's not always the case.
You're absolutely right, however, we can't ignore the fact that...
We totally disagree.
Sorry to interrupt, but how about...?

1b An informal letter/e-mail

Plan

GREETING

- **Greet the person you're writing to.**
  - *Dear Kevin,* • *Hi Bill!* • *Hello Mary,* • *Hey Phil!*
  - *Dear Mom,* • *Dear Uncle Greg,*
  - *Dear brother/friend/cousin*

OPENING PARAGRAPH

- **Begin your letter/e-mail and say why you're writing. Use set phrases like:**
  - *How's it going? I hope everything's OK.*
  - *How are you (keeping)?*
  - *Thanks for your last letter/e-mail.*
  - *It was nice to hear from you again.*
  - *I'm writing to tell you / let you know...*
  - *Sorry I didn't reply sooner, but...*
  - *It's taken me ages to reply, but...*
  - *I've been meaning to get back to you, but...*
  - *Sorry I haven't written for so long, but...*

MAIN PART (1-3 paragraphs)

- **Mention everything you want to include in your letter/e-mail.**

CLOSING PARAGRAPH

- **State anything you want to emphasize and end your letter/e-mail. Use phrases like:**
  - *I have to go now.*
  - *Well, I'd better finish off here.*
  - *That's all for now.*
  - *Say hello to everyone.*
  - *E-mail me when you get the chance.*
  - *Get back to me soon.*
  - *Keep me posted.*
  - *Drop me a line and let me know how you're doing.*
  - *I'm looking forward to hearing from you.*

SIGNING OFF

- **Use a signature ending and your first name below that.**
  - *Yours,* • *Take care,* • *Bye for now,* • *Love,* • *Keep in touch,*
  - *All the best,* • *Best wishes,* • *See you soon,* • *Write back soon,*

2b A story

Plan

INTRODUCTION

Describe the setting of the story (time, place, weather, etc.) and introduce the main character(s).

MAIN PART (2-3 paragraphs)

Mention what happened, what the character(s) did, saw, heard, said, etc. and how they felt.

CONCLUSION

Describe what happened in the end and make a short comment.

3b An article describing a place

Plan

TITLE
Think of an interesting or catchy title.

INTRODUCTION
- Give some general information about the place.
- Refer to what makes the place so interesting or why you are going to write about it.

MAIN PART (1-2 paragraphs)
- Describe the place, the sights and any other attractions.
- Give your impression of the place and/or describe your feelings.

CONCLUSION
Sum up your opinion by making a general comment about the place or by expressing your feelings.

10b An article describing an event

Plan

TITLE
Think of an interesting or catchy title.

INTRODUCTION
Give some general information about the event:
- name
- where and when it takes/took place
- what the event is/was for (celebration, festival, ceremony, fund-raiser)
- who takes/took part (could also be included in the main part)

MAIN PART (2-3 paragraphs)
Develop the important features of the event:
- preparations for the event
- what activities take/took place
- what happens/happened after the event

CONCLUSION
Give your overall opinion of this event or make a general comment.

9b A book review

Plan

INTRODUCTION
Give some general information about the book (title, author, type of book, etc.). Use phrases like:
- ... is a bestseller/timeless classic by...
- The book is/was written by...
- ... is a historical novel / an autobiography / a crime novel / an action adventure, etc.
- It was published in...

MAIN PART (2 paragraphs)
1 Give a brief summary of the plot. Don't include too many details and don't reveal the ending. Use the Present Simple and phrases like:
- The book tells the story of...
- It is set / takes place in...
- The main character...
2 Comment on the interesting features of the book. Use phrases like:
- The book is well-known for...
- The book has vivid descriptions of...
- The author does a great job of...
- The author never fails to...
- One of the features that make this book... is...

CONCLUSION
State your opinion and make a recommendation. Use phrases like:
- You will find it hard to put down.
- It's definitely (not) worth reading.
- It's sure to appeal to all ages.
- It's suitable for adults who are interested in...
- It's a good read, especially for...
- It's a real page-turner!
- If you are a... fan, don't forget to put it on your list of books to read.
- Overall, I found...
- It's nothing special.
- It's a waste of time and money.
- It was better than I expected.
- If you haven't read it yet, make sure you get a copy.
- I recommend it to all... fans.
- I would recommend it to readers who...

11b A letter (to the editor) expressing an opinion

Plan

GREETING

Use a formal greeting.
- *Dear Sir/Madam,*
- *Dear Editor,*

OPENING PARAGRAPH
- **Say why you are writing the letter.**
- **Refer to specific points of the article you are responding to (topic, title).**

MAIN PART (1-2 paragraphs)
- **Focus on one or two aspects of the issue/problem.**
- **Give your opinion and provide justification and examples.**
- **Make any relevant suggestions.**

CLOSING PARAGRAPH

Summarize your points and end your letter politely.

SIGNING OFF
- **Use an appropriate signature ending.**
  - *Yours truly,*
  - *Yours sincerely,*
- **Sign underneath and print your full name below your signature.**

12b An informal e-mail giving advice

Plan

GREETING

OPENING PARAGRAPH

Begin your e-mail appropriately, refer to the problem and express concern or sympathy. Use phrases like:
- *I'm sorry to hear that you're having problems with...*
- *I understand what you're going through.*
- *I know how you feel.*
- *I know the feeling.*
- *Here are some tips to help you deal with your problem.*
- *I hope the following advice will help you.*
- *I've given your problem a lot of thought and I've come up with a solution.*

MAIN PART (1-2 paragraphs)

Say what you think may be causing the problem, give your advice and make various suggestions. Use phrases like:
- *Maybe you should/could...*
- *If I were you, I'd...,*
- *If I were in your position, I'd...*
- *If I were in your shoes, I'd...*
- *First of all, you'd better (not)...*
- *Perhaps it would be a good idea to...*
- *How/What about...?*
- *Why don't you...?*
- *Have you ever thought of...?*
- *Something else you can try is...*

CLOSING PARAGRAPH

Make a final comment. Use phrases like:
- *I hope everything goes well. Good luck!*
- *Let me know how everything turns out.*
- *Everything will be just fine.*
- *Don't worry. You'll get over it in no time.*
- *I hope I've been of some help to you.*

SIGNING OFF

An informal e-mail

An informal e-mail is usually sent to a friend, a relative or an acquaintance. Note the layout below:

Subject: a brief phrase that indicates what the content of the e-mail is.

Greeting: on the left-hand side of the page. Put a comma after the name.

Paragraphing: write in blocked paragraphs leaving a blank line in between the paragraphs.

Signing off: on the left-hand side of the page. Use your first name.

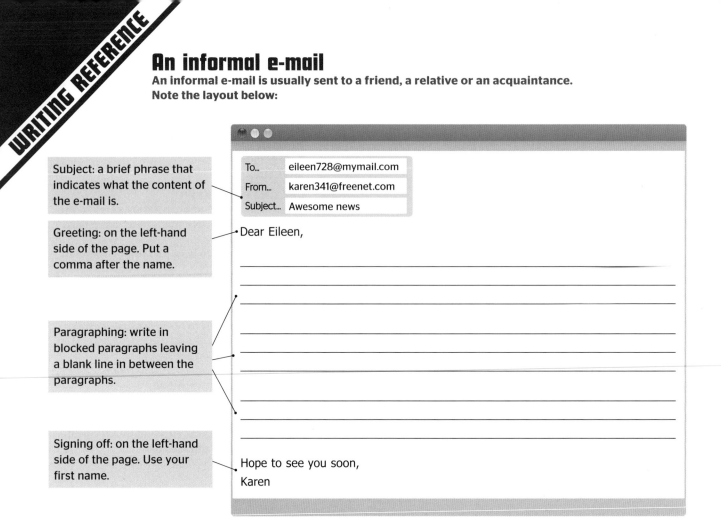

To... eileen728@mymail.com
From... karen341@freenet.com
Subject... Awesome news

Dear Eileen,

Hope to see you soon,
Karen

An informal letter

An informal letter is a personal letter usually written to a friend, a relative or an acquaintance. Note the layout below:

Greeting: on the left-hand side of the page. Put a comma after the name.

Indent paragraphs: start the first line of each paragraph under the comma.

Signing off: towards the right-hand side of the page (e.g. Yours, Best wishes). Don't forget the comma followed by your first name written underneath.

Your address: on the right-hand side of the page (not always necessary).

Date: below the address.

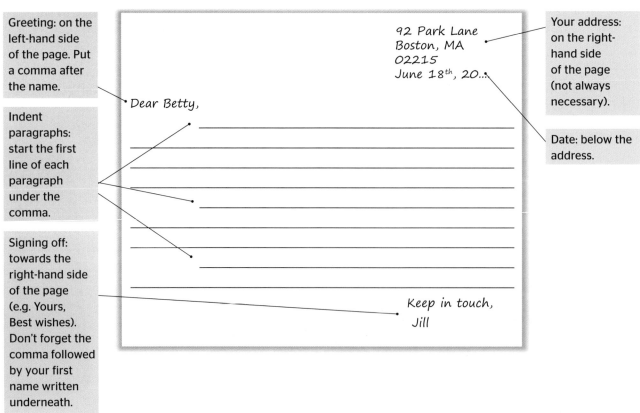

92 Park Lane
Boston, MA
02215
June 18th, 20...

Dear Betty,

Keep in touch,
Jill

A formal letter

A formal letter is written to someone you don't know personally and it is usually of a business nature. Note the layout below:

Position of the person you are writing to and/or name of company (start one line below the date).

Address of the person or company you are writing to.

Greeting: on the left-hand side of the page (leave a blank line before and after the greeting).

Signing off: on the left-hand side of the page, followed by a comma.

Your signature and your full name clearly written underneath.

Your address: on the right-hand side of the page (without your name).

Date: below the address, leaving a blank line in between.

Paragraphing: You can indent or write in blocked paragraphs leaving a blank line in between the paragraphs. Note that when using blocked paragraphs, everything begins on the left-hand side of the page, except your address and the date.

> 92 Park Lane
> Boston, MA
> 02215
>
> June 18th, 20....
>
> Human Resources Manager
> Jacksonville Swimming Pool
> 72 Albany Ave.
> Chicago, IL 60616
>
> Dear Sir or Madam, / Dear Mr. Jones,
>
> _____
> _____
> _____
> _____
> _____
> _____
> _____
> _____
> _____
>
> Yours truly, / Yours sincerely,
>
> Jill Thomas (Ms.)

TIP

In a formal letter/e-mail, when you don't know the name of the person you are writing to, begin with Dear Sir/Madam. When you are writing to a woman and are unsure of her marital status, begin with Dear Ms. + last name.

Phonetic symbols

Vowel sounds			
/iː/ read	/ɪ/ did	/ɛ/ next	/æ/ back
/ɑː/ bottle	/ɔː/ boring	/ʊ/ good	/uː/ food
/ʌ/ butter	/ɜː/ bird	/ə/ father	/eɪ/ player
/oʊ/ boat	/aɪ/ nine	/aʊ/ about	/ɔɪ/ point

Consonant sounds					
/p/ pet	/b/ book	/d/ doctor	/k/ kid	/g/ grandson	/tʃ/ chair
/dʒ/ large	/f/ first	/v/ vet	/θ/ theater	/ð/ that	/s/ space
/z/ has	/t/ take	/ʃ/ shop	/ʒ/ usually	/h/ whole	/m/ man
/n/ neat	/ŋ/ thing	/w/ wear	/l/ lips	/r/ room	/j/ yellow

Modules 1-3

A. Read the text and choose a, b, c or d.

A Unique Vacation on Water

My wife and I had gotten tired **1** ____ beach vacations, so last year we decided to try something different. After some research, we **2** ____ decided to go to Stockholm, a city with many cultural attractions and beautiful countryside nearby. We stayed somewhere very unusual: on the the Gustav Af Klint steamship, which **3** ____ on the water near Stockholm's Old Town. Nowadays, it is a hostel with several cabins that can **4** ____ up to 24 guests. Our double cabin was certainly not luxurious, but it was a real **5** ____. It's difficult to find inexpensive accommodations in such a great **6** ____, and with such a great view. It has easy **7** ____ to public transportation, and there's a lot to see and do in the neighborhood. **8** ____ our stay there, we took a guided **9** ____ of places featured in books by the famous Swedish writer, Stieg Larsson. Our vacation was **10** ____ fascinating than we had ever expected. The only **11** ____ was that I felt a little seasick on the boat when it was windy. However, if you can cope **12** ____ your bed rocking a little, I definitely recommend this hostel in Stockholm.

1. a. with	**b.** of	**c.** over	**d.** on
2. a. currently	**b.** eventually	**c.** wisely	**d.** directly
3. a. blows	**b.** lands	**c.** slides	**d.** floats
4. a. accommodate	**b.** provide	**c.** put	**d.** treat
5. a. discovery	**b.** shock	**c.** bargain	**d.** landmark
6. a. surroundings	**b.** landscape	**c.** scenery	**d.** location
7. a. access	**b.** introduction	**c.** connection	**d.** distance
8. a. While	**b.** When	**c.** During	**d.** Whether
9. a. excursion	**b.** tour	**c.** expedition	**d.** voyage
10.a. the most	**b.** as	**c.** the more	**d.** more
11. a. development	**b.** highlight	**c.** drawback	**d.** struggle
12.a. for	**b.** on	**c.** with	**d.** in

B. Complete the text with the correct form of the words in capitals.

Extreme Breath-Holding World Record

When David Blaine held his breath under water for 17 minutes and 4 seconds in 2008, it made an **1** _____ on people all over the world. It was an extraordinary **2** _____. Blaine prepared himself for months in advance, with the help of experienced **3** _____. He had also taken part in similar tests of **4** _____ before, so he knew what to expect. However, many **5** _____ doubted that Blaine's attempt would be successful. Some people still wonder if it was real. We spoke to Dr. Alan Sharp who gave us an **6** _____ of how it is possible. "Under the right conditions the human body can survive for a long time without air. The key is to get your mind to control your body. The **7** _____ of people can hold their breath for about 2 minutes but, with practice, there is a **8** _____ of increasing that time. People who take part in such tests relax their bodies so that everything slows down and they need less oxygen. They even try to think less and stay calm. Of course, you need to be very healthy, too."

IMPRESS
ACHIEVE
TRAIN
ENDURE
JOURNAL

EXPLAIN

MAJOR

POSSIBLE

C. Complete the second sentence so that it has a similar meaning to the first sentence, using the word given. Do not change the word given. You must use between two and five words, including the word given.

1. The weather was warmer than we expected.

   The weather _____ we expected.

   `cold`

2. Every day Ryan is improving his English.

   Every day, Ryan is getting _____ at English.

   `and`

3. Using the printer is easy once you get used to it.

   Using the printer is easy once _____ It.

   `hang`

4. I want to know how you're doing abroad, so let me know, OK?

   I want to know how you're doing abroad, so _____, OK?

   `posted`

5. Jenny attended every lecture last semester.

   Jenny _____ any lectures last semester.

   `out`

6. Kevin didn't use to be so impatient.

   Kevin is _____ to be.

   `than`

7. The last time I saw Greg was in 2010.

   I _____ 2010.

   `seen`

8. We might go to Italy next year.

   We _____ to Italy next year.

   `thinking`

9. I'm really annoyed with this weather!

   I'm really _____ this weather!

   `up`

10. He couldn't find a cheaper tablet.

    That was _____ he could find.

    `the`

11. You should accept the idea of working overtime every day.

    You should _____ of working overtime every day.

    `used`

12. Tina started doing housework three hours ago and she still hasn't finished.

    Tina _____ three hours and she still hasn't finished.

    `been`

D. Complete the blanks in the text with one word.

Add Some Color to Your Home

Last month I I _____ sitting in my living room with my husband when I realized that our home needed a change. The walls were dark and the furniture looked worn 2 _____ and old. I turned to him and said, "We 3 _____ to have such a nice house when we got married, but look at it now! Do you know 4 _____ the last time we redecorated it was?" That was when we finally decided to do something about it. Over the past few weeks, I have 5 _____ researching home design. The problem is that once you get started, there is no end to what you can do to improve your home. I wasn't aware 6 _____ the fact that the colors we choose for our home can affect our mood. Now I know all about the colors that can make me feel happy and I 7 _____ decided to paint the kitchen bright yellow. As for the living room, well, what can I say? As 8 _____ as we changed the furniture, it felt like we had moved into a new home. Even my mother noticed the difference when she dropped 9 _____ yesterday. Now I finally understand what people mean when they say "There's no place 10 _____ home!"

Modules 4-6

A. Choose a, b, c or d.

1. You are not _____ to work as an accountant.
   a. qualified   **b.** literate   **c.** spontaneous   **d.** effective

2. Did you read the _____ I sent you by e-mail?
   a. encyclopedia   **b.** document   **c.** warning   **d.** deadline

3. Don't worry. You can _____ me to keep your secret.
   a. refer   **b.** notify   **c.** trust   **d.** reveal

4. Stop _____ about other people all the time! What they do in their personal lives doesn't concern you.
   a. mentioning   **b.** arguing   **c.** complaining   **d.** gossiping

5. Please carry this box with extreme _____.
   a. caution   **b.** progress   **c.** manner   **d.** protection

6. Teenagers are often _____ about their appearance and think they don't look good enough.
   a. irrelevant   **b.** impractical   **c.** immature   **d.** insecure

7. By the time you come home, the children _____ to bed.
   a. will have gone   **b.** have gone   **c.** will go   **d.** would go

8. I used to work with a guy _____ father was a politician.
   a. whose   **b.** who   **c.** who's   **d.** that

9. If you _____ us the truth, we'll be able to help you.
   a. are told   **b.** told   **c.** will tell   **d.** tell

10. Your car is so old. If I were you, I _____ a new one.
    a. might buy   **b.** 'll buy   **c.** 'd buy   **d.** bought

11. That _____ be Tina's mother. She looks young enough to be her sister!
    a. couldn't   **b.** can't   **c.** mustn't   **d.** shouldn't

12. Look out! You _____ that window with the football.
    a. must have broken   **b.** could have broken   **c.** shouldn't break   **d.** can't have broken

B. Complete the blanks in the text with one word.

A new beginning

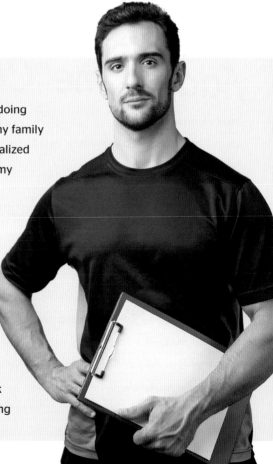

What job **1** _____ you do if you could change your career?
I always wanted to be a lawyer ever since I was young. But after 12 years of doing
the same job, I felt I wasn't satisfied. I was working long hours, I never saw my family
and I felt like I wasn't really helping people. Besides **2** _____, I realized
that spending my life in an office wasn't going to make me happy. One day, my
boss, **3** _____ was a couple of years away from retiring, said
something that got me thinking about my life and my career. He said:
"There **4** _____ to be more to life than this!" I was sure I'd feel
the same way in 40 years **5** _____ I did something about it.
So that's when I **6** _____ the decision to go **7** _____
another dream of mine. I had always enjoyed working **8** _____
and I had noticed that everybody looked happy and relaxed during
fitness class. So, I **9** _____ myself a new goal; to become
a personal trainer. I quit my job as a lawyer and took a personal trainer
course. Now I work part-time at a gym, **10** _____ I help people
get in shape and feel good about themselves. You **11** _____ think
I was out of my mind, but you know what? **12** _____ last, I'm doing
a job that I absolutely love!

C. Complete the second sentence so that it has a similar meaning to the first sentence, using the word given. Do not change the word given. You must use between two and five words, including the word given.

1. I don't think that they will hire the girl if she doesn't have experience.

   I think that _____, they won't hire her. **unless**

2. Parking on this side of the street is not allowed.

   It _____ on this side of the street. **forbidden**

3. It's a good idea not to be late for the job interview.

   You _____ for the job interview. **better**

4. The most logical explanation is that someone stole your cell on the bus.

   Someone _____ on the bus. **must**

5. Trevor thought of a way to solve the problem.

   Trevor _____ to solve the problem. **came**

6. The town where I grew up is in the mountains.

   The town _____ is in the mountains. **in**

7. It's illegal to drive without a license.

   It's _____ without a license. **law**

8. They don't let children enter the site.

   Children _____ the site. **allowed**

9. I will move to Canada before the end of the year.

   By the end of the year, _____ to Canada. **have**

10. I work long hours so it's impossible for me to start a new hobby.

    I'd start a new hobby _____ long hours. **if**

11. It wasn't a good idea to shout at your boss.

    You _____ at your boss. **should**

12. Have you decided where we're going to go tonight?

    Have you _____ where we're going to go tonight? **mind**

D. Complete the blanks with the correct form of the words in capitals.

GENERATION Y

Generation Y (Gen Y), also known as the Millennial Generation, consists of the people who were born during the 1980s up until about the early 2000s. **1** _____ believe that this generation has specific characteristics that are different from previous generations, and define the way these people communicate, the way they work as well as their relationships with others.

RESEARCH

Gen Y grew up with technology and rely on it 24/7. They find it is totally **2** _____ and **3** _____ not to use technology to perform a job better. Gen Y also uses smartphones, tablets, social media and the Internet to **4** _____. They prefer communicating through e-mail or text messages rather than face-to-face communication. Gen Y will reply **5** _____ to a text message, but might leave the phone unanswered.

PRACTICAL
CONVENIENT
SOCIAL

INSTANT

In **6** _____, people belonging to Gen Y are also known for growing up with the **7** _____ that they have a strong possibility of becoming rich, famous or successful. They are confident and **8** _____. They prefer jobs where teamwork is encouraged and where they can use their skills and **9** _____. However, their top priority in life is family and friends.

ADD
BELIEVE
AMBITION
CREATE

Finally, **10** _____ for Gen Y is not being able to go after their dreams.

FAIL

Modules 7-9

A. Complete the blanks in the text with one word.

EcoFads is an eco-fashion brand that takes the protection of the environment 1 _____ consideration when making and selling clothes. Eco-fashion is a new trend that is becoming more and more popular and which is based 2 _____ the idea that clothes should 3 _____ created in ways that are environmentally friendly.

EcoFads uses cotton that 4 _____ grown without pesticides, materials that have been reused or recycled and avoids all types of leather. Priscilla Wells, the founder of Ecofads, points 5 _____ that most fashion companies use methods to make clothes that can harm the environment in the 6 _____ run. "I had been looking 7 _____ techniques eco-fashion uses because I didn't want to end 8 _____ harming the environment with my business, too," she says. "That's why I always stick to environmentally-friendly ways of manufacturing, while producing clothes that appeal 9 _____ young people and are stylish." Will more fashion companies get interested in eco-friendly ways of making clothes before it's too late? Only time will 10 _____.

B. Choose a, b, c or d.

1. You can order it online and have it sent to your home. _____ is free of charge.
   a. Substance   c. Stock
   b. Shipping   d. Swamp

2. The percentage of child _____ is increasing in many countries because of junk food.
   a. obesity   c. disease
   b. muscle   d. nausea

3. Cheese, milk and butter are _____ products.
   a. grain   c. dairy
   b. artificial   d. vivid

4. The _____ got into the house by breaking the window and then threatened to shoot the owners.
   a. companions   c. victims
   b. intruders   d. vendors

5. I'm absolutely _____. I haven't eaten anything since this morning.
   a. astonished   c. starving
   b. hilarious   d. marvelous

6. The scientists _____ an experiment in Antarctica.
   a. conducted   c. cooperated
   b. charged   d. combined

7. By the time they reached the station, the train _____.
   a. had been leaving   c. had left
   b. left   d. leaves

8. People who _____ large amounts of fat are more likely to suffer from heart disease.
   a. consume   c. bother
   b. attack   d. absorb

9. Danny _____ outside for over an hour when his mother called him to come in.
   a. has been playing   c. is playing
   b. played   d. had been playing

10. I spent a summer in Mexico, where I learned _____ Spanish.
    a. speak   c. spoken
    b. to speak   d. speaking

11. All participants will _____ a prize at the end of the race.
    a. give   c. be giving
    b. given   d. be given

12. Do you remember _____ Carol last week?
    a. meet   c. meeting
    b. to meet   d. to meeting

C. Complete the text with the correct form of the words in capitals.

MAKING GREENSBURG GREEN

In May 2007, a 1 _____ tornado struck Greensburg. **DEVASTATE**
The tornado, which covered an area larger than the city itself, resulted in the
2 _____ of 95% of the buildings there and the death of **DESTROY**
13 people. After that, most of the residents left the city, because they had
nowhere to live. Emergency services arrived as well as volunteers from nearby
towns to help, providing the residents with food and mobile homes. The
3 _____ buildings that were destroyed couldn't prevent the **COUNT**
residents from planning a new future for their town. The plan was to rebuild
Greensburg.

During the summer that followed, residents held weekly meetings to decide on
what they were going to do for their town. 4 _____, all the **INITIAL**
residents couldn't agree and many people 5 _____ of some of the plans because they believed **APPROVE**
they were not 6 _____ under the circumstances. However, not only did they manage to **AFFORD**
7 _____ the problems, but they also turned Greensburg into one of the nation's greenest **COME**
towns.

Now, people from all over the world visit Greensburg, where many homes, public buildings and businesses
have been built according to the latest energy-saving and environmentally-friendly design technology. This
strategy is helping the environment and also it is 8 _____ believed that it is helping all the **GENERAL**
residents as well. This is because wind turbines were installed, which produce enough electricity for all the
homes, businesses and town facilities in Greensburg.

Today, Greensburg is proving to be an example for other towns and cities around the world as well, which are
also trying to use renewable energy and eco-friendly designing to make greener cities.

**D. Complete the second sentence so that it has a similar meaning to the first sentence, using the word given.
Do not change the word given. You must use between two and five words, including the word given.**

1. I don't often go to work by car, because it harms the environment.   avoid

   I _____ by car, because it harms the environment.

2. They have informed all the passengers about the delay.   been

   All the passengers _____ about the delay.

3. Many people think that skydiving is dangerous.   thought

   Skydiving _____ dangerous.

4. Everyone knows that eating too much sugar is bad for your health.   common

   It is _____ eating too much sugar is bad for your health.

5. Brenda doesn't really like reading poetry.   rather

   Brenda _____ poetry.

6. Billy doesn't have much money so he borrowed some from me.   short

   Billy _____ so he borrowed some from me.

7. Victor decided to stop eating so much red meat.   cut

   Victor decided _____ red meat.

8. We drove around for an hour and then realized our car was almost out of gas.   been

   We _____ an hour before we realized our car was almost out of gas.

9. I felt terrible when I heard that Tina had moved away.   sorry

   I was _____ Tina had moved away.

10. I can't wait to go to Greece on vacation.   forward

   I'm _____ to Greece on vacation.

143

THREE... TWO... ONE... JUMP!

Modules 10-12

A. Complete the blanks in the text with one word.

I had an experience last month that completely blew my mind. I went bungee jumping! Steve, a friend of mine, suggested going to the Angeles National Forest in California 1 _____ bungee jump from a bridge over a river. Initially, I jumped 2 _____ the chance, but when we reached the meeting point, my jaw dropped as I watched a man jump off the bridge. 3 _____ of us had ever done it before, so the sight of him dropping down kind of scared us. When my turn came, I wished I 4 _____ never signed up for this, but I went ahead with it. The instructors gave me a special suit to wear and attached the elastic cords to it. As I was looking down from a height of 120 feet, my heart was in my mouth. That's when everybody started the countdown. Three... Two... One! The moment I jumped off the bridge was the most thrilling in my life. I closed my eyes as I felt gravity pulling me down at an enormous speed and just as I thought I was going to crash onto the surface of the river, the elastic cords pulled me back up again. I went up and down a few times and eventually stopped. I hung there for a few moments, 5 _____ of breath, as the instructors slowly lowered me down to a boat, where another instructor was waiting for me. 6 _____ Steve hadn't suggested doing this, I would never 7 _____ tried it on my own. When we were going home, I could still feel the adrenaline rush. Even 8 _____ it was an incredible experience, I don't think that I would do it again!

B. Choose a, b, c or d.

1. Is something bothering you? You seem ____.
   a. irritating   c. distracted
   b. delightful   d. energized

2. That book has a lot of ____. I found it hard to put down.
   a. suspense   c. admission
   b. perfection   d. evolution

3. As we ____ the house, we saw a light on in the living room.
   a. improvised   c. aimed
   b. approached   d. anticipated

4. I'm sorry, that name doesn't ____ a bell.
   a. spill   c. dial
   b. ring   d. roll

5. Lots of people ____ up at the charity event so lots of money was raised.
   a. kept   c. stayed
   b. turned   d. brought

6. Ted, I'll be gone for half an hour. Please stay ____.
   a. in trouble   c. in order
   b. out of trouble   d. out of order

7. The security guard asked me ____ in my bag.
   a. what I have   c. what I had
   b. if I had   d. what do I have

8. I've found two coats that I like. The problem is that both ____ a fortune!
   a. coat cost   c. coats cost
   b. coat costs   d. coats costs

9. I pulled a muscle ____ I did stretching exercises before I started working out.
   a. despite   c. in order to
   b. in spite of   d. even though

10. A: What did Kelly and Mary argue about?
   B: I don't know. I haven't spoken to ____ since yesterday.
   a. both of them   c. either girls
   b. both girls   d. either of them

11. If I ____ my studies, I probably would have become a reporter.
   a. didn't give up   c. hadn't given up
   b. haven't given up   d. wouldn't give up

12. I wish I ____ you, but I'm in a hurry.
   a. helped   c. can help
   b. had helped   d. could help

C. Complete the second sentence so that it has a similar meaning to the first sentence, using the word given. Do not change the word given. You must use between two and five words, including the word given.

1. We were having dinner when, unexpectedly, Charlie got up and left. `blue`

   We were having dinner when, _____, Charlie got up and left.

2. Although I work out often, I haven't lost any weight. `despite`

   I haven't lost any weight _____ often.

3. Bill regrets not going to Madrid to visit his cousin last week. `wishes`

   Bill _____ to Madrid to visit his cousin last week.

4. I can't buy those shoes because they're too expensive. `only`

   If _____ those shoes.

5. Jake was sick; that's why he didn't come to the meeting today. `have`

   Jake _____ to the meeting today if he hadn't been sick.

6. Climbing this mountain is very easy for experienced climbers. `piece`

   Climbing this mountain _____ for experienced climbers.

7. I used your computer because I wanted to send an e-mail. `so`

   I used your computer _____ an e-mail.

8. In the end, Nancy didn't visit the museum and Susan didn't either. `nor`

   In the end, _____ the museum.

9. Stop complaining because you're starting to really annoy me, OK? `nerves`

   Stop complaining because you're starting _____, OK?

10. "Don't go rollerblading without a helmet," the instructor told us. `not`

    The instructor told us _____ without a helmet.

11. In spite of being very sleepy, Andy went to the gym. `although`

    Andy went to the gym _____ very sleepy.

12. I wrote down the doctor's phone number because I didn't want to forget it. `order`

    I wrote down the doctor's phone number _____ it.

D. Complete the blanks with the correct form of the words in capitals.

An Amazing Act of Kindness

Yesterday, something 1 _____ happened at the Maplewood Orphanage. A 2 _____ man walked in with a plain, white envelope and said that he would like to make a 3 _____ to the orphanage. He gave it to the receptionist, requested to remain anonymous and left in a flash.

BELIEVE
MYSTERY
DONATE

The receptionist didn't think much of the event until a few moments later when she opened the envelope. Inside was a check for $20,000. When the receptionist saw the 4 _____ amount of money, she quickly informed some of her colleagues, but when they ran outside, he had already driven away. Cathy Crawford, who is in charge of the orphanage, says, "Nobody has ever shown up and given such a large amount of money without telling us who they are. It's truly 5 _____! It is 6 _____ for people to want to remain anonymous, but we didn't even get the chance to thank him."

ASTONISH

REMARK, REASON

This act of kindness couldn't have come at a better time for Maplewood Orphanage. Cathy says, "The past few months have been quite 7 _____ for us. The government funds we receive are 8 _____ and we would soon have had to close down the orphanage. This saved us. Thank you, sir, whoever you are!"

CHALLENGE
ADEQUATE

Module 1

) Present Simple vs. Present Progressive

Present Simple

I work	He sleeps
Do you work?	Does she sleep?
They don't work	It doesn't sleep

Present Progressive

I'm working	He's sleeping
Are you working?	Is she sleeping?
They aren't working	It isn't sleeping

We use the Present Simple:	We use the Present Progressive:
• for permanent states. *Ted lives in Boston.* • for habits or actions that happen regularly. *We always have breakfast at eight.* • for general truths. *The earth goes around the sun.*	• for temporary states. *I'm taking driving lessons this month.* • for actions happening at the moment of speaking. *Lucy is sleeping now.* • for situations which are changing or developing around the present time. *Air pollution is increasing in our city.* • for future arrangements. *We're flying to Acapulco tonight.*

Time Expressions	
Present Simple	**Present Progressive**
usually, always, often, etc. every day/week, etc. in the morning/spring, etc. on Mondays/Monday morning, etc. on the weekend, etc. once/twice/three times, etc. a week/day, etc.	now, right now, at the moment, today, these days, this week/year, etc. tonight, tomorrow, etc. next week/year, etc.

) Stative Verbs

The following verbs are usually **not** used in progressive tenses:

- **Verbs of the senses:**
  see, feel, hear, smell, taste, seem, look (=seem), notice, appear, etc.

- **Verbs of emotion:**
  like, dislike, love, hate, want, need, prefer, mind, etc.

- **Verbs of perception and opinion:**
  know, mean, think (=believe), understand, agree, mean, remember, forget, imagine, hope, believe, etc.

- **Other verbs:**
  be, have (= possess), own, belong, cost, etc.

> The verbs *see, hear, smell, taste* and *feel* are commonly used with **can** to indicate an action happening now.
> *I can hear a strange noise coming from the kitchen.*

> Certain stative verbs can be used in progressive tenses when they express actions rather than states but with a difference in meaning:
> - think (= consider)
>   *I'm thinking of buying a car.*
> - have (= drink, eat, taste)
>   *Greg is having lunch at the cafeteria right now.*

) Question words

Question words	We ask about	Examples
Who	people (subject or object)	*Who is your best friend?* *Who are you talking to?*
Which	people or things (limited choice)	*Which students will participate in the survey?* *Which of these sweaters do you like best?*
What	things (unlimited choice), actions and activities general descriptions specific information	*What did you buy?* *What happened?* *What is your brother like?* *What kind of cars do you like driving?*
Whose	possession	*Whose are these sneakers?*
Why	reason, purpose	*Why did she call you?*
When	time	*When are your parents coming?*
Where	place	*Where would you like to go tonight?*
How	manner specific information quantity someone's health frequency	*How did you fix this?* *How far is it to the station?* *How long are you staying?* *How much coffee is left?* *How's your sister?* *How often do you travel?*

) Subject - Object Questions

- **Subject Questions:** When we use the question words **who**, **which** and **what** to ask about the subject of the verb, we form the question without auxiliary verbs (**who / which / what** + **verb** in the **affirmative form**).
  Who saw the accident?   Tom (saw the accident).
  What happened outside?   An accident (happened).

- **Object Questions:** When we use the question words **who**, **which** and **what** to ask about the object of the verb, we form the question with auxiliary verbs (**who / which / what** + **verb** in the **question form**).
  Who did you see at the restaurant?
  (I saw) Tom and June.

  What are you eating?
  (I'm eating) Chinese food.

❯ Indirect questions

We use indirect questions when we ask for information.
Indirect questions begin with phrases like:
Can/Could/Would you tell me...?
Can/Could/Would you inform me...?
Can/Could/Would you let me know...?
Do you know...?
I'd like to know...
I was wondering...

Direct Question
Where *is the post office?*

Indirect Question
*Can you tell me **where** the post office is?*

Direct Question
Is the museum open today?

Indirect Question
*Do you know **if/whether** the museum is open today?*

- If the direct question begins with a question word, the indirect question also begins with **the same question word**.
- If the direct question does not begin with a question word, the indirect question begins with **if/whether**.
- In indirect questions, the word order is the same as in affirmative sentences and the tenses do not change.

Module 2
❯ Past Simple

I worked	He slept
Did you work?	Did she sleep?
They didn't work	It didn't sleep

Irregular verbs in the Past Simple don't take **-ed**.
For a list of irregular verbs go to page 157.

We use the **Past Simple** for:

- actions that started and were completed at a specific time in the past.
  We bought our house five years ago.
- habitual or repeated actions in the past.
  I always went to bed early when I lived with my parents.
- completed actions that happened one after the other in the past.
  I made a sandwich, turned on the TV and watched the game.
- permanent situations in the past.
  I lived in London for 20 years.

The Past Simple of the verb *can* is ***could***.
The Past Simple of the verb *to be* is ***was/were***.

TIME EXPRESSIONS
yesterday / yesterday morning, etc.
in + years / centuries
last night / month / Friday / summer, etc.
two days / a week ago

❯ used to

I used to work	He used to sleep
Did you use to work?	Did she use to sleep?
They didn't use to work	It didn't use to sleep

used to + **base form** is used:

- to describe permanent past states.
  I used to be overweight when I was younger.
- to describe past habits.
  My father used to drive to work, but now he walks.
- to describe repeated actions in the past, that no longer happen.
  We used to go out every day, but we don't anymore.

❯ Past Progressive

I was working	He was sleeping
Were you working?	Was she sleeping?
They weren't working	It wasn't sleeping

We use the **Past Progressive**:

- for actions that were happening at a specific point of time in the past.
  I was watching TV at 7 o'clock yesterday evening.
- to set the scene in a story.
  Jill was walking in the forest and it was raining.
- for actions that were happening at the same time in the past. In this case, we usually use **while** or **as**.
  While I was watching TV, my father was cooking.

❯ Past Simple vs. Past Progressive

- We use the **Past Progressive** and the **Past Simple** in the same sentence when one action interrupted another in the past. We use the **Past Progressive** for the longer action and the **Past Simple** for the shorter action. In this case we usually use **while, when** or **as**.
  As/While I was driving, I saw a cat in the street.
  I was sleeping when the telephone rang.

We use **as soon as** with the **Past Simple**.
As soon as they left, we started cleaning up the house.

Module 3
❯ Present Perfect Simple

I have worked	He has slept
Have you worked?	Has she slept?
They haven't worked	It hasn't slept

We use the **Present Perfect Simple**:

- for actions which happened in the past, but we don't mention when exactly.
  I've traveled to Colombia twice.
- for a state which started in the past and continues up to the present.
  Mark has had this car since September.
- for actions which happened in the past and finished, but their results are obvious in the present.
  I'm tired. I've just finished studying.
  Look! Jerry has broken his leg!

For a list of irregular verbs go to page 157.

TIME EXPRESSIONS
always, ever, never, before, once, twice, many times, so far, just, recently, lately, for, since, already, yet, etc.

have been to = have visited and come back
have gone to = have not returned yet
I've been to the mall twice this week.
John isn't here; he's gone to the mall.

Present Perfect Simple vs. Past Simple

We use the Present Perfect Simple:	We use the Past Simple:
• for actions that happened in the past, but we don't say when exactly. *I have tasted Mexican food.* • for actions that started in the past and are still happening in the present. *Ted has worked as a waiter for two years. (=he is still working).*	• for actions that happened at a definite time in the past. We say when. *I tasted Mexican food last night.* • for actions that started and were completed in the past. *Ted worked as a waiter when he was a student.*

We use **for** and **since** for actions that started in the past and continue up to the present.
for + a period of time
I've had this car for 5 years.
since + a specific point in time
I've had this car since 2004.
Present Perfect Simple + since + Past Simple
Julia has changed jobs three times since she came to Lakewood.

Present Perfect Progressive

I have been working	He has been sleeping
Have you been working?	Has she been sleeping?
They haven't been working	It hasn't been sleeping

We use the **Present Perfect Progressive** for:

• a repeated action or state which started in the past and continues up to the present.
They have been using the Internet for more than two hours now.

• an action which was happening over a period of time in the past and may have finished, but its results are obvious in the present.
He's very tired. He's been studying all night.

TIME EXPRESSIONS
for, since, how long, all day/week, etc.

Present Perfect Simple vs. Present Perfect Progressive

We use the Present Perfect Simple:	We use the Present Perfect Progressive:
• to emphasize the result of an action. *Lucy has typed eight letters since 10:30.*	• to emphasize the duration of an action. *Lucy has been typing letters since 10:30.*

Adjectives / Adverbs of manner

• Adjectives describe nouns.
• Adverbs of manner describe how something happens.

We form most adverbs of manner by adding -ly to the adjective.	quiet → quietly careful → carefully
Adjectives ending in a consonant + -y, drop the -y and take -ily.	easy → easily
Adjectives ending in -le, drop the -e and take -y.	terrible → terribly

IRREGULAR ADVERBS
good → well fast → fast hard → hard late → late early → early

Comparatives and superlatives of adjectives and adverbs

• We use the **comparative** of adjectives and adverbs when we compare two people, animals or things. Adjectives and adverbs are usually followed by **than**.
Peter is taller than James.
Living with your family can be easier than living on your own.

• We use the **superlative** of adjectives and adverbs when we compare one person, animal or thing with several of the same kind. Adjectives and adverbs always take the definite article **the** and are usually followed by the prepositions **of** or **in**.
That's the most interesting book I've ever read.
My brother drives the most carefully of all of us.

All one-syllable and most two-syllable adjectives take **-er/-est**	short - shorter - the shortest happy - happier - the happiest big - bigger - the biggest
Adjectives with three or more syllables and some two-syllable adjectives take: **more + adjective / most + adjective**	interesting - more interesting - the most interesting
All one-syllable adverbs and **early** take **-er/-est**	fast - faster - the fastest early - earlier - the earliest
Adverbs with two or more syllables take: **more + adverb / most + adverb**	carefully - more carefully - the most carefully

Irregular Comparative and Superlative Forms

Positive Form	Comparative form	Superlative form
good/well	better	the best
bad/badly	worse	the worst
little	less	the least
far	farther/further	the farthest/furthest
many/much	more	the most

> Some two-syllable adjectives form comparative and superlative forms in both ways.
> *clever - cleverer / more clever - cleverest / most clever*
> *common - commoner / more common - commonest / most common*
> *narrow - narrower / more narrow - narrowest / most narrow*
> *simple - simpler / more simple - simplest / most simple*

❯ Other forms of comparison

- **less + adjective/adverb + than** (to show inferiority)
  The sweater is less expensive than the shirt.
  Terry sings less terribly than his sister.
- **the least + adjective/adverb + of/in** (to show inferiority)
  This is the least interesting book in the world!
- **as + adjective/adverb + as** (to show similarity)
  The skirt is as colorful as the shirt.
  Kelly runs as fast as Sheila.
- **not as/so + adjective/adverb + as** (to show difference)
  The sweater isn't as expensive as the shirt.
  Kelly doesn't run as/so fast as Sheila.
- **comparative + and + comparative** (to indicate continual increase or decrease)
  The car was going faster and faster.

> To emphasize a comparative we use the words **much, a lot, rather, a little, even** and **far**.
> *She's much prettier than her friend Sally.*

Module 4

Modals I
❯ must / have to / need

- We use **must + base form** to express **personal obligation** in the present/future.
  I must finish this by tonight. (= I say so)
- We use **have to + base form** to express **external obligation** in the present/future.
  You have to drive on the left when you're in England. (= It's the law)

> We use **have to** to form all the other tenses, expressing either personal or external obligation.
> *When I was at school, I had to wake up at 7 o'clock every morning.*
> *We'll have to work really hard to finish this project.*

- We use **need to + base form** to express **necessity** in the present or future.
  I need to know how many people will be at the seminar.

❯ mustn't / can't

- We use **mustn't/can't + base form** to express **prohibition**.
  You mustn't / can't park here. (= You aren't allowed to)

❯ don't have to / don't need to / needn't

- We use **don't have to / don't need to / needn't + base form** to express **lack of obligation/necessity** in the present or future.
  You don't have to call us again. (= It isn't necessary)
  She doesn't need to buy us presents.
  You needn't worry. Everything is under control.
- We use **didn't have to / didn't need to + base form** to express **absence of necessity** in the past (something wasn't necessary, but it is not clear if it was done or not).
  I didn't have to/didn't need to pick up the kids from school.

> **Need** means that something is necessary. It is used:
> - as a **main verb** in all tenses, in the affirmative, negative and question form. It is followed by **to + base form** and forms the negative and question form with auxiliary verbs.
> - as a **modal verb** only in the negative and question form of the **Present Simple**. It is followed by a **base form** and forms the negative and question form without auxiliary verbs.
>
> | Affirmative | Questions |
> |---|---|
> | I need to go.
He needs to go. | Do I need to go? / Need I go?
Does he need to go? / Need he go? |
>
> | Negative | |
> |---|---|
> | I don't need to go. / I needn't go.
He doesn't need to go. / He needn't go. | |

❯ should / ought to

Should / Shouldn't + base form refers to the present or future and is used:

- to ask for or give **advice**.
  Should I apologize to John for shouting at him?
  You shouldn't eat so much sugar.
- to express an **opinion**.
  She should be more careful when she drives.
- to make a **suggestion**.
  You should go to that new restaurant. It's fantastic!
- to express mild **obligation**.
  You should go to work on time.

> **Should** can be replaced with **ought to** in all of the above examples.
> *You ought to go to that new restaurant. It's fantastic!*
> *You ought not to eat so much sugar.*

should(n't) + have + past participle

- We use **should + have + past participle** to express **regret** about something that didn't happen in the past.
  We should have come home earlier.

  It's also used to express **criticism** about somebody's behavior.
  You should have called me and let me know you weren't coming.

- We use **shouldn't + have + past participle** to express **regret** about something that happened in the past.
  I shouldn't have borrowed money from Larry.

  It's also used to express **criticism** about something somebody has done.
  Danny shouldn't have told you that. It was supposed to be a secret.

had better

We use **had better + base form** to give strong advice. It often expresses **threat** or **warning** and it's stronger than *should/ought to*. It refers to the present or future, not the past. Its negative form is **had better not**. In spoken English the short form is commonly used (I'd better, you'd better, etc.).
You'd better ask a doctor about it.
You'd better not lie to me again.

Modals II

may / might / could

- We use **may / might / could + base form** to express possibility in the present or future.
  He could/may/might be at home now.

- We use **may not / might not + base form** to express improbability in the present or future.
  We may not/might not go to the meeting tomorrow.

may / might / could + have + past participle

- We use **may/might + have + past participle** to express possibility in the past.
  I may/might have seen the movie, but I'm not sure.

- We use **could + have + past participle** to express that something was possible in the past but didn't eventually happen.
  You were lucky. You could have been hurt.

must / can't

- We use **must + base form** to express a **positive deduction** about the present or future. We are almost certain that something is true.
  My parents must be at work now.

- We use **can't + base form** to express a **negative deduction** about the present or future. We believe that something is impossible.
  You can't be over 20 years old. You just finished school!

must / can't / couldn't + have + past participle

- We use **must + have + past participle** to express a **positive deduction** about the past. We are almost certain that something happened in the past.
  I must have left my wallet at home.

- We use **can't/couldn't + have + past participle** to express a **negative deduction** about the past. We are almost certain that something didn't happen.
  You can't/couldn't have met their parents. They live in the U.K.

Module 5

Relative pronouns (who, which, that, whose)
Relative adverb (where)

The relative pronouns *who, which, that, whose* and the adverb *where* introduce relative clauses.

	Pronouns	Examples
PEOPLE	who/that	The woman who/that is driving that sports car is my aunt. The teacher (who/that) I like the most is Mrs. Robbins.
THINGS ANIMALS IDEAS	which/that	The bag which/that is on the table is mine. The movie (which/that) I watched last night was terrible.
POSSESSION	whose	That's the woman whose son I go to school with.

	Adverb	
PLACE	where	The place where I live is beautiful.

Relative clauses

Defining relative clauses give information which is needed to understand the meaning of the sentence. They are not separated from the main clause by commas.
She's the girl who/that lives next door.
The book (which/that) you bought is on the desk.

- **Who**, **which** and **that** can be omitted when they are the object of the verb in the relative clause. **Whose** and **where** cannot be omitted or replaced with **that**.

- In **formal language** prepositions appear at the beginning of the relative clause.
  In **informal language** they appear at the end of the relative clause.
  The chair on which I'm sitting isn't very comfortable. (formal)
  The chair (which/that) I am sitting on isn't very comfortable. (informal)

Non-defining relative clauses give extra information about the person, thing or idea they refer to. They are always separated from the main clause by commas.
Mr. Brown, who is our Geography teacher, is really old.
Our car, which cost us a lot, keeps breaking down.

- **Relative pronouns/adverbs** cannot be omitted in non-defining relative clauses; neither can we use **that** instead of them.
- Prepositions usually appear at the beginning of non-defining relative clauses.
  This box, in which I keep my old toys, hasn't been cleaned for ages.
- **Which** may also refer to a whole sentence.
  He offered to give me a ride, which was very kind of him.

Module 6

) Future *will*

I'll work	He'll sleep
Will you work?	Will she sleep?
They won't work	It won't sleep

The **Future *will*** is used:
- to make predictions about the future, usually with **perhaps** and **probably** or after the verbs **believe, think, hope, expect, be sure**, etc.
  She'll probably be here tomorrow.
- to talk about on-the-spot decisions.
  We've run out of milk; I'll go and buy some.
- for promises.
  I'll be on time, don't worry!
- for offers and requests.
  I'll do the dishes after dinner.
  Will you help me clean my room?
- for threats and warnings.
  I won't speak to you again!

) Future *be going to*

I'm going to stay	He's going to leave
Are you going to stay?	Is she going to leave?
They aren't going to stay	It isn't going to leave

The **Future *be going to*** is used:
- to talk about future plans.
  My brother is going to study Biology.
- to make predictions based on evidence.
  Look out! You're going to trip over that chair.

TIME EXPRESSIONS
tomorrow, tonight, next month/year/week/Tuesday, etc. this month/year/week/Tuesday, etc. in an hour/year, etc. soon

We use the **Present Progressive** for planned future actions related to personal arrangements.
I'm traveling to Detroit tomorrow.

) Future Perfect

I'll have worked	He'll have slept
Will you have worked?	Will she have slept?
They won't have worked	It won't have slept

The **Future Perfect** is used:
- to talk about actions that will be completed before a specific time or another action in the future. The verb describing the second action is in the **Present Simple**.
  She'll have returned by the time you leave.

TIME EXPRESSIONS
by + a point in time (e.g. Sunday), by the time, by then, before, etc.

) Zero Conditional

if-clause	Main clause
If/When + Present Simple	Present Simple

The **Zero Conditional** is used to talk about general truths/facts.
If/When you press the button, the machine starts.

) Conditional Sentences Type 1

We use **Conditional Sentences Type 1** for something which is likely to happen in the present or future.

if-clause	Main clause
if + Present Simple	• Future *will*
	• Modal Verbs (may, might, can, should)
	• Imperative

If I find the book, I'll buy it for you.
If you go to the gym early, you might see him there.
If you see her, ask her about the meeting.

) Conditional Sentences Type 2

We use **Conditional Sentences Type 2** for unreal or imaginary situations which are unlikely to happen in the present or the future.

if-clause	Main clause
If + Past Simple	would/could + base form

If I had money, I would buy a farm in the country.
You could lose some weight if you went on a diet.

- In Conditional Sentences Type 2 **were** is often used instead of **was** in the if-clause in all persons.
  If I were rich, I would live in a luxurious house.
- We use **If I were you** to express an opinion or to give advice.
  If I were you, I wouldn't buy it.
- **Unless** can be used instead of **if... not...** in all conditional sentences.
  I won't buy this car unless you agree (= I won't buy this car if you don't agree).
- When the **if-clause** comes before the **main clause**, the two clauses are separated by a **comma**.

Module 7

) Past Perfect Simple

I had worked	He had slept
Had you worked?	Had she slept?
They hadn't worked	It hadn't slept

The **Past Perfect Simple** is used:

• to describe an action which was completed before a specific point of time in the past.
My mom had done the dishes by midnight.

• to describe an action that was completed before another action in the past. We use the **Past Perfect Simple** for the action that happened first and the **Past Simple** for the action which followed.
The movie had already started when we got to the movie theater.

> For a list of irregular verbs go to page 157.

TIME EXPRESSIONS
before + point in time
by + point in time
before, after, when, by the time
already, ever, never, just

) Past Perfect Progressive

I had been working	He had been sleeping
Had you been working?	Had she been sleeping?
They hadn't been working	It hadn't been sleeping

The **Past Perfect Progressive** is used:

• to emphasize the duration of an action that took place before another action in the past.
He had been living in California for 15 years when he moved to Boston.

• to refer to an action whose duration caused visible results at a later point of time in the past.
They were tired because they had been cleaning the house all day.

TIME EXPRESSIONS
before + point in time
by + point in time
before, after, when
how long, for, since
by the time

) Articles (a/an/the)

• The indefinite article **a** is used before singular countable nouns when we mention them for the first time or when we don't refer to a specific item. We use **a** when the next word begins with a consonant sound and **an** when the next word begins with a vowel sound.
There is a lamp in the room. There isn't an armchair in the room.

a + consonant sounds	an + vowel sounds
a **d**esk, a **Eu**ropean country, a **u**niversity, a **h**ospital, a **b**lue umbrella	an **a**pple, an **e**gg, an **o**range, an **u**mbrella, an **h**our, an **e**xciting vacation

• The **definite article *the*** is used before uncountable nouns and countable nouns in the singular and the plural.

the is used:

• before something specific or already mentioned.
I have to go to the dentist.
I bought two T-shirts and a dress. The dress is white.

• for things that are unique.
The sun heats the Earth.

• for things that are defined.
The house which is next to ours is 300 years old.

• with the superlative of adjectives/adverbs.
Joan is the best student of all.

• before names of **seas, oceans, rivers, canals, coasts, gulfs, deserts, groups of islands, mountain ranges** and **countries in the plural**.
the Black Sea, the Indian Ocean, the Thames, the Panama Canal, the Blue Coast, the Gulf of Mexico, the Kalahari Desert, the Azores, the Alps, the U.S.A.

• before nationalities when we refer to the whole nation.
The Chinese invented paper thousands of years ago.

• before people's last names when we refer to the whole family.
The Simpsons came to see us last night.

• with buildings: **hotels, restaurants, theaters, museums, institutions**.
the Hilton, the Pasta House, the National Theater, the Museum of Modern Art, the British Council

• with **newspapers, services** and **organizations**.
the Washington Post, the police, the United Nations

• with adjectives referring to classes of people.
the old, the blind, the poor

• before **musical instruments**.
My son plays the drums.

the is not used:

• before countable and uncountable nouns which refer to something general or not mentioned before.
He loves chocolate.
Whales are mammals.

• before names of **people, streets, cities, countries, continents, islands** and **mountains**.
Maggie Smith, Park Street, Mexico, Italy, Asia, Corsica, Mount Everest

• before the **days of the week** and **months**.
on Monday, in June

• before names of **squares, parks, lakes** and **falls**.
Madison Square, Central Park, Lake Winnipeg, Niagara Falls

• before the names of **magazines, sports, games, colors, school subjects** and **languages** (when they are not followed by the word *language*).
Newsweek, tennis, bingo, white, Math, Spanish

• with meals (**breakfast, lunch, dinner**).
What did you have for breakfast?
But: When we talk about a specific meal, we use **the**:
I didn't enjoy the dinner on the plane.

• before the words **bed, court, home, prison, school, college, work** when they are used for the purpose for which they exist.
Thomas went to college to study engineering.

But: *Peter went to the college to visit his professor.*
• before **names of airlines** or **companies**.
Delta, BMW

Module 8
▶ Passive Voice I
Use
We use the **Passive Voice** to emphasize the action rather than who or what is responsible for it.

Formation
The Passive Voice is formed with the verb **to be** in the appropriate form and the **past participle** of the verb of the sentence.

> The person who causes or carries out the action is called an **agent** and is preceded by the preposition **by**. We usually omit the agent:
> • when the action interests us more than the agent.
> • when we don't know the agent.
> • when it is easy to figure out who the agent is.
> *My bag was stolen! (by someone who we do not know)*
> *BMW cars are made in Germany. (by factory workers)*

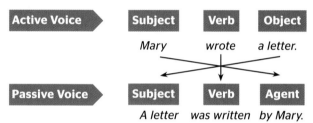

Present Simple	Past Simple
I am called Are you called? They aren't called	I was called Were you called? They weren't called

Present Perfect Simple	Past Perfect Simple
I've been called Have you been called? They haven't been called	I'd been called Had you been called? They hadn't been called

Future Will	Modal Verbs
I'll be called Will you be called? They won't be called	I may be called Should you be called? They mustn't be called

> For a list of irregular verbs go to page 157.

▶ Passive Voice II
• We form the **Progressive tenses** in the Passive Voice with the appropriate form of the verb **to be + being + the past participle of the main verb**.

Present Progressive	Past Progressive
I am being called Are you being called? They aren't being called	I was being called Were you being called? They weren't being called

• Verbs such as **know**, **believe**, **say**, **think**, **consider**, **expect**, **report**, etc. are often followed by a *that* clause in the Active Voice and can be used to make general statements.
People believe that he is very rich.

The Passive Voice can be formed in two ways:
• **It + passive form of verb + that clause**
It is believed that he is very rich.
• **subject + passive form of verb + to + base form**
He is believed to be very rich.

Module 9
▶ Infinitives
We use the **full infinitive** (**to** + base form of the verb):
• to express purpose.
He called to tell me the news.

• after certain verbs: *afford, agree, appear, arrange, choose, decide, forget, hope, learn, manage, need, offer, plan, pretend, promise, refuse, seem, tend, try, want, would like, would love,* etc.
Laura needs to buy a new car.

• after the objects of certain verbs: *advise, allow, encourage, expect, invite, order, persuade, remind, teach, tell,* etc.
It was Glen who persuaded me to apply for this job.

• with **too** and **enough**.
The soup is too hot to eat.

• after the structure **it + be + adjective**.
It's difficult to read his handwriting.

• after certain adjectives: *afraid, surprised, free, happy, ready, sorry, pleased.*
At last he was free to do what he wanted.

• after verbs followed by a **question word** (who, what, which, where, how, **but not** why)
Have you decided where to go for your vacation?

We use the **bare infinitive** (base form of the verb **without to**):
• after modal verbs (*can, could, will, would, should, may, might, must*).
Can you tell me what's wrong?
We may go out tonight.

• after the verbs **let** and **make** (in the Active Voice).
Fay always makes me laugh.
My brother doesn't let me drive his car.

• after **would rather** and **had better**.
I'd rather buy the red car.
You'd better tell me the truth.

> We can use the verb **help** with a bare or full infinitive.
> *I always help my mother **clean** the house.*
> *I always help my mother **to clean** the house.*

▶ -ing form
We use the **-ing form** (base form of the verb + *-ing*) as a noun. We use *-ing* forms:
• as the subject of a verb.
Fishing can be very relaxing.

- after certain verbs: *like, love, hate, enjoy, prefer, consider, continue, stop, finish, start, keep, avoid, begin, imagine, practice, suggest, risk, spend (time),* etc.
  Ken just finished washing the car.

- after certain expressions: *don't mind, can't stand, be interested in, it's worth, How/What about..?, look forward to, be good at, can't help, feel like, there's no point in, it's no use, it's no good, be/get used to,* etc.
  Louis is interested in taking up a language course.

- after prepositions (*for, of, about, without,* etc.).
  Helen is thinking of buying a new car.
  That knife is for cutting meat, not cheese.

- after the verb **go** to indicate physical activities.
  We go skiing every year.

> - The verbs **like**, **dislike**, **love**, **hate**, **start**, **begin**, **continue**, are followed by a **full infinitive** or an **-ing form** without any significant difference in meaning.
>   *I like playing/to play the guitar in the evening.*
> - The verbs **remember** and **forget** are followed either by a **full infinitive** or an **-ing form**, but with a different meaning:
>   - We use **remember/forget + ing** when we refer to something that has already happened.
>   *I remember returning the book.*
>   *I'll never forget meeting them.*
>   - We use **remember/forget + full infinitive** when we remember/forget something before doing it.
>   *I'll remember to go to the grocery store.*
>   *Don't forget to lock the door.*

) prefer, would prefer, would rather

To express **preference** in the present or future we can use the following structures:

Structures	Examples
prefer + noun (preference in a particular situation)	*I prefer chocolate ice cream.*
prefer + -ing + to + -ing (general preference)	*Ted prefers swimming to scuba diving.*
prefer + full infinitive + rather than + bare infinitive (general preference)	*Mary prefers to travel by plane rather than (travel) by car.*
would prefer + full infinitive + rather than + bare infinitive (preference in a particular situation)	*I'd prefer to go out for dinner rather than stay home.*
would rather (not) + bare infinitive (preference in a particular situation)	*I'd rather go to Ibiza this year.*
would rather + bare infinitive + than + bare infinitive (general preference, preference in a particular situation)	*He'd rather work overtime on weekdays than work on Saturdays.*

Module 10
) Reported Speech (Statements)

In **Direct Speech**, we repeat the exact words that someone said. We usually use the verb **say** and the words of the speaker are put in quotation marks.
Irina said, "Tina is on the phone."

In **Reported Speech**, we report the meaning of what someone said, without using their exact words. We use a reporting verb, usually **say** or **tell**, followed by **that** (which can be omitted) and the reported statement.
Irina said that Tina was on the phone.

> - We use **say** when there is no indirect object.
>   *"I'll be there," he said.*
>   *He said that he would be there.*
> - We use **tell** when there is an indirect object.
>   *"I'll call you, Mark," she said.*
>   *She told Mark she would call him.*

- When we change a sentence from Direct to Reported Speech, pronouns and possessive adjectives change according to the meaning of the sentence. Also, the verb **come** changes to **go**.
  "You look great in your new dress," said Kate.
  Kate said that I looked great in my new dress.
  Kelly said, "I'll come to the mall with you."
  Kelly said she would go to the mall with me.

- When the reporting verb (say or tell) is in the Past Tense, we usually make the following changes:

Present Simple → Past Simple
Sue said, "I want to go bowling."
Sue said (that) she wanted to go bowling.

Present Progressive → Past Progressive
Beth said, "I'm reading a novel."
Beth said she was reading a novel.

Past Simple → Past Perfect Simple
Pete said, "Mom made some sandwiches."
Pete said his mom had made some sandwiches.

Present Perfect Simple → Past Perfect Simple
Jo said, "I've worked hard today."
Jo said she had worked hard that day.

Present Perfect Progressive → Past Perfect Progressive
Andy said, "I've been waiting for an hour."
Andy said he had been waiting for an hour.

will → would
Sean said, "I'll be there soon."
Sean said he would be there soon.

can → could
Jane said, "I can help you with your homework."
Jane said she could help me with my homework.

may → might
Frank said, "I may buy her a pair of shoes."
Frank said he might buy her a pair of shoes.

must → had to
Mom said, "You must be home early."
Mom said I had to be home early.

Conditional Sentences Type 1 → Conditional Sentences Type 2
Diane said, "If we take a taxi, we'll get there quicker."
Diane said if they took a taxi, they would get there quicker.

now → then
Tina said, "I'll call him now."
Tina said she would call him then.

here → there
Eric said, "I saw it here."
Eric said he had seen it there.

ago → before
Bill said, "I bought this house two years ago."
Bill said he had bought that house two years before.

today, tonight → that day, that night
Martha said, "We're having pizza for lunch today."
Martha said they were having pizza for lunch that day.

yesterday → the previous day / the day before
Dad said, "I visited the doctor yesterday."
Dad said he had visited the doctor the previous day.

this morning/year, etc. → that morning/year, etc.
Beth said, "I haven't bought anything this year."
Beth said she hadn't bought anything that year.

tomorrow → the next day / the following day
Lynn said, "I'm flying to Mexico tomorrow."
Lynn said she was flying to Mexico the following day.

last week/month, etc. → the previous week/month etc. / the week/month, etc. before
Colin said, "I met her last year."
Colin said he had met her the previous year.

next week / month, etc. → the following week/month, etc.
Bob said, "I'll finish the report next week."
Bob said he would finish the report the following week.

- These changes cannot be made when the sentence expresses a general truth or the reporting verb is in the Present, Future or Present Perfect Simple.
  "I enjoy cooking," Ted said.
  Ted said (that) he enjoys cooking.
  "I will move to Chicago next year," Eric says.
  Eric says he will move to Chicago next year.
- The Past Perfect and the verbs *could, might, should, would* and *used to* do not change in Reported Speech.
- The Past Progressive usually doesn't change but when it does, it changes to Past Perfect Progressive.
- Conditional Sentences Types 2 and 3 do not change in Reported Speech.
- Apart from *say* and *tell*, other verbs can also be used to introduce reported statements: *explain, inform, add*, etc.

) Reported Speech (Questions)

- We usually introduce reported questions with the reporting verbs **ask, wonder** and the expression **want to know**.
- Reported questions follow the word order of affirmative sentences.
  "Why did he come back?" he asked.
  He asked me why he had come back.

- If the direct question begins with a question word, the reported question also begins with the same question word.
  *"**What** are you doing?" she asked.*
  *She asked me **what** I was doing.*
- If the direct question does not begin with a question word, the reported question begins with *if/whether*.
  "Did you enjoy the meal?" he asked.
  *He asked me **if/whether** I had enjoyed the meal.*
- When we change questions from Direct to Reported Speech, pronouns, tenses, adverbs, etc. change in the same way as when we report statements.

) Reported Speech (Commands - Requests)

- We commonly use **tell** or **order** when we report commands and **ask** when we report requests.
- The Imperative changes to **to + base form** or **not + to + base form**.
  "Stay there," said the man.
  The man told me to stay there.
  "Don't take this away, please," she said.
  She asked me not to take that away.

When the request is in question form, in Reported Speech it usually changes to *to + base form*.
"Will you lend me that book, please?" Kate asked me.
Kate asked me if/whether I would lend her that book.
Kate asked me to lend her that book.

Module 11
) Clauses of Concession

We use **Clauses of Concession** to express contrast or opposition to the main clause.

- **although / even though + subject + verb**
  Although / Even though he was starving, he didn't take any of the food they offered him.
- **in spite of / despite + noun / -ing form**
  Despite the heavy rain, it was very hot.
  In spite of feeling afraid, Jim went on the roller coaster.
- **in spite of / despite + the fact + that-clause**
  He went out in spite of / despite the fact that he had a terrible headache.

) Clauses of Purpose

We use **Clauses of Purpose** to show the purpose of an action.

- **so as (not) to / in order (not) to + base form**
  She spoke quietly in order not to / so as not to wake up the baby.
- **so that + can / may / will** (present / future time reference)
  You should work hard now so that you can take some time off in the summer.
- **so that + could / might / would** (past time reference)
  Henry took his car to the garage so that the mechanic could take a look at it.

All / Both / Neither / None / Either

- **All** is used for more than two people or things. It is used in affirmative sentences and takes a plural verb.
  Anna, Mary and Kate are going to attend a seminar. They are all very excited. / All of them are very excited.

- **Both** is used for two people, things, etc. It is used in affirmative sentences and takes a plural verb.
  Bill and Ted are cousins. Both of them are on a team. / They are both on a team.

- **Neither** is used for two people, things, etc. It is used in affirmative sentences and gives them a negative meaning. It takes a singular or plural verb.
  Patty and Monica want to get a cat. Neither of them have/has had a pet before.

- **None** is used for more than two people, things, etc. It is used in affirmative sentences and gives them a negative meaning. It takes a singular or plural verb.
  All my friends love coffee. None of them likes/like tea.

- **Either** is used for two people, things, etc. It means one or the other (it doesn't matter which of the two).
  A: Should we order Italian or Chinese?
  B: Either. I don't mind.

both... and... / either... or... / neither... nor...

Double conjunctions (**both... and...**, **either... or** and **neither... nor...**) link two words or phrases in the same sentence. They are used only in affirmative sentences.

- **Both... and...** is used when something is true for two people, things, etc. It always takes a plural verb.
  Both my sister and my brother go to high school.

- **Either... or...** is used when something is true for one of two people, things, etc.
  Either she was too busy or she didn't want to come.

- **Neither... nor...** is used when something is not true for two people, things, etc. The verb can be singular or plural.
  Neither Mary nor Jim like/likes tennis.

Module 12

Conditional Sentences Type 3

if-clause	Main clause
If + Past Perfect	would/could/might + have + past participle

Conditional Sentences Type 3 are used:

- to talk about unreal or imaginary situations in the past.
  If they had hired me at the computer company, I would have left my current job.

- to express regret.
  If I hadn't gone to bed so late last night, I would have woken up on time this morning.

- to criticize somebody/something.
  If you had completed your Master's degree, you might have found a better job.

Wishes and Unreal Past

Sometimes we use the Past Simple when referring to the present or future. This is called the **Unreal Past**.

- We use **wish / if only + Past Simple** to make a wish about a present or future situation which we would like to be different.
  I wish you didn't have to go tomorrow. (= But you have to).
  I wish I had a bigger house. (= But I don't).

> - In the Unreal Past we usually use *were* instead of *was*. *I wish I were older.*

- We use **wish / if only + could + base form** to express regret about something we cannot do at present.
  I wish I could speak Italian.
  I wish I could come with you on Friday.

- We use **wish / if only + Past Perfect Simple** to express regret about something that happened or didn't happen in the past.
  I wish I had taken a flashlight with me. I can't see a thing.

Base form	Past Simple	Past Participle	Base form	Past Simple	Past Participle
be	was/were	been	lie	lay	lain
beat	beat	beaten	light	lit	lit
become	became	become	lose	lost	lost
begin	began	begun	make	made	made
bite	bit	bitten	mean	meant	meant
bleed	bled	bled	meet	met	met
blow	blew	blown	mow	mowed	mowed/mown
break	broke	broken	pay	paid	paid
bring	brought	brought	put	put	put
build	built	built	read	read	read
burn	burned/burnt	burned/burnt	ride	rode	ridden
burst	burst	burst	ring	rang	rung
buy	bought	bought	rise	rose	risen
catch	caught	caught	run	ran	run
choose	chose	chosen	say	said	said
come	came	come	see	saw	seen
cost	cost	cost	sell	sold	sold
cut	cut	cut	send	sent	sent
deal	dealt	dealt	set	set	set
dig	dug	dug	shake	shook	shaken
do	did	done	shine	shone/shined	shone/shined
draw	drew	drawn	shoot	shot	shot
drink	drank	drunk	show	showed	shown
drive	drove	driven	shut	shut	shut
eat	ate	eaten	sing	sang	sung
fall	fell	fallen	sink	sank	sunk
feed	fed	fed	sit	sat	sat
feel	felt	felt	sleep	slept	slept
fight	fought	fought	smell	smelled/smelt	smelled/smelt
find	found	found	speak	spoke	spoken
fly	flew	flown	spell	spelled/spelt	spelled/spelt
forget	forgot	forgotten	spend	spent	spent
freeze	froze	frozen	spill	spilled/spilt	spilled/spilt
get	got	gotten/got	spread	spread	spread
give	gave	given	stand	stood	stood
go	went	gone	steal	stole	stolen
grow	grew	grown	stick	stuck	stuck
hang	hung	hung	sting	stung	stung
have	had	had	swim	swam	swum
hear	heard	heard	take	took	taken
hide	hid	hidden	teach	taught	taught
hit	hit	hit	tell	told	told
hold	held	held	think	thought	thought
hurt	hurt	hurt	throw	threw	thrown
keep	kept	kept	understand	understood	understood
know	knew	known	wake	woke	woken
lead	led	led	wear	wore	worn
learn	learned/learnt	learned/learnt	win	won	won
leave	left	left	withdraw	withdrew	withdrawn
lend	lent	lent	write	wrote	written
let	let	let			

spelling

American English	British English
airplane	aeroplane
analyze	analyse
apologize	apologise
behavior	behaviour
canceled	cancelled
center	centre
check	cheque
chili pepper	chilli pepper
civilization	civilisation
color	colour
cozy	cosy
favor	favour
favorite	favourite
gray	grey
humor	humour
jewelry	jewellery
lasagna	lasagne
license	licence
liter	litre
marvelous	marvellous
memorize	memorise
meter	metre
mold	mould
mustache	moustache
neighborhood	neighbourhood
omelet	omelette
organization	organisation
organize	organise
parlor	parlour
percent	per cent
practice (v)	practise
realize	realise
recognize	recognise
skillful	skilful
socialize	socialise
sympathize	sympathise
theater	theatre
tire	tyre
traveler	traveller

grammar and usage

American English	British English
January 16th	16th January
do well on	do well in
on the team	in the team
on the weekend	at the weekend
Turn right/left onto a street.	Turn right/left into a street.
It's ten after six.	It's ten past six.
learned	learnt, learned
spelled	spelt, spelled

words and phrases

American English	British English
across from	opposite
aluminum	aluminium
anchorman	newsreader
apartment	flat
apartment building	block of flats
appetizers	starters
bill	note
blond (hair)	fair (hair)
bulletin board	noticeboard
candy	sweets
carry-on	hand luggage
cell	mobile
check	tick
coffee shop	café
cookie	biscuit
couch	sofa
crosswalk	zebra crossing
do/wash the dishes	do the washing-up
do the laundry	do the washing
doctor's office	doctor's surgery
downtown (area)	city centre
eggplant	aubergine
elementary school	primary school
elevator	lift
faucet	tap
flashlight	torch
(French) fries	chips
gas	petrol
give sb. a ride	give sb. a lift
go to the movies	go to the cinema
grade	mark
have a fever	have a temperature
high school	secondary school
highway	motorway
horseback riding	horse riding
last name	surname
license plate	number plate
line	queue
mad	angry
Math	Maths
mom	mum
motorcycle	motorbike
movie	film
movie theater	cinema
neat	tidy
newsstand	newsagent's
pants	trousers
parentheses	brackets
period	full stop
pharmacy, drugstore	chemist's
ping-pong	table tennis
potato chips	crisps
principal	head teacher
purse	handbag
refrigerator	fridge
register	till
résumé	CV
roommate	flatmate
RV (Recreational vehicle)	camper
salesperson	shop assistant
Science major	Science student
sick	ill
sidewalk	pavement
sneakers	trainers
soccer	football
stay in shape	stay fit
store	shop
stove, oven	cooker
streetcar	tram
subway	underground
sweater	jumper
talk show	chat show
the check	the bill
track and field	athletics
trash, garbage	rubbish
truck	lorry
trunk	boot
vacation	holiday
windshield	windscreen
yard	garden
zip code	post code

Module 1

1.

A: So, how's your new place, Will?

B: Well, it's a lot better than the dorm we used to live in, that's for sure.

A: Anywhere's better than that place. Are you near your parents?

B: No, I couldn't live there. The suburbs are full of big houses, and I needed somewhere small.

A: So, did you find somewhere near the college?

B: No, I'm right in the middle of the city. I live on the tenth floor and the view is amazing.

A: I'll drop by some day and see for myself.

2.

A: Hey, Julie! Where are you?

B: Hi, Susie. Actually, I'm in your neighborhood. I just went to the bank.

A: I was wondering if you would like to come over for a coffee.

B: I guess I can drop by before I go to the supermarket.

A: OK.

3.

A: So Pam, how long have you been living in the countryside now?

B: A year.

A: Wow. Are you used to life out here now?

B: Definitely. The first month was difficult because it was a big change from city life, but after a couple more months, I was settled in, and now I can't imagine moving back to the city, to be honest.

A: Who would've thought of it?

4.

A: Could you just sign here, sir?

B: Certainly. By the way, I'd like to speak to the manager, please.

A: I'm afraid he's not here at the moment.

B: Could you tell me when he'll be back?

A: At around six, I think.

B: That's no good. Our plane leaves at five. Anyway, could you pass on a message? Just tell him we've had a wonderful time here, and he runs an excellent hotel.

A: He'll be pleased to hear that. I'll also need your room key.

B: Of course. Here it is.

5.

A: Hello?

B: Hello. I'm calling about the apartment you're renting on Dale Street.

A: Actually, there are two, one on the first floor and the other on the fifth.

B: Well, I'm interested in the one on the fifth floor. Would you please tell me how many bedrooms there are?

A: There's a big bedroom and a smaller one, but they both have a beautiful view of the park.

B: Great. I'd also like to know if the apartment is furnished.

A: Well, the person who was renting it left a couch in the living room and a bookcase and some other stuff, but if that's a

problem, I can empty it out completely for you.

B: Actually, I can't afford a lot of furniture at the moment, so I'd appreciate it if you'd leave the stuff.

A: Sure.

6.

A: So, tell me about your neighbor.

B: I can't tell you much. She doesn't really talk a lot.

A: Well, do you know what she does for a living?

B: I know she's a piano teacher and that she often plays the piano.

A: Really? That must be pretty annoying.

B: No, she only plays during the day, when I'm at work, so it's fine.

A: So, you haven't been over for coffee or anything?

B: No. I've been over a few times to borrow things. It's really nice to know there's someone there, just in case.

A: Yeah, that's true.

1b

Speaker 1

I came to Japan to work as an English teacher but it was pretty difficult to adjust in the beginning. I had difficulty even in everyday situations. For instance, when you meet a person, you usually bow to show respect instead of shaking hands. And another thing, back home it's normal to use your cell phone on the bus. In Japan, it's not considered polite. Also, you should never be late for an appointment, because it shows that you don't respect the other person. Anyway, I wasn't aware of these things in the beginning, but now I feel like I know a lot about life in Japan.

Speaker 2

When my boss sent me to Venice to work for two years, I was full of enthusiasm. After a few weeks, though, I started missing my old life, my family and friends, and I didn't feel like doing much in my new city. When my friends back home asked me how things were, they didn't believe me when I told them how I felt. One day, though, a colleague of mine insisted we go for a coffee and I did. This helped me meet other colleagues, and I slowly started making friends. I also signed up at a language school to learn Italian, which is helping me socialize even more. Venice may not feel like home yet, but I think it's a unique experience.

Speaker 3

Being used to living in a big city like New York, you can understand how shocking it was to move to a small town in Sweden with my husband when he was offered a new job. It's a beautiful town, but I felt kind of isolated with no big supermarkets or malls around. So, to fill my spare time I took up a hobby. I started making jewelry. Whenever my husband's colleagues or neighbors came over, they were really fascinated by my creations and wanted to buy them. That is how I opened up a jewelry store. Now, I know almost everyone in the town, I am doing something I like, and I actually prefer this place to the big

city I used to live in.

Module 2

2a

A: Good evening. Three years ago tomorrow, a young man survived an airplane crash and then lived ten days in the jungle before he was rescued. It's an incredible story, and here to tell it is the man himself, Conrad Mendez.

B: Hello, it's good to be here.

A: So, Conrad, tell us your story. You were on the plane to Peru, right?

B: Right. You see, my father, who is from the States, is a zoologist and spends most of his time in Peru. That's where he met my mother. She is actually from Brazil, and I was flying from Rio to meet my father when the accident happened somewhere over the Bolivian rainforest.

A: So, what happened to the plane?

B: We were flying through a terrible storm. There was a lot of turbulence and I couldn't see outside; it was so dark. Suddenly I saw a flash of lightning and then the wing caught fire. Within minutes, it broke apart and the plane started going down. As you can imagine, I was terrified. Suddenly, I realized I was not in the plane anymore and I was flying down towards the jungle, still strapped to my seat. I thought I was going to die. What are the chances of surviving a plane crash, right? But I did! Luckily, the trees are very thick in that part of the rainforest and they broke my fall. Also, I was falling backwards so my injuries weren't that bad. I just had a broken collarbone and a bad cut on my arm.

A: That's amazing. But then, you still had to deal with the jungle.

B: I wasn't too scared of that. I've spent a lot of time in the jungle with my father, and I recognize the dangers. My first thought was to find other passengers, but I was unsuccessful. In fact, I couldn't find any survivors, or even the plane. They must have been miles away.

A: What about food or water?

B: I came across a river, so at least I had water to drink. As for food, I was able to find some fruit in the jungle. But after a few days, I was really weak. I was starting to give up hope when I heard rescue helicopters overhead. They were looking for the plane, I guessed, but the trees were so thick that they couldn't see me, so I wasn't rescued then. The following day, I decided to follow the river as far as I could. I thought that maybe I could find a village or something. A few miles down the river, I spotted a boat and decided to wait there. Later that day, two fishermen found me unconscious, but alive, by their boat.

A: Where did they take you?

B: They took me to the nearest hospital, which was 7 hours away. There, I found out that out of the 87 passengers on the plane, I was one of the lucky survivors along with eight other people. Amazingly, they had survived the crash, too. But they were all badly injured and only lasted a couple of days. In the end, I was the only survivor.

A: That's just terrible. Have you been back there since?

B: Actually, I'm going back for the first time next month, as part of a documentary Channel 5 is making. I'm going to visit the site of the plane crash and meet up with the fishermen who saved me. It's strange, because it was such a terrifying experience for me, but for some reason, I can't wait to return. It's a part of my life that I just can't forget.

A: Well, it's a fascinating story, that's for sure. Now, we're going to take a break...

2b

Before the race

Tim Hello, this is Tim Carter reporting live from the Extreme Bicycle Race. It's another year at the exciting ultimate challenge for cyclists from all around the world, who ride a total of 800 miles in 10 days. Today is the final day of the event and with us, just an hour before the race, is Alex Tyler, who came in second place two years ago.

Alex Hello, everyone.

Tim So Alex, only 80 more miles today to the finish line. How do you feel?

Alex What can I say? I'm thrilled to be here.

Tim You didn't participate last year, due to a knee injury, from what I've heard.

Alex That's right. Two months before the Extreme Bicycle Race, I was competing in a race in Australia. When the unfortunate incident happened, I was devastated. You can't imagine how much I wanted to be here. After the surgery, I started training and practicing again and here I am.

Tim Well, you seem to be in great shape, and there's a good chance you may be the winner this year.

Alex I hope so. It's my dream!

Tim Good luck, Alex! And now we are going over to ....

During the race

Tim This is Tim Carter and we're back from the break.

Patrick And this is Patrick Hunt. The race is almost over. In just a few minutes we will know who the winner is.

Tim That's right. We can see the cyclists riding into the last mile. In the lead is last year's winner, Daniel Kent, who is one of the best bike riders in the world.

Patrick But will he be the winner today? Right behind him is Michael Phillips. It's hard to believe that he was an amateur rider two years ago, riding just for the fun of it.

Tim Yeah, wasn't he studying to become a doctor?

Patrick Yep. I guess he changed his mind.

Wow! Look at Alex Tyler speeding up from fifth place!

Tim He's third now right behind Michael Phillips. What a race! There's just one last corner till the finish line, with Daniel Kent still leading.

Patrick What a surprising turn of events! Tyler just passed both of them! He's in the lead, just a few yards before the finish line! Unbelievable!

Tim And yes! He is now the new champion of the Extreme Bicycle Race, taking the title from Daniel Kent!

After the race

Tim Right next to me is the winner of the 10th annual Extreme Bicycle Race. So, how does first place feel?

Alex Much better than second place, that's for sure!

Tim And this is your first time winning in the ten years you've been competing, right?

Alex Actually, this is my first time winning in the Extreme Bicycle Race, but I've also won another two races; a local race back home in Ireland and a Road Bicycle Race in Canada.

Tim Oh yes, Canada. I remember that. That was about five years ago.

Alex Four to be exact, but it wasn't a very big event.

Tim So, what is your next step in your cycling career? The Tour de France?

Alex Well, I'm thinking of taking a break from competitions, at least for a while. My dream is to create a cycling club. A place where I can teach young cyclists everything I know about how to succeed in competitions and help them train.

Tim Sounds interesting Alex.

Module 3
3a
1.

A: Hello, Highland Airlines. How can I help you?

B: Hello, I'd like to book a flight to Sydney on March 15th.

A: Of course, ma'am. Which city will you be leaving from?

B: Melbourne.

A: Well, let me see. I'm sorry, but there aren't any flights available on that day. What about the previous day, March 14th? Or the following day, March 16th?

B: No, the 14th isn't any good, because I'm working. Can you check the following day?

A: One moment. Yes, there is a morning flight that day.

B: OK, I'll book that one.

2.

A: Did you check the train schedule for Saturday?

B: Yes. The departures are at 4:45, 5:30 and 7:00.

A: Well, I finish work at 6:00, so I can't make it earlier than that.

B: So, I guess we only have one choice, then.

3.

Your attention, please. This is an announcement for passengers on platform 2 waiting for the 2:45 train to Chicago. We apologize for the delay. Thank you for your patience. The train will be arriving shortly at platform 1. So, will all passengers traveling to Chicago please proceed to platform 1. Sorry again for the inconvenience.

4.

A: What do you think we should do today?

B: Well, it's our first day in the city so we should do some sightseeing.

A: How about renting bicycles and exploring the city on our own?

B: But I wanted to take the bus that goes on a tour of the whole city. It has a guide who gives information about the sights and it also makes stops if you want to eat or go shopping.

A: Not a bad idea, but we can do that another day. It's such a nice day and we need some exercise.

B: You're right.

5.

A: What am I supposed to do now?

B: Calm down. I'm sure the airport employees will solve the problem!

A: This has never happened to me before! I have so many important things in my suitcase, like the presentation I prepared and all my clothes, of course!

B: Well, things like this happen. Did you get any travel insurance?

A: Yes, I did. Do you think that will help?

B: Sure it will. They might give you money and you can buy some clothes to wear until they find your suitcase. In the meantime, we can start working on a new presentation.

A: OK.

6.

Hello. My name is Bradley West and I'm flying to Tokyo with you next week. My reference number is TY345 556... No, no I'm traveling alone... Well, I'm calling because I heard about the cancelations to some of your flights and I was a little worried... Ah, so that's why they were canceled. And my flight isn't affected?... Oh, that's great news. Thank you.

3b

Pilot *Cabin crew, prepare for take-off...*

A: So, is this your first trip to Beijing?

B: Yes, and you?

A: No, I'm a frequent visitor. I go there on business often. What about you? Business or pleasure? Or perhaps you're visiting friends?

B: No, I'm not. It's just somewhere I've always wanted to go.

A: I see. Well, there are lots of wonderful places you shouldn't miss.

B: I know. I downloaded this app which has all the famous sights and it tells you where the closest tourist attraction to you is. I can even store my photos.

A: That's handy. Have you ever used it?

B: Well, I used a similar one in Moscow last

year and it worked great.

A: Well, there's much more to the city than just tourist sights, you know. I have a friend who takes me to the most fascinating places. If you want to see the real Beijing, you need someone to show you around.

B: Well, I have an app for that, too.

A: Really?

B: Yes, look.

A: Should you be using that app on the plane?

B: It's OK, it works offline. Look, I've entered information about when and where I'm staying and it's given me a list of places where I can go and eat.

A: Chao Ming's! My friend takes me there all the time.

B: Well, there you go. It seems to be working.

A: You certainly are very organized. I need to get some of those apps, I think.

B: I'm not the person who plans everything to the last detail, but since I got this smartphone, everything's changed. This app here has been the most useful. I downloaded it a month ago and it's helped me prepare for my trip so much. It's ideal for someone like you because it remembers previous trips you've gone on and you can use the reminders for your next trip.

A: I have to get that app for sure. What's it called?

B: Umm... Let me see...

Module 4
4a

1.

A: Did you hear what happened?

B: No, what?

A: Danny was fired this morning!

B: Really? That's terrible! But, now that I think of it, it doesn't surprise me.

A: Why do you say that? He was a nice hard-working guy.

B: Well, he might not have been the type that sat around doing nothing, but he was hardly ever on time the past month. Didn't you notice?

A: Not really. I heard he was looking for a new job.

B: Exactly. He was probably going to interviews or something. And he might not have arrived on time once again today. You know how punctual our boss is.

A: At least I hope he's found a new job.

2.

A: How's the job hunting going, Bill?

B: Well, I've applied for a few positions and tomorrow I have an interview at a firm downtown.

A: That's great news! You've been unemployed for a while now. I hope you make a good impression tomorrow.

B: I hope so, too. Finding a job is harder than I thought. I shouldn't have quit before finding a new one.

A: Well, don't give up now. Just do your best. Any other job interviews in the

near future?

B: Well, a cousin of mine might arrange an interview for me. He told me that there's a job opening at his company. I shouldn't forget to call him later.

A: Well, good luck.

3.

A: So, James, your résumé looks very impressive. I'm sure you could find a job in a much bigger company. Why did you choose to have an interview with us?

B: Well, I'll be honest. I've had offers from other companies with larger salaries, but that wasn't what I was looking for.

A: I see. And you do realize that with this job, you may have to work late?

B: Yes, I'm OK with that. Basically, I was worried that if I went to a bigger company, I'd be stuck in the same position for years, whereas your advertisement states that there are opportunities for better positions in the future.

A: Absolutely! And we encourage people to be positive and to...

4.

A: What do you do for a living, Mark?

B: I'm a part-time reporter for an online news website. I have been working for a few months.

A: How's it going?

B: Not bad. It's the first time I've worked as a reporter. Their offices are on the outskirts of the city. It takes me about an hour to drive there.

A: That must be a big problem for you!

B: For some people it may be. But I don't mind, because I enjoy this type of work and I couldn't find another job closer to home. The pay isn't much unfortunately, but I get along with my colleagues and my boss, even though I haven't known them for long. Hopefully, I'll get a raise by the end of the year.

A: Well, I hope so, too!

5.

A: So, how's it going with your new assistant, Susan?

B: OK, I guess.

A: You don't sound very enthusiastic.

B: Well, it's just that...

A: What? Don't tell me she's not helpful, like the other one?

B: Not at all. Actually, she's very eager to learn and help out.

A: So, what is it then?

B: Well, how can I say this? She has all the required knowledge and qualifications. I mean she has a degree in Software Engineering and everything, but she hardly has any experience and that makes her kind of slow.

A: Oh, I see. Well just give her some time to learn.

6.

A: Hello, I need some information about the volunteer program in Bolivia.

B: Yes, we've had quite a bit of interest in that program.

A: I'm thinking about Bolivia because I can

speak Spanish. Does that help?

B: It's not required, but it will definitely be useful.

A: It says in the advertisement that I will have to pay for my travel expenses but that you can find me somewhere to stay.

B: That's correct. There are some very nice youth hostels in the area where we put up our volunteers.

A: That sounds good. There's just one more thing...

4b

Speaker 1

I've been running my own business for many years, but it's been a struggle. I know it's a competitive world out there, but I always had a feeling I was doing something wrong. I have a cousin who is much more successful than me, so I asked him to be honest and tell me what I was doing wrong. He took one look at my office and realized what the problem was right away. He told me to sort out all my papers, and to install a computer program that would do a lot of the work for me. Not only did it feel good to clean out everything, but my business is now doing much better. I even look more professional now. I don't know why I didn't think of it earlier.

Speaker 2

All my friends from college and I started our careers soon after we graduated. Throughout college, I was the one who was organized, and I always knew what to do next. When I got my first job, though, I was really nervous and afraid of making mistakes. About a year later, my friends were doing so much better than me. I just couldn't understand why. My best friend told me I needed to change my attitude, be more creative, and try different ideas without worrying too much. So I did, and it improved my work very much. I learned a lot from my mistakes and everything is much better now.

Speaker 3

The other day I remembered some excellent advice my first boss had given me: "Good things come to those who wait," he said. And it really had worked for him, because he was a successful businessman. He believed that it's a mistake to make quick decisions without thinking. He thought it was better to just let things take their course. I should have listened to him and done the same. However, when I started my own business last year, I was too ambitious and in a hurry to become someone. I rushed into things and it all went wrong. I guess I need to start over again, but I'll take it easy this time.

Speaker 4

This advice was given to me by an old colleague who was very successful in her career. I always thought her success came from her being more intelligent than me, but it's not true. As I was starting out, she said to me, "Never eat alone." I know, it sounds ridiculous, but she was trying to tell me how important networking is. It's all about the people you know, the contacts you have and having people around who think the same way you do. You may not need them right away, but in the future, you never know. It's been a big help for me, and the main reason for my success.

Module 5

5a

A: Hey, what happened to you? I wanted to send you a funny video yesterday and you'd disappeared from my contact list.

B: Yeah, I know.

A: Did you unfriend me or something?

B: No, I deactivated my account.

A: Really? You hadn't mentioned anything about doing that. Why did you deactivate it?

B: Well, for a few reasons.

A: Did you spend too much time on there? I know I do. I could spend all day chatting and sending funny pictures.

B: No, it was the opposite. I was spending less and less time because it's just full of garbage.

A: What? But you can keep in touch with so many people. I mean, all our old school friends are on there.

B: I know, but let me explain. I don't really want to stay in touch with them all. Maybe one or two, and I usually call them or send them e-mail. The rest just send me useless messages all day and night. Also, there are lots of people on there who write about every little detail of their lives. You know what? I don't care if you're at the store... and they don't have bananas!

A: OK, don't yell. We're not arguing, you know. Personally, I don't know what I'd do without it. I send all my messages through there, I make arrangements to go out, I found my roommate and I even arranged for over 100 people to meet at Kilburn Park to clean it up. Remember?

B: Yeah. There are many benefits, I'm sure. But since I gave it up, I don't miss it at all.

A: What about the news? It's the best place to find out about breaking news stories.

B: Oh, come on. There are plenty of websites I can visit to check the news in my own time. So what if I learn about it half an hour later?

A: Anyway, you have to see this video I found.

B: E-mail it to me.

A: OK, I will.

5b

1.

A: OK, when you see a post office, turn left.

B: Are you sure? There isn't one around here.

A: There! You missed it! You're going too fast.

B: No, I'm not.

A: Yes, you are. Look at the sign. The police will stop us, and we'll get a ticket.

B: Maybe you're right. Let me turn here and we can go back.

2.

A: I'm really glad we came to the museum today.

B: Me too.

C: Excuse me! I'm afraid that's not permitted in here.

B: I'm sorry, I didn't know.

C: Well, there are clear signs all over the museum.

B: Is there anywhere where it is allowed?

C: Not inside the building.

B: Who wants to see a picture of the outside of the building?

A: Just leave it, Steve.

3.

A: There's the opera house, look. What a beautiful building!

B: Where?

A: Over there. Stop the car here so I can take a picture.

B: I can't.

A: Why not? There's plenty of room.

B: Can't you see the sign?

A: Oh. Then turn left here and stop somewhere so I can get out.

4.

A: It's a nice day to be outside, isn't it?

B: Yes, and it would be even nicer if you weren't smoking. We'd be able to breathe some nice fresh air.

A: Come on, give me a break.

B: Let's go and sit over there.

A: We're not allowed, look.

B: That's a shame. Let's go and sit on that bench, then.

A: OK.

5.

A: Excuse me! Where are you going?

B: I'm looking for somewhere to park.

A: Well, you can't enter this area. Didn't you see the sign?

B: The sign?

A: It's for your own safety. There's a parking lot not far from here.

B: Really? Where?

A: Just turn left here and it's at the end of the road near the park.

B: OK, thanks.

Module 6

6a

Psychologist Hello, my name is Dr. Tammy Morris and I am a psychologist. I am here today to discuss how studies have shown that it is possible to predict whether people will be successful or not in their lives. Successful people seem to have specific characteristics that can be spotted from a very young age. A study which took place in the 1960s and 1970s managed to change the way we had understood the concept of success up until then. It was called the "Marshmallow Experiment," a funny name for an experiment, but you'll understand why it was called that in a minute.

It turns out that successful people aren't just intelligent, as most of us would think, but they also have the ability to control themselves and delay gratification. What do I mean by "delay gratification"? It is the ability a person has to refuse a reward now and be patient enough to wait for a bigger or greater reward later. It's a simple idea and after I tell you about the experiment, I'm sure you will have understood it clearly.

So, let's go on to discuss the experiment. It involved a group of four-year-olds that had to sit in a room with only a table and a chair in it. The psychologists showed each child a marshmallow and told them that they had two options. The first was that they could eat the marshmallow at any time they wanted to. But if they were impatient and ate it right away, they wouldn't get another one. The other option? If they waited for 15 minutes, they would get a second marshmallow to eat. The psychologists then left the room and left the children alone to decide. I know it sounds like a long time for young children to wait. You might say that even 5 minutes would be long enough. However, the results showed that it wasn't an impossible task for some. About one out of three children managed to wait the appropriate amount of time and get a second marshmallow.

The psychologists then asked themselves. "What will happen to these children in the future?" The amazing thing is that they contacted the children after about 15 years and investigated whether they could be considered successful or not. What did the psychologists discover? It turns out that the ones who were able to delay gratification were indeed the ones who got better grades in school, had better relationships with their teachers, parents and friends and also showed a greater ability to cope with stress and other problems, proving that they were more successful than the others.

This experiment has been conducted in many other countries and ...

6b

A: Welcome back. Liz is here with me to check the answers to our Record Breakers quiz. I think I got all the answers right this time.

B: OK. Let's see what you got. What is the longest distance traveled on a bike in 24 hours without the rider's feet touching the ground?

A: Well, I was going to put 5,533.5, but then I realized that that's longer than the Tour de France, a race which lasts for 21 days. So I chose 553.15.

B: Well done! What about the next one?

A: The longest beard? Well, they all seem pretty amazing to me. But I went for 4.7 ft.

B: I'm afraid you're wrong.

A: Was it only 2.7 ft? I say "only" but that's very long as well. Not that I would know. I've never tried to grow a beard.

B: No, it's actually 7.7 ft.

A: Get out of here! That's taller than the

tallest basketball player.

B: I know, it's pretty unbelievable, don't you think? OK, on to the next one. How many records were broken at the London Marathon in 2011?

A: Now, this one confused me a little, because there are only a few winners, so there can't be 35 records broken. I'm going to say zero, because I think it's a trick question.

B: Well, it is a trick question. There were 35 records broken, but they were mainly for being the fastest wearing a particular costume, or running backwards, that kind of thing.

A: I see. Well, I couldn't know that. What about the underwater wedding question?

B: What did you guess?

A: Well, I didn't actually guess. I remember seeing it on TV when it happened.

B: That's cheating!

A: No. I just happen to know the answer. Anyway, there were only about 130 people at my wedding, and I thought that was a lot. So, how they managed to get 275 people in that lake, all with scuba gear, was pretty amazing.

B: On to the last question. How many T-shirts did Sanath Bandara wear at once?

A: I have no idea about this one. But I'm guessing 357 is way too many. Let's say 257.

B: You're right!

A: He must have been pretty hot in there.

B: No doubt.

Module 7
7a

Hi, I'm Jack Fuller and this week on *Wild World* we're exploring the seas and oceans of the world and discovering why the Earth is known as the blue planet.

Here I am on Ascension Island, right in the middle of the Atlantic Ocean, 1,000 miles off the coast of Africa and 1,400 miles from the coast of South America. And here, every year from about November to May, green sea turtles visit the island to lay their eggs deep in the sand. They are huge creatures, about 5 feet long, sometimes weighing more than 700 pounds. As you can see, it is night now, and if we're lucky, we'll be able to see some baby turtles come out of the sand and head towards the water. This is the most dangerous time of their lives, as seagulls and crabs attack and eat them. And once in the water, they have to avoid fish, too. Only a few will survive, and those lucky enough to reach adulthood in twenty or more years' time, will return here to lay their eggs. Some travel 1,600 miles to find the exact beach where they were born.

At the moment, I am at a depth of 12,000 feet in the Atlantic Ocean. I'm inside a submersible, specially designed for deep-sea diving. It is completely black down here, the temperatures are close to freezing and the pressure is enormous. However, there are living creatures down here. And if I'm lucky, I should be able to

see what I'm looking for. There it is! An anglerfish! The reason we can see this animal is because it has a light coming out of its head. Anglerfish use this light to attract other fish and eat them. It is a very useful thing to have at this depth. Of course, this isn't the deepest part of the ocean. For that, you need to travel to the Mariana Trench in the Pacific Ocean. There, the depth is 35,000 feet, and very little is known about the bottom of the trench, where very few people have ever been. In fact, more people have been on the surface of the moon than the sea floor of the Mariana Trench. But, amazingly, you can still find small life forms down there.

I'm sitting in a boat off the coast of North America and I'm waiting to see one of my all-time favorite animals. The blue whale is simply the largest creature that has ever existed on our planet. It can measure 100 feet long and weigh up to 200 tons whereas the heaviest dinosaur was only 90 tons. Just to give you an idea of what we're talking about, a blue whale's heart is the same size as a small car. These creatures can also swim very fast, reaching speeds of 46 miles per hour. Before they began to be hunted, there were about 240,000 blue whales in the Antarctic alone. Today, sadly, they are an endangered species and their population worldwide is estimated to be between 5,000 and 12,000. Wait! I think I see something. Yes! There's one.... Wow! Look at that!

7b

A: Hello, this is Jeff Atkins. Today on our show we have a special guest, Tom Summers, who is here to tell us about World Water Day. What is World Water Day, Tom?

B: On World Water Day lots of events are organized around the world to raise awareness about water issues. Many of us take water for granted, but there are millions of people around the world who don't have access to clean water. So, every year on March 22nd, World Water Day turns our attention to this constantly growing problem.

A: It is a big problem, Tom. What does World Water Day try to achieve, though?

B: Basically, its goal is to inform people about the problem of water shortage. It is getting bigger because of the increasing world population, changes in our lifestyles, pollution and climate change and, unfortunately, it leads to a shocking number of deaths around the world. This year, many events will take place in cities all around the world, including ours. Speakers will educate us on how we can save water.

A: What kind of events take place on World Water Day?

B: Well, one example is the Walk for Water event. In many countries, women and children have to walk as far as 4 miles to find water every day. The Walk for Water event is a great way to show people the importance of water. It's an event mostly for schools, however, anybody can take part. Participants walk 4 miles

while carrying a backpack filled with 12 pints of water. Last year, 350,000 people "walked for water" in cities all around the world.

A: Wow, that's a large number. Do you have any advice for our listeners? How can they help out?

B: Well, first of all we should all try to decrease our water footprint, which shows how many gallons of water we use every day, not just by brushing our teeth and showering, but also the water we consume based on the food we eat and the products or services we use. For instance, 1,000 pints of water are used just to produce 1 pint of milk! And for 1 pound of beef, you need 12,000 gallons of water. A vegetarian for instance, consumes less water daily than somebody who eats meat. In fact, up to hundreds of gallons less.

A: That's interesting. How can we learn more about World Water Day?

B: On our official website you can find out how we can help out in different countries, and watch videos of World Water Day events from last year. It's also a great place to find out details about future events.

A: Well, sounds great. Now, let's go to a break...

Module 8
8a

A: Good afternoon. Yesterday the government announced that a wind farm will be built just outside Winterdale. This was not a popular decision with some local residents, who are totally against the idea, and there are already social media groups trying to change the decision. On the line I have Emily Taylor from the Environmental Protection Agency. Hello, Ms. Taylor.

B: Good afternoon.

A: What exactly will this wind farm be like?

B: Well, 15 turbines will be built on the hills just outside the town. They will provide 20% of the town's total electricity.

A: So, we will still rely mainly on fossil fuels for our electricity.

B: That's true, but we will be using fossil fuels less which is a step in the right direction.

A: Now, some residents aren't happy at all about the wind farm, in particular farmers.

B: Well, what farmers need to realize is that these wind turbines will be on the top of the hills, where the strongest winds are. There are no farms and hardly any farmland up there. Also, I would like to mention something that is possible and has been done elsewhere. You can have a wind farm, grow crops and have animals all in the same field. There's nothing stopping you from sharing the land.

A: What about birds? Some bird protection organizations are worried that these huge turbines will kill a lot of them.

B: It's true that turbines sometimes kill birds accidentally, but compared to other man-made structures, the number is very small. Power lines kill about 150 million birds every year in the U.S., and cars kill about 70 million. But wind turbines only kill about 20 thousand.

A: Now, another thing to consider is the beautiful countryside surrounding Winterdale. Isn't this wind farm going to be an ugly addition to the hills? I mean we'll be able to see them for miles around.

B: I've heard lots of stories in the media about this problem, but our research says that it's just not true. Most people aren't worried about what the land will look like. They are more interested in how beneficial to the environment this project will be.

A: What about those who live nearby? They say the value of their house will go down because of the wind farm, which is probably true. What can you do about that?

B: Well, a scheme is being set up, as in Denmark, where you can claim money from the government if the value of your house reduces because of the wind farm. But I can't really see house prices going down just because 15 wind turbines will be built in the area..

A: OK, thank you, Ms. Taylor. Now let's go over to...

8b

1.

A: Hi, Jason. Is that your dinner?

B: Yeah.

A: Have you given up with your diet, then?

B: What do you mean?

A: Look at the size of that steak! It's huge.

B: I see no problem with a little bit of protein. And I have some spinach and carrots, too. Delicious!

A: And no fries?

B: Well, I'm not going to lose weight eating fries, bread and cakes, am I? It's just empty calories.

A: Whatever you say.

2.

A: So, Mr. Anderson, how are you feeling?

B: Very well. I haven't had any stomachaches for a while. So, I think the diet is working.

A: Are you eating a lot of meat?

B: Not really, but I'm trying to increase the amount of calcium in my diet.

A: Yes, make sure you get a lot of calcium but I also think you could do with a little more meat.

B: OK, doctor.

3.

A: Hello, would you like fish or beef?

B: Umm, what do they come with?

A: The beef comes with potatoes and cauliflower and the fish has a green salad.

B: OK. The beef, I suppose.

A: There you go.

B: I saw someone with pasta over there.

A: Yes, that's the vegetarian meal. Would you like that instead?

B: Yeah, that would be much better for me.

A: Jean! Do we have any vegetarian meals left? No?

B: It's OK. Don't worry about it. I'm fine with this.

4.

A: OK, the chicken is looking very nice there in the oven. Let's get to work on the dessert.

B: What are you going to prepare, Erica?

A: My summer fruit salad. It's a recipe from my new book, and all you need is a variety of fruit to get different types of vitamins. Here we have some pears, apricots and I always like to add a few strawberries. It would have been nice if we had some watermelon, but don't worry. It'll be just as refreshing. OK, first we cut our lovely fresh pears and put them in a bowl.

B: Can I help with that?

A: Sure, go ahead.

5.

Man You can become overweight or obese when you eat more calories than you use. Your body needs energy to function and to be active. But if you take in more energy than your body uses, you will gain weight. Many factors can play a role in becoming overweight or obese. These factors include behavior patterns, such as not eating healthily or not getting enough physical activity, environment and culture, or sometimes it can simply be in your genes.

6.

A: Excuse me. Can you help me out? What's this dish here on the menu?

B: Stuffed eggplant? That's eggplant with chopped tomatoes, mushrooms and grated parmesan cheese on top, baked in the oven. It's delicious.

A: And the eggplant special?

B: Well, that's stuffed eggplant but it also includes shrimps.

A: And mushrooms?

B: Yes, unless you don't like them and you want to replace them with something else.

A: Well, I'm not a big fan. Can we just leave them out?

B: Of course, no problem. So, one eggplant special...

Module 9
9a

1.

A: How can I help you?

B: I'm thinking about getting a tablet, but I'm not sure.

A: Well, what would you like to do with it?

B: I don't know, just check my e-mail, maybe watch a movie.

A: Do you have a laptop?

B: Yes, and I use that most of the time for my work, and for watching movies. But I'd prefer something that's more convenient and up to date.

A: Well, have you considered a smartphone? You can do amazing things with them these days.

B: Yeah, I have one. That's why I'm looking for something in between.

A: Well, then I think you only have one choice. Let me show you this model, here...

2.

A: Have you decided on anything?

B: Well, I really like these black shoes but I'm short of cash. Is there an ATM nearby?

A: There's one about two blocks away.

B: Umm, I don't think I have enough time.

A: It's only 6 o'clock. We don't close for another hour.

B: I know, but I need to be somewhere in half an hour.

A: Why don't I hold on to them and you can pick them up tomorrow?

B: That'll be great! Thank you. What time do you open?

A: Eight o'clock.

3.

A: So, let me see what you got.

B: There, what do you think?

A: That's a nice coat. How much was it?

B: Well, it was 125 dollars, but I got it for a hundred.

A: A hundred dollars for a coat like that. That's a steal!

B: I also got these gloves to go with it. They were fifty dollars but I got them half price.

A: 50% off? They're nice too.

B: I'm telling you, they have some great bargains down there.

4.

Today's special offers at Digiworld! All our headphones have up to a 40% discount. We have a huge selection of TVs. If you buy one, you get a second one for free! Don't miss our 3 for 2 offer on all USB memory sticks, today only! There are also half-price deals on CDs, DVDs and computer games. So, what are you waiting for? Get down to Digiworld today!

5.

A: So, what do we need to do today?

B: Well, we need to go to the mall and get some gifts.

A: Again?

B: Why? What do you want to do? Sit on the couch and watch TV all day?

A: No, I'd just prefer to do something else, that's all.

B: Well, if you're worried about the soccer game, we can go shopping in the morning if you like. That way, you can still go to the game in the afternoon.

A: That's not what I had in mind. Take a look at this invitation.

B: A car exhibition? How thoughtful of you! That way I can choose which one to buy.

A: Well, we'll see about that.

9b

A: Hello?

B: Good afternoon, Mr. Thompson.

A: It's Tompkins, actually.

B: Oh, I'm sorry. My name's Sophie and I'm calling from Globofone. I understand you've made a request to cancel your contract with us and move to another company. Is that right?

A: Yes.

B: Can I ask you the reason why?

A: Well, there are a few actually.

B: Perhaps I can persuade you to change your mind. We have some great offers at the moment, and I can get you a good deal on a smartphone.

A: I have a smartphone, and I'm not canceling my account because it's expensive.

B: Please tell me why then.

A: Well, to be honest, I'm pretty dissatisfied with your level of service.

B: Oh.

A: I mean, I've called countless times to change the name on my bill, but you get it wrong every time.

B: Well, there must be some misunderstanding, but that is something I can correct right now. It's Mr. Thompson, right?

A: It's Tompkins.

B: Oh, yes, sorry again.

A: And another thing, whenever I need help and call the customer service helpline, I usually have to wait for half an hour before I speak to anyone.

B: What time of day do you usually call?

A: Does it matter? You advertise that you have a 24-hour customer service helpline.

B: You're right about that but...

A: And what's more, I have no signal on my phone at my work. Everyone that doesn't have Globofone has no problem, but I have to go onto the roof to make a call.

B: Well, we are improving the system at the moment and most areas with problems will be fine in the near future.

A: I'll believe that when I see it. But you know, the thing that really annoys me is that people from Globofone keep making endless calls and offering me special deals. I know you're trying to help but it gets so annoying sometimes.

B: It seems like you've made up your mind. I'm sorry to have bothered you, Mr. Thompson.

Module 10

10a

1.

A: Hey, Mary. I ran into Jenny this afternoon.

B: Yeah, where? At the gym?

A: No, at the mall. But she told me she was going to the gym later.

B: She must be there now. She goes almost every day after work, you know. She was there yesterday and the day before.

A: Good for her!

2.

A: Riverside Sports Center. How can I help you?

B: Hello, could you give me some information about the tennis lessons?

A: Yes, there are lessons every weekday at 6 and 8 p.m.

B: What about the cost?

A: It's 15 dollars per lesson or a monthly fee of 75 dollars.

B: Do you have private instructors?

A: Yes, but it works out to be a little more expensive.

B: More than 75 dollars?

A: It's 50 for...

B: For a month?

A: No, that's per hour.

B: I see. OK, I think I'd like to sign up for...

3.

A: Ow!

B: Are you OK, Linda? What's up?

A: I think I've pulled a muscle in my leg.

B: Well, that's enough for you today. Sit down over here.

A: Thanks.

B: You really should do some warm-up exercises before you start, you know.

A: I do, every time. But I think I've been overdoing it lately.

B: Yes, I've seen you here almost every day. When your leg gets better, maybe you should take it easy. Come in every other day so your body can recover.

A: I think you're right.

4.

A: I don't know, Fiona.

B: Come on, you really need some exercise.

A: I used to do weight training at college. Maybe I could take that up again.

B: That was a long time ago. Anyway, I think you need to move around more and do something a little more energetic if you want to lose weight.

A: Yeah, I suppose so.

B: Listen, you don't have to go every day of the week. You can go on Tuesday, Thursday and Friday evenings, while I'm at my aerobics class. The park is nice at that time of day.

A: OK, maybe I'll start this Tuesday.

5.

A: What happened to you? Is it broken?

B: No, I just pulled a muscle, but it really hurts.

A: How did it happen? You can barely walk. Here, hold my arm.

B: Well, Gary called and asked if I wanted to play basketball with him and his friends. They were missing a player so I accepted.

A: Did it cross your mind that you haven't exercised in years?

B: I know, but I wanted to play. You should have seen me play.

A: You're lucky you didn't injure your back.

10b

A: Hello, and welcome to *Entertainment Now*. Video games are becoming more and more popular, and many people believe they will challenge movies and music to become the number one choice for entertainment. To learn a little bit more about just how much work goes into making a video game, I have with me today Julian Fellows of Digi-star, a company famous for games such as Star Gaze, Glass Planet and Tales of Simiaz. Welcome, Julian.

B: Hi, there.

A: So, what is the first stage in making a video game?

B: Well, every game begins with a story. The ideas for these come from game designers or outsiders, but more and more games are based on other forms of entertainment, like popular movies. Once the idea is there, writers and artists work together to make rough drawings of each scene of the game.

A: Much like a movie.

B: Yes, but a movie has a single story. Video games can have thousands of outcomes.

A: I see.

B: The next stage is to design the characters. It is important at this stage for artists to create the characters paying great attention to detail, because it's costly to change them later. The artists' sketches are transformed into a 3D character and after about 5 days, we have a character that we can control and move around. In many games, designers study the movements of real people, so that the game is very realistic. Designers also pay a lot of attention to the environment that the characters move around in.

A: What about sound?

B: Again, the quality of the sound is as important as in a movie. In fact, it is common to use famous actors for the voices of the characters of a game. Of course, the quality of acting depends on the scriptwriters. This is something that video games have been attacked for in the past, but game designers have realized that realistic sounds and acting is important for the overall game.

A: So, what's the next step?

B: Next begins the real hard work. Computer programmers and engineers basically put everything together to make the game work. In modern games, it is a huge task and needs very powerful computers. Finally, after that comes the testing stage, where game testers play the game checking every outcome, to make sure there are no problems.

A: And then the game is ready for the stores?

B: Not quite yet. Then comes marketing and advertising. As with movies, games

and advertising. As with movies, games have trailers and teasers to advertise the game and get people excited before a game is released.

A: It's no wonder that many people consider video games to be the future of entertainment. Thanks for coming in today and....

Module 11
11a
Joey
I had a vivid dream about my old school. At first, everything was nice and all my friends were there. Then I realized I had Chemistry class, but I didn't know where I was supposed to go. Suddenly, the schoolyard was empty. I was anxious about getting to class but none of my friends were there so that I could ask them where to go. Then, I realized it was near the end of the school year and that I should be preparing for my exams. Not only that, but I realized I had missed almost all the classes that year, and there was no way to learn everything in such a short time. I was so stressed I didn't know what to do! That's when I woke up. Apparently, it's a very common dream, especially when you've started something new in your life. So, maybe the fact that I have a new job is what caused that dream. I certainly hope I don't have it again.

Tonia
I was looking out of my bedroom window when I saw a gate at the end of the yard, hidden behind a bush. I had never noticed it before, so I went to check it out. On the other side of the gate was a field running down to a small lake. On the other side of the lake was a horse. At first I thought it was a statue, but then it moved its tail. I love horses, so I decided to go and see it up close even though it was pretty far away. I walked and walked but it was taking ages, so I decided to run. I ran and ran but for some reason, I couldn't get close to the lake. It was so annoying! Then I woke up. The following day, I went to the local stables and signed up for horseback riding lessons.

Ryan
I was at the airport in order to pick up a friend who was arriving. Suddenly a man came up to me and said: "Your friend isn't coming. I advise you to get out of here." I was totally confused. Then I noticed two men in black jackets pointing at me. I started running through a crowd of people so that the two men would lose me. But they were right behind me. So, I decided to find somewhere to hide. I saw an open office door, ran inside, shut the door and hid behind a bookcase. I could hear their voices outside the door. It was really scary! Then, the door opened and the room filled with light. That's when I woke up because my brother had opened the curtains in my room and told me I was late for work. More

stress, but at least I wasn't being chased anymore.

Kylie
I dreamed about a camping vacation. I was in the woods in this huge tent with, like, ten friends of mine. The top of the tent was open and we could see the stars. It was cool, but also a little weird. Although it was after midnight, I was still awake playing a game on my cell phone while everyone else was asleep. Suddenly, I saw a huge snake next to one of my friends. I tried to scream, but I could neither make a sound nor move. I was completely terrified. The next thing I knew the snake turned and looked at me, and slowly started coming towards me. I still couldn't do anything, but luckily I woke up. It took me a while to recover from the shock and I couldn't get back to sleep again. It's not the first time I've had this dream, and it probably won't be the last.

11b
Good afternoon and welcome to the Talworth Planetarium. Let's start from the beginning, the very beginning. The universe is about 14 billion years old, and since the beginning it has been expanding, and it still is. About 4.5 billion years ago, our solar system was formed, including the Sun and its planets and, of course, the Earth.

The universe is big, really big. It's difficult to comprehend just how big it is. Standing on the Earth's surface and looking at the night sky, it is full of stars. On a clear night, if you look up in the sky, you can see about 2,500 stars, but there are over 100 billion in our galaxy alone. And just how many stars are there in the universe? A trillion? Are there more stars in the universe than grains of sand on a beach? Well, actually there are more stars than all the grains of sand on all the beaches in the world. In comparison, the number that we can see at night is just a small handful of sand. And when you look at the stars, you are actually looking back into the past. The light from stars takes thousands, even millions of years to reach the Earth. That means you are seeing what they were like millions of years ago. In fact, they might have exploded thousands of years ago, and we wouldn't know, because we can still see their light.

Along with the stars, you can see the fifth largest natural satellite in the solar system, also known as the moon. The Earth only has one moon, which is a pretty weak effort, compared to Uranus which has 27 and Jupiter which has 63. And even though we have a good relationship with our moon, it is moving away from us at about an inch and a half every year. But don't worry, it won't have time to fly away completely from the Earth. In 5 billion years, the Earth won't be able to support any life whatsoever, because the Sun will have grown very large. Eventually, the Sun will eat up the Earth, along with the other planets in the solar system. A terrifying thought, I know, but this is something that happens all the time in the universe.

Module 12
12a
1.
A: Greg? Greg Ridgewell! Long time no see!
B: Well, well, hello, Nancy. How have you been?
A: Not bad. I just arrived. I'll be here for a week.
B: Oh, that's right. You live and work somewhere abroad.
A: Uh-huh, in Madrid. It's been three years now.
B: I wish I had done the same. I had the opportunity but didn't take it.
A: Well, you should have. I'm glad I did. If I hadn't accepted, I would have missed out on a once-in-a-lifetime experience.
B: Listen, I have some time to kill. How about continuing this over coffee?

2.
A: I thought you were going to play tennis today.
B: I was.
A: And? Did Steve cancel on you again? You should find another tennis partner, you know.
B: It's not that. I wanted to practice on my own, but I couldn't.
A: Oh, the rain. It started so suddenly, didn't it?
B: I didn't leave because of that. They had some kind of tournament and were using all the courts.
A: Oh, I see.

3.
A: Do you want to come to the mall with me?
B: Why? Don't tell me you're going to return that black dress you bought yesterday?
A: What dress? I didn't get it in the end.
B: Why not? You said it was really beautiful.
A: I would have bought it if I'd had my purse with me. But I'd left it at home.
B: You're so forgetful sometimes!
A: I think stupid is the word. I spent all afternoon searching for it in all the stores I'd been to, I notified security and asked them if anyone had found my purse. Basically, I made a fool of myself because when I returned home, my purse was lying on my bed.
B: Come on, let's go, but don't forget your purse this time.
A: Very funny.

4.
A: Kevin? Don't tell me you missed it?
B: Well, since I'm not on it, yeah, I missed it.
A: How come? You had plenty of time when you left the house. Did you get stuck in traffic?
B: There was a lot of traffic on the roads but the taxi driver managed to avoid it. Anyway, I got there and went to get myself a snack. I had my ticket and everything so I thought there was plenty of time, right? I wish I had paid more attention to the announcements.

They changed the platform and I didn't find the correct one until it was too late.

A: If only you'd grow up and be more responsible!

B: Well, at least I asked about the ticket. They won't give me a full refund but I'll get some money back.

5.

A: There he is! Morning, Danny! Did you sleep well?

B: Well, one thing's for sure. Camping is not for me!

A: I told you so! If only you'd listened to me and gone to the campground. Free camping is not that easy.

B: I am staying at the campground.

A: Oh. Then is there something wrong with your brother's tent?

B: No, it's fine. It's just that this type of vacation is not very comfortable. There are a lot of bugs, and someone was playing a guitar till 4 a.m.

A: You wouldn't have had such a terrible night if you had checked into a hotel, like me.

B: Yeah, maybe I need to rethink my accommodations for this vacation.

6.

A: Hi, Jenny. How did the job interview go?

B: Don't ask. I just wish I could turn back time!

A: That bad? Why didn't you call me?

B: I've been at my sister's all afternoon discussing how bad it went.

A: Your sister? She's not the best person to get advice from, is she?

B: On the contrary, she was really helpful.

A: So, what conclusion did you come to?

B: That I should have done some research about the company and the position I was applying for so that I could answer their questions.

A: Well, better luck next time.

12b

A: Welcome back to *Top of the Morning*. I'm Bob Simmons.

B: And I'm Cathy Harper.

A: And we're taking a look at the newspapers this morning. Did you see that amazing story about those twins?

B: What twins?

A: It's a little tragic I must say, but amazing nonetheless. There were two identical twins who died terribly on the same day in northern Finland, both riding a bike on the same road during a blizzard!

B: That's unbelievable! But why were two kids riding bikes in a blizzard?

A: They weren't exactly kids, Cathy. They were seventy years old! What makes the story even more unbelievable is that they were both hit by trucks, but not at the same time. Each brother was riding his bike alone and they were killed within about a two-hour difference.

B: So, the second twin can't have known his brother had died while he was riding.

A: No, the police hadn't informed the family yet.

B: Imagine if they had gotten hit by the same truck driver as well. That would have been a pretty spooky coincidence!

A: Indeed, it would've!

B: It reminds me of another amazing story I heard a while ago, but fortunately this one is much more cheerful. There were two identical twins who, despite being separated at birth, had almost identical lives!

A: What do you mean by identical lives?

B: Well, after they were born, they were adopted by two different families. So, they grew up without knowing they were twins. What is amazing is that they were both given the name James, without the other family knowing.

A: Wow!

B: But the coincidences don't stop there. They both got married to women whose name was Linda and both twins had jobs in Law.

A: You're kidding, right? What are the chances of that happening?

B: You tell me! It's interesting because research has been done to discover if identical twins have similar lives. Many studies have shown that identical twins who have had similar childhoods, often go on to lead completely different lives. But here, exactly the opposite happened! They led very similar lives and they even had similar likes and dislikes, for example school subjects.

A: Well, that is indeed incredible! And I just remembered another fascinating story about two identical twins who came from my hometown.

B: I'm all ears.

A: Ashley and Angie, I think their names were. They were happily married and they found out they were pregnant within the same week.

B: Don't tell me they both had twins, too.

A: Exactly, and not just that! They gave birth on the same day, within an hour of each other.

B: That's what I call a coincidence!

Task: Modules 3 & 4

Tour 1

We currently have three tours available around Croatia. Our Grand Tour is ideal for first-time visitors as it covers the most important sights in the company of one of our excellent guides. However, there are also some long distances, so older travelers may find this tour a little too tiring. It includes visits to the fascinating cities of Dubrovnik, Split and Zagreb where you can shop, visit museums and palaces, and even go to a concert. What's more, you are given the opportunity to sail around five beautiful islands.

Tour 2

For nature lovers, I would definitely recommend our Nature Tour. You will be able to enjoy the spectacular natural environment that Croatia offers, like mountain areas and national parks. This tour also includes a guided tour of the extraordinary Plitvice Lakes and waterfalls,

organized by experienced local guides. It's a great way to learn about the many different species of animals and birds that live there.

Tour 3

If you're looking for a more educational experience, I recommend our history tour that takes you to the most important historical sights and museums in the company of one of our excellent guides. A highlight of the trip is a visit to Pula, the largest city in the region of Istria, famous for the Roman ruins and extraordinary amphitheater in the town center.

Task: Modules 7 & 8

There are many ways to save water in our daily lives. Leaky faucets or toilets waste a lot of water. For example, a leaky toilet wastes over 200 gallons of water a day! So, it can really help to check your house for leaky faucets and toilets and fix them right away. A faucet that leaks about 20 drops per minute does not seem like a big deal. However, if you knew that this faucet can waste 700 gallons of water a year, I'm sure you'd consider fixing it.

Also, changing a few things in our daily habits can help save a great deal of water! We have all been told not to brush our teeth or wash our face and leave the water running. Just imagine that by turning off the faucet while brushing your teeth, you can save up to 200 gallons of water a month. Additionally, taking shorter showers can also help save water. Experts say that if we could make our showers 5 minutes shorter, we would be able to save over 350 gallons of water each month.

Using the dishwasher is much more efficient than washing the dishes by hand, but only if you fill it up. If you use the dishwasher for only a few plates or glasses, you will end up wasting more water. So, always remember to run your dishwasher as well as your washing machine only when they are full. That way you can save up to 1,000 gallons a month!

Task: Modules 9 & 10

Does your car need a wash? Well, instead of going to your regular car wash, or even washing it yourself, get down to Lumsden College this weekend where they are having a charity car wash. The event will take place at the college parking lot where the students will be washing cars for a good cause. All day on Saturday the 4th, from eight in the morning till eight in the evening you can have your car washed by an expert team of cleaners. And the prices are pretty good, too - just ten dollars for the exterior of your car and eight dollars for the interior. If you want the full service, exterior and interior, it will cost you only fifteen dollars. That's not too bad. But the main thing is that all the money raised will go to homeless people in the area. The students are aiming to raise a thousand dollars, so if your car is dirty, you know where to take it this weekend.

Module 1
cover (p.7)

A home away from home
Feels like home
Have a roof over your head
Home is where the heart is
Home sweet home
Live out of a suitcase
Make yourself at home
There's no place like home

1a (pp. 8-9)

access (n.)
admire
belongings
cope with
cramped
currently
dorm
drawback
drop by
expenses
face (v.)
fill up
furnished
get tired of
get used to
groceries
heating
houseboat
inviting
isolated
lighthouse
location
loneliness
luxurious
narrow
out of one's mind
peace and quiet
permanent
recreational
regret (v.)
residence
settle in
spacious
stairway
temporary
tower
wisely

1a (pp. 10-11)

bungalow
campus
check in
check out
cottage
county
inform
lane (=street)
move in
move out
outskirts
put sb. up
rural
suburb
suburban
urban

1b (pp. 12-13)

adjust
anxiety
appreciate
bakery
become aware of
catch up on
cause (v.)
community
discovery
enthusiasm
fascinated
frustrated
get down to business
get involved
get over
get rid of
get to know
homesickness
impatient
initial
loved ones
miss out on
native (language)
no longer
observe
obtain
occur
period of time
phase
remind
shock
sign up
study (=research)
surroundings
turn into

1b (pp. 14-15)

as well (=too)
bicycle lane
consider
get the hang of sth.
ideal
option
pleased
run (for buses)
shoreline
suitable
university

Phrases

All the best
Best wishes
Drop me a line
E-mail me when you get the chance
Get back to me soon
How are you keeping?
I haven't told you the latest, have I?
I'd better finish off here
It's taken me ages to reply
I've been meaning to...
Just thought I'd drop you a line
Keep me posted
Let me fill you in
Personally, I believe...
Very true, but...
You have a point

Module 2
cover (p.17)

bungee jump
endurance
go without food
hold
hold one's breath
rope
run a marathon

2a (pp. 18-19)

abandoned
against all odds
barely
branch
breathe
catastrophic
coconuts
cover (=travel a distance)
crawl
damage (v.+n.)
dig
drag
drop (temperature)

drown
eventually
extreme conditions
float (v.)
footprint
force (v.)
form (v.)
harm (v.+n.)
hiker
igloo
injure
one by one
oxygen
passerby
ranger
recover
ruin (v.)
several
shelter
signal (v.)
spot (v.)
strike (tsunami)
stunned
supplies
survivor
trapped
treat (v.) (at hospital)
wave (v.)

2a (pp. 20-21)

ambulance
block (v.)
bystander
emergency services
jungle
land (v.)
overturn
possibility
resident
skid
slide (v.)
violent

Words related to the weather

blizzard
blow
boiling
breeze
chilly
clear skies
drizzle (v.)
dull
foggy
freezing
icy
lightning

mild
overcast
pour (v.)
shine
shower
snowstorm
thunder

2b (pp. 22-23)
amateur
annual
assist
assistant
attendant
breathtaking
challenge (n.)
compete
competitor
contestant
conventional
cyclist
distance
due to
edit
editor
endure
extraordinary
fatal
finalist
finish line
incident
instructor
journal
journalist
land (n.)
landscape
lead (v.)
leader
loser
majority
measures
mud
organizer
participant
participate
professional (n.)
quad
race (v.)
racer
rally
reality
remain
sand dune
security
specifically
spectator

test (v.)
tough
trainer (person)

2b (pp. 24-25)
bandage (v.)
be in luck
be in shock
be over
bear
camp (v.)
chase (v.)
cliff
edge
fog
hang
hold on
in the middle of nowhere
light a fire
relieved
scared stiff
shake with fear
signal
swollen
thick
Phrases
Oh my!
What's up with you?

Module 3
cover (p. 27)
broaden the mind
globetrotting

3a (pp. 28-29)
accommodations
achievement
adventurer
article
attempt (n. + v.)
benefit (n.)
brave
circle (v.)
complete (v.)
courage
crew
cruise
despite
development
entire
excursion
expedition
globe
globetrotter
hitchhiking
hold the record
journey

presentation
prove
provide
publish
remarkable
sail (v.)
sailor
set sail
solo
succeed
unfamiliar
voyage
wear sth. out

3a (pp. 30-31)
accommodate
achieve
advertise
announce
announcement
application
apply
campground
cancelation
confirm
connect
connection
description
destination
develop
exotic
explanation
exploration
guided tour
improvement
inexpensive
insurance
introduction
on board
platform
present (v.)
reservation
reserve
safari
scenery
stress-free
transport (v.)
wildlife

3b (pp. 32-33)
access (v.)
anxious
app
arrival
bargain (n.)
car rental
come across

come up
compare
count on
currency
delay
departure
directly
do without sth.
domestic flight
essential
fed up with
flexible
frequent
handy
hassle (n.)
illegal
impressed
interactive
journal
landmark
legal
leisure
major
offline
once (sth. happens)
record (v.)
right (n.)
schedule (n.)
section
store (v.)
streetcar
struggle (n.)
unique
update (n.)
upload (v.)

3b (pp. 34-35)
botanical garden
colorful
educational
enjoyable
fascinating
from up close
get seasick
highlight (n.)
impression
magnificent
massive
mouth-watering
once in a lifetime
opportunity
palm tree
peaceful
pond
private
recommendation

species
spectacular
square (adj.)
suggestion
sweet-smelling
the public
tropical
typical
unforgettable
weird
wonder (n.)

Phrases
I'd prefer (not) to...
I'd rather (not)...
See for yourself

Module 4
cover (p.37)
balance (n.)
prospects
salary

4a (pp.38-39)
advise
at last
be willing to
career break
creature
delighted
eager
encourage
enthusiastic
fairly
greet
hopefully
income
interact
motivated
on one's mind
overtime
plenty of
principal
résumé
rewarding
rise
sanctuary
sleepless
somehow
staff
teens

Collocations with "make"
make a decision/guess
make a difference
make a good/bad
  impression
make a mistake
make a suggestion/an
  arrangement
make an effort
make plans
make sense
make the most of sth.
make up one's mind

Collocations with "do"
do a project
do an experiment
do as you please
do business
do my hair
do one's best
do research
do sb. a favor
do some exercise
do well/badly

4a (pp.40-41)
applicant
careless
earn a living
experience (work)
get fired
hire
knowledge
position
previous
qualifications
quit
raise (n.)
react
rent
tell sb. off

Phrases
I didn't mean to...
I don't have any excuses for
  my behavior
I would strongly advise you
  to...
That was thoughtless of you
That wasn't very wise of
  you
Why on Earth did you do
  that?

4b (pp.42-43)
affect
come up with
concern (n.)

deadline
emotions
express (v.)
extrovert
freedom
get along with
imagination
introvert
issue
medical care
role model
solution
take one's time
technician
trust (v.)

Jobs
academic
accountant
consultant
detective
engineer
interior designer
lawyer
marketing manager
mechanic
politician
public speaker
researcher
veterinarian

Personality adjectives
ambitious
artistic
courageous
disorganized
honest
imaginative
musical
patient
rational
reliable
sociable
spontaneous
strict
well-organized

4b (pp.44-45)
apart from that
argument
bulletin board
by mistake
candidate
delete
document
dress (v.)
exchange program
furthermore

give a talk
in addition
internship
job fair
promote
promotion
registration
senior (year)
to begin with
what is more

Phrases
I bet...
I doubt it
It's hard to say...
It's probable that...
It's very (un)likely that...
My guess is...

Module 5
5a (pp.48-49)
accidentally
be around
beneficial
commonplace
compulsory
effective
encyclopedia
foreigner
generation
gesture
hill
hilly
mist
mountainous
mystery
origin
pass down
pick sth. up (learn)
practice makes perfect
rare
separate (adj.)
sign language
speech
take control
take over
valley
whistle (v.)
widely
yell

Collocations with "tell"
tell a joke
tell a lie
tell a secret
tell a story
tell the difference
tell the truth

tell time

Collocations with "say"

say hello

say so

say sorry

say sth.

say thank you

say yes

5a (pp. 50-51)

argue

care (v.)

chat

complain

costly

face-to-face

gossip (v.)

inconvenient

instantly

mention

outdated

place (v.)

portable

practical

refer

socialize

time-consuming

time-saving

up to date

user-friendly

Words/Phrases related to technology

account (e.g. e-mail)

attach

crash

data

deactivate

drag and drop

function

gadget freak

install

instant messaging

key

keyboard

post (v.)

press

scroll

select

shut down

tap (v.)

touchscreen

virus

Phrases

Anyway, as I was saying...

Can I add something?

Could I say something

before you continue?

Hold on. Are you saying that...?

May I interrupt you for a second?

Now, what was I saying?

Now, where was I?

Sorry to interrupt, but...

5b (pp. 52-53)

against the law

at all times

be located

be supposed to

behave

beware of

caution

circle (n.)

construction worker

evacuate

evacuation

exit (v.)

fire extinguisher

handle (n.)

hazard (n.)

in case of

in progress

keep off

keep out

manner

notify

obtain

owner

passenger car

permission

permit (v.)

protection

protective

qualified

required

(building) site

strictly forbidden

suspicious

track

unaffected

warn

warning

wave (n.)

5b (pp. 54-55)

get off (work)

ice-cream parlor

seminar

shift

Directions

Could you give me directions to...?

Cross at the crosswalk/ footbridge

Do you happen to know where the...is?

Go along... Street.

Go past/towards...

Go straight for another hundred yards.

It's on the corner of...

Keep going for two blocks.

Take the first/second/etc. left/right onto...

Turn... at the intersection.

You'll find it on the left/ right-hand side.

Phrases

Does that make sense?

I didn't catch/get that

I hope that's not too confusing

I hope you're making sense of what I'm saying

I'm not following you

Is everything clear?

Were my directions clear enough?

What was that again?

Module 6
cover (p.57)

make history

well-educated

6a (pp. 58-59)

award

barefoot

blame (v.)

by nature

candle

concept

developing country

doubt (n.)

exist

fable

fall in love

go after (a dream)

investigate

irrational

laughter

make fun of

president

realistic

response

reveal

risk (v.)

satisfying

seed

set a goal

unrealistic

victory

6a (pp. 60-61)

accomplish

affected

ambition

illiterate

illogical

immature

impolite

impractical

inappropriate

incorrect

inexperienced

insecure

intelligence

intend

irregular

irrelevant

irresponsible

literate

logical

marshmallow

mature

psychologist

relevant

secure (adj.)

unaware

unkind

unprofessional

unreliable

unsuitable

unwilling

6b (pp. 62-63)

altitude

anger

approximately

awareness

be named

belief

break a record

briefly

cave

creativity

darkness

depth

fame

fearless

feat

gain

growth

height

kindness

laziness
leap (v.)
mission
parachute
passion
popularity
properly
relief
responsibility
sadness
set a record
similarity
slow down
speed
strength
therefore
thought (n.)
unhurt
weakness
weight

6b (pp.64-65)

all in all
appealing
besides that
demanding
devote
devotion
disappointment
energizing
escape from
extensive
failure
in conclusion
in the first place
injury
lack of
last but not least
let sth. go to waste
maintain
maintenance
moreover
on the one hand
on the other hand
on the whole
outweigh
patio
the pros and cons
to sum up
turn professional
unappealing

weather dependent
while (=contrast)
work out (exercise)

Module 7
cover (p.67)

running water
sparkling water
tap water
water cooler
water fountain
water pollution

7a (pp.68-69)

attack (v.)
be about to
beak
beast
blind
companion
cry (n.)
enormous
feather
for an instant
force (n.)
gaze (v.)
giant
gigantic
grab
head (v.)
knock over
legend
liquid
marine
monster
myth
obvious(ly)
order (n.)
overcome
overhear
repair
rush (v.)
squid
stare
struggle (v.)
surface
swallow
tears
violence
weapon

7a (pp.70-71)

cause (n.)
disease
endangered species
extinct

hunting
national park
Animals
beetle
cheetah
koala
octopus
penguin
rhinoceros (rhino)
toad
turtle
whale
Geographical features
bay
canal
canyon
desert
falls
gulf
mountain range
peak
rainforest
volcano
Phrases
I can't say for sure but...
I could be wrong but I
   believe...
I have no doubt that...
I know for a fact that...
I suppose...
I'm absolutely certain
I'm positive
I'm very/fairly/completely
   confident that...
It seems unbelievable but...

7b (pp.72-73)

agriculture
at risk
average
bother (v.)
congratulate
consume
cooperate
decrease
depend
flush toilet
for instance
germs
in motion
increase
insist
instant coffee
limited
link (v.)
muscle

nausea
percentage
raise awareness
rely
source (of life)
suffer from
supply (n.)
swamp
take sth. for granted
total amount
trillion
use up
vomit
water shortage

7b (pp.74-75)

astonished
be out of luck
binoculars
die down
dot
fall overboard
filthy
furious
gentle
gorgeous
hilarious
just in time
lifeboat
marvelous
miserable
on the horizon
rock (v.)
rough
row (v.)
sink (v.)
starving
think to oneself
thrilled
tiny
treasure
unconscious
wounded
Phrases
I get it
I nearly jumped out of my
   skin
I went red as a beet
In other words,...
It was too good to be true
The next thing I knew...
There was no hope left
Within minutes...
Without thinking...

Module 8
8a (pp.78-79)

a series of
absorb
artificial
attack (n.)
carbon dioxide
completion
criticism
damaging
decade
destruction
devastating
dust (n.)
enemy
expanding
global warming
habitat
intruder
loss
man-made
Only time will tell
outcome
process
rate
result in
scarce
speed up
traffic congestion
valuable

8a (pp.80-81)

acid rain
alternative energy
ban (v.)
carpool
chemicals
close down
coal
commercial
cut down (trees)
deforestation
exhaust fumes
factory
fine (n.)
firewood
fossil fuels
gases
layer
leak (v.)
materials
mixture
monuments
oil spill
pass a law
poisonous

pump into
recycling plant
reuse
severe
smog
spread (v.)
substance
tanker
threat
toxic waste
wind turbine

Phrases
I couldn't agree more
It is a fact that...
It is common knowledge
    that...
It is (generally) believed
    that...

8b (pp.82-83)

balanced diet
blood pressure
calcium
carbohydrates
cholesterol
cut down on
cut sth. out (of a diet)
dairy products
diabetes
end up
exclude
fat (n.)
fiber
function (v.)
grains
immune system
in the long run
iron
look into
matter (n.)
minerals
nutrients
nutritious
obese
obesity
point out
prevent
protein
replace
stick to
vegan
vegetarianism
vitamin

Food
apricot
cauliflower

eggplant
grapefruit
lamb
lentils
noodles
oatmeal
peanuts
pear
pumpkin
shrimp
spinach
watermelon

Phrases
Don't get me wrong

8b (pp.84-85)

affordable
beverages
calorie
cancer
carbonated drink
crops
diet / regular drink
food poisoning
food stand
highly (toxic)
insect
organic food
soil
three-course meal
vendor
whereas

Module 9
cover (p.87)

brand
preference
slogan

9a (pp.88-89)

analyze
be based on
bombard
brain
conduct (an experiment)
conservative
countless
factor
indicate
influence (v.)
initially
instinct
limit (v.)
measure (v.)
misery
necessarily

no matter how
pick (=choose)
range (n.)
selection
spam e-mail
take sth. into consideration
tend
unimportant

9a (pp.90-91)

be broke
be on a tight budget
be short of cash
beanbag
browse
cheat sb. out of sth.
cost a fortune
game console
model
on sale
out of stock
refund (n.)
sale
shop around
shopaholic
spare some cash
special offer
storage box
vacuum cleaner

Phrases
If it were up to me,...
It doesn't matter
It's a rip-off
Money is no object
My first choice would be...
That's a steal

9b (pp.92-93)

accent
adore
amusing
burst out laughing
can't be bothered
case (=container)
charge (a service)
combine
complaint
contract
disapprove
dishonest
disrespect
dissatisfied
endless
gag
hopeless
in stock

inflatable
label (n.)
misbehave
misinform
mislead
misleading
misplace
misspell
misunderstand
overpriced
play a joke on sb.
plug (v.)
pop (out)
pretend
set up
shipping
slight
spray (n.)
tricky
try out
typewriter
wireless
worthless

9b (pp. 94-95)

a good read
a page-turner
account (=story)
author
autobiography
award-winning
be set in
bestseller
biography
chapter
character
classic
complicated
cookbook
dull (=boring)
fantasy
fiction
graphic novel
gripping
hero
heroine
killer
murder (v.+n.)
non-fiction
ongoing
perfection

plot
poetry
predict
question (v.)
reader
suspect (n.)
suspense
timeless
trilogy
twists and turns
universe
unoriginal
victim
vivid

Phrases

It appeals to all ages
Make sure you get a
  copy
Overall, I found...
You will find it hard to
  put down

Module 10
cover (p. 97)

be a bit of a downer
be bored stiff
be thrilled to pieces
get a kick out of sth.
get on one's nerves
have a whale of a
  time
make one's day
wind sb. up

10a (pp. 98-99)

a flight of steps
backflip
blow sb. away
can't help (doing sth.)
come back to sb.
cover (v.)
elastic band
evolution
examine
gather
give sth. a shot
halfway
hand sth. over
in one's youth
judge (v.)
jump at the chance
look sb. up and down
original
sb.'s mouth fell open
somersault
springs
transform

trick (n.)
witness (v.)

**Prepositional
  phrases**

in a row
in charge of
in general
in need
in particular
in person
in/out of control
in/out of danger
in/out of order
in/out of shape
in/out of sight
in/out of trouble
in/out of use
out of breath
out of date
out of one's reach
out of the ordinary
out of the question
out of work

10a (pp. 100-101)

every other day
gentle
lift weights
move (n.)
overweight
persuade
pull a muscle
run into
sign (v.)
stretch
stretching exercises
treadmill
warm up
weight training
workout

Phrases

a piece of cake
cross one's mind
grab a bite to eat
I can't take it anymore
I'll pass
kill two birds with one
  stone

10b (pp. 102-103)

approach
bow and arrow
cautiously
compared to
controls
dismount

dragon
drawing
guard
imaginary
lose a life
lose contact
lose interest in
lose one's patience
lose one's temper
miss a meal
miss a meeting/
  appointment
multiplayer
no time to lose
proceed
purpose
reflexes
script
scriptwriter
sequel
soldier
stage
step by step
summarize
surround
sword
tail
tale
trail (n.)
trap (n.)
trick (v.)
walkthrough
wander
windmill
wing

10b (pp. 104-105)

admission
assure
ceremony
charity
city hall
disabled people
donation
entertaining
everything goes
  according to plan
exhibit
fancy dress
fee
for a good cause
fund-raiser
funds
glow
hand out
improvise

name tag
necklace
on display
raise money
refreshments
roll (v.)
rollerblades
rollerblading
sculpture
set (sun)
skater
skates
stray (v.)
support
venue
wristband

Module 11
cover (p. 107)

comet
early bird
night owl
satellite

11a (pp. 108-109)

adequate
adjustment
alert
be up all night
behind the wheel
concentrate
constantly
consult
cure (v.)
depressed
diary
disorder
distracted
energized
fall behind
figure out
get sb. down
give up
insomnia
long-term effect
medical condition
physician
schedule (v.)
sleepiness
specialist
sunlight
symptom
take a nap
treatment
uncontrollable

11a (pp. 110-111)

bring up
call up
cough
dial
give up
hang up
heart attack
heater
hurt one's feelings
keep up
make up
mental health
nightmare
physical health
pill
sleep in
stay up
turn up

11b (pp. 112-113)

anticipate
astonish
astonishing
brighten
challenging
cultural
curtain
delight (n.)
delightful
explosion
first-hand
fjord
fox
generate
glow (n.)
impress
in awe
in search of
indigenous people
luxury
meet up
mysterious
(natural)
   phenomenon
planetarium
powerful
(un)predictable
profession
release
remark (n.+ v.)
snowmobile
spectacle
thrilling
treat (v.)
view (v.)

11b (pp. 114-115)

aim (v.)
at all costs
burglary
commit a crime
concerned
criminal
garbage collector
garbage truck
inadequate
lot (n.)
mayor
nonsense
outrageous
patrol officer
pedestrian
poor
priority
switch off
take action
threaten
unemployment
vacant
vandalism

Phrases

As a consequence...
As I see it...
For this reason...
I'm writing in
   response to...
Our main concern
   should be...
This is due to the fact
   that...

Module 12
cover (p. 117)

**Phrases with
"chance"**

a second chance
by chance
fat chance
given half the chance
last chance
leave nothing to
   chance
not stand a chance
slim chance
take my chances

12a (pp. 118-119)

antibiotic
bacteria
bookmark
cell (biology)
chemist

experiment (v.)
flame
glue (n.)
inspection
irritating
lab
make a profit
mankind
match (n.)
mold (n.)
numerous
on the contrary
patent
penicillin
picky
progress (v.)
remove
reputation
scrap paper
slice (v.)
slippery
stick (n.)
stick (v.)
thanks to
vase

12a (pp. 120-121)

Phrases with "time"

for the time being
from time to time
have no time for sth.
have time to kill
in no time
in time
in one's own time
of all time
on time
turn back time

Phrases

Better late than never
Better luck next time
I know the feeling
It's better than
   nothing
It's never too late
Look on the bright
   side
What a pity!
What a shame!
You win some, you
   lose some

12b (pp. 122-123)

coincidence
come over sb.
envelope
give a sigh of relief

give birth
hesitate
identical twins
knock
odd
sealed
send a shiver down
   my spine
slam (v.)
spooky
toss and turn
Idioms
a pain in the neck
all ears
blow one's mind
can't make heads or
   tails of sth.
in a flash
on top of the world
one's heart was in
   one's mouth
one's jaw dropped
out of the blue
ring a bell
sleep like a log
spill the beans

12b (pp. 124-125)

behind one's back
circle of friends
clear one's head
expand
feel rejected
friendship
handle (v.)
jump to conclusions
put money aside
reasonable
throw money around
work out differences
Phrases
If I were in your
   position,...
Let me know how
   things turn out

Pioneer Intermediate B1
American edition
Student's Book
H. Q. Mitchell - Marileni Malkogianni

Published by: **MM Publications**
www.mmpublications.com
info@mmpublications.com

Offices
UK China Cyprus Greece Korea Poland Turkey USA
Associated companies and representatives throughout the world.

Copyright © 2014 MM Publications

All rights reserved. No part of this publication may be reproduced, stored in a retrieval system or transmitted in any form or by any means, electronic, mechanical, photocopying, recording or otherwise, without permission in writing from the publishers.

The publishers have tried to contact all copyright holders, but in cases where they may have failed, they will be pleased to make the necessary arrangements at the first opportunity.

Produced in the EU

ISBN978-4-7647-4160-7

C2005005042-17471